The Women's Institutes' Book of Favourite Recipes

The Women's Institutes' Book of Favourite Recipes

Edited by Norma MacMillan

BB Bounty
Books

First published in Great Britain in 1980
Reprinted 2006, 2007, 2008

This edition published in 2010 by Bounty Books,
a division of Octopus Publishing Group Ltd
Endeavour House, 189 Shaftesbury Avenue,
London WC2H 8JY
www.octopusbooks.co.uk

An Hachette UK Company
www.hachette.co.uk

Reprinted 2011
Copyright © 1980 WI Books Ltd.

ISBN: 978-0-753719-56-5

A CIP catalogue record for this book is available from
the British Library

Printed and bound in China

Contents

Introduction

The recipes in this book have been collected over many years from members of Women's Institutes throughout England and Wales. Some have been published in cookbooks now long out of print. Others have come to us through the many cookbooks produced by the sixty-five County and Island Federations of Women's Institutes. Still others have appeared in *Home and Country*, the official magazine of the NFWI.

This book is a mixture of the traditional and the new. A special section has been compiled which consists of fifty prizewinning recipes, all original to WI members, and selected from those submitted as competition entries. The National Federation of Women's Institutes wishes to record its appreciation of the help it has received from the County Federations and its grateful thanks to the many members who have made this book possible.

The National Federation of Women's Institutes is the largest national organization of country-women in the world. Its 400,000-strong membership includes experts on cookery, home crafts and gardening, many of whom lecture at the NFWI's college of adult education where courses are available in a wide range of subjects.

If you are a woman aged sixteen or over, you can join the WI for a small annual contribution. For further details, write to: The General Secretary, National Federation of Women's Institutes, 39 Eccleston Street, London SW1W 9NT.

Anne Ballard

Anne Ballard
General Secretary
National Federation of Women's Institutes

Tuna Cocktail

Serves 4

150 ml/¼ pint natural
   yogurt
1 × 5 cm/2 inch piece
   cucumber, peeled and
   grated
1 teaspoon tomato purée
juice of 1 lemon
shredded lettuce
200 g/7 oz canned tuna
   fish, drained and flaked
paprika

Mix together the yogurt, cucumber, tomato purée and lemon juice. Make a bed of lettuce in each of four serving dishes and divide the tuna fish between them. Top with the yogurt sauce and sprinkle with paprika.

Pork and Liver Pâté

Serves 10

450 g/1 lb belly pork
450 g/1 lb pig's liver
1 small onion
salt
pepper
1 egg, beaten
1 tablespoon sherry
   (optional)
6 streaky bacon rashers,
   rinded and stretched

Mince the pork, then mince again with the liver and onion. Add salt, pepper, the egg and sherry, if used, and beat well.

Line an oval pâté dish with 3 of the bacon rashers. Spoon in the pork mixture and smooth the top. Cover with the rest of the rashers. Place the dish in a roasting tin of hot water and bake in a preheated moderate oven (180 C/350 F, Gas Mark 4) for about 1 hour. When done, the pâté will have shrunk a little from the sides of the dish and there will be a lot of liquid around it. Do not pour this away: the pâté will absorb it as it cools.

7

Hare Pâté

Serves 6–8

1 hare, cut into pieces
100 g/4 oz butter
1 parsley sprig
1 thyme sprig
3 bay leaves
4 peppercorns
salt
stock or water
50 g/2 oz mushrooms,
* sliced*
1 thick slice of bread,
* soaked in milk*
2 egg yolks
6 tablespoons brandy or
* Madeira*
pepper

Melt 40 g/1½ oz of the butter in a frying pan and fry the hare pieces until they are lightly browned on all sides. Transfer them to a saucepan, packing them in closely. Add the parsley, thyme, 2 of the bay leaves, the peppercorns and salt and just cover with stock or water. Bring to the boil and simmer gently for 2 to 3 hours or until the hare is very tender.

Drain the hare, reserving the liquid, and take the meat from the bones. Chop the meat. Strain the liquid.

Melt 15 g/½ oz of the remaining butter in the frying pan and fry the mushrooms for 3 minutes. Add to the hare meat. Squeeze the slice of bread to remove the excess milk and add to the mixture. Mince or blend to a smooth purée.

Moisten the purée with a little of the reserved liquid, then beat in the remaining butter, the egg yolks, the brandy or Madeira, salt and pepper.

Put the remaining bay leaf in the bottom of a pâté dish and spoon in the hare mixture. Smooth the top, then cover and steam for 3 hours. This pâté will keep for several weeks in the refrigerator.

Chicken Liver Pâté

Serves 6

75 g/3 oz streaky bacon,
* rinded and diced*
1 medium onion, chopped
225 g/8 oz chicken livers
salt
pepper
2 garlic cloves, crushed
1 egg, beaten

Fry the bacon and onion in a frying pan until the onion is softened and the bacon has rendered its fat. Add the livers, salt and pepper and continue cooking gently for 10 minutes.

Pass the liver mixture through a fine mincer twice, then beat in the garlic and egg. Turn into a straight-sided basin, or baking tin. Cover tightly and steam for 1 hour, or place the tin in a roasting tin of hot water and bake in a preheated cool oven (150 C/300 F, Gas Mark 2) for 1 hour. Cool before serving.

Seafood Cocktail

Serves 4–6

4 tablespoons mayonnaise
3 tablespoons natural
  yogurt
1 tablespoon tomato
  ketchup
pinch of cayenne pepper
shredded lettuce
2 tomatoes, quartered
1 small green pepper,
  cored, seeded and
  chopped
225 g/8 oz shelled prawns
100 g/4 oz cooked,
  shelled mussels
lemon slices, onion rings
  and unshelled prawns
  to garnish

Mix together the mayonnaise, yogurt, ketchup and cayenne. Put the lettuce, tomatoes and green pepper in a shallow serving dish, or individual dishes, and pile the prawns and mussels on top. Pour over the dressing. Chill well and serve garnished with lemon slices, onion rings and unshelled prawns.

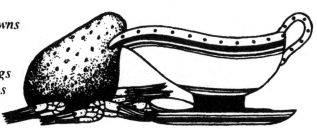

Simple Terrine

Serves 6–8

100 g/4 oz streaky bacon
  rashers, rinded and
  stretched
450 g/1 lb liver
1 small onion
1 garlic clove
450 g/1 lb pork
  sausagemeat
salt
pepper
2 hard-boiled eggs,
  chopped
1 teaspoon dried mixed
  herbs
1 bay leaf
flour and water paste
approx. 300 ml/½ pint
  jellied stock

Line a small earthenware dish with the bacon rashers. Mince together the liver, onion and garlic, then mix with the sausagemeat. Add salt, pepper, the eggs and mixed herbs and combine thoroughly. Spoon into the dish, smooth the top and put the bay leaf on top.

Cover the dish with the lid and seal with the flour and water paste. Place the dish in a roasting tin of hot water and cook in a preheated moderate oven (180 C/350 F, Gas Mark 4) for 1½ hours.

Remove from the oven and take off the lid. Put a weight on top (not more than 1 kg/2 lb) and leave overnight.

The next day, melt the jellied stock and pour enough into the dish to fill up the sides. Leave until set, then turn out to serve.

Liver and Bacon Pâté
Serves 6–8

275 g/10 oz streaky bacon rashers, rinded
450 g/1 lb pig's liver
1 large onion
2 cloves garlic
½ teaspoon dried mixed herbs
salt
pepper
1 egg, beaten
4 tablespoons red wine
sliced stuffed olives to garnish

Stretch half the bacon rashers with the back of a knife, then use to line a greased 500 g/1 lb loaf tin. Leave the rashers hanging over the edge of the tin.

Mince the rest of the bacon twice with the liver, onion and garlic. Add the herbs, salt, pepper, egg and wine and beat well together. Spoon into the tin and smooth the top. Fold over the ends of the bacon rashers on top of the pâté.

Place the tin in a roasting tin of hot water and bake in a preheated moderate oven (180 C/350 F, Gas Mark 4) for 1½ hours. Cool slightly, then place a weight on top and leave until cold. Turn out to serve, garnished with sliced olives.

Pheasant and Pork Pâté
Serves 8–10

brace of pheasants, cleaned
1 small onion
1 celery stalk
2 bay leaves
salt
pepper
25 g/1 oz gelatine
225 g/8 oz fat pork
clarified butter

Put the pheasants into a saucepan and cover with cold water. Bring to the boil, then drain and skin the pheasants. Return to the pan, cover with fresh cold water and add the onion, celery, bay leaves, salt and pepper. Bring to the boil and simmer for 1 hour.

Remove the pheasants from the pan and strip the meat from the carcasses. Return the meat to the pan and simmer for a further 1 hour.

Remove the pheasant meat and strain the cooking liquid. Reserve 150 ml/¼ pint of the liquid and dissolve the gelatine in it. When completely dissolved, add to the remaining liquid.

Mince the pheasant meat with the fat pork and stir into the gelatine mixture. Turn into a baking dish. Cover with buttered paper and bake in a preheated moderately hot oven (200 C/400 F, Gas Mark 6) for 1½ to 2 hours.

Allow the pâté to cool, then cover the top with clarified butter.

Stuffed Eggs
Serves 6

6 hard-boiled eggs,
  halved
1 tablespoon natural
  yogurt
½ teaspoon dry mustard
1 tablespoon grated
  Parmesan cheese
1 teaspoon chopped fresh
  oregano or marjoram
chopped parsley and
  tomato quarters to
  garnish

Remove the yolks from the egg whites, keeping the whites intact, and mash the yolks with the yogurt, mustard, cheese and herbs. Fill the egg white halves with the yolk mixture and arrange on a serving plate. Sprinkle with chopped parsley and garnish with tomato quarters.

Orange or Grapefruit Tuna Pâté
Serves 4

200 g/7 oz canned tuna
  fish, drained and flaked
grated rind and juice of 1
  orange or grapefruit
50 g/2 oz fresh
  breadcrumbs
1 egg, beaten
salt
pepper

Mix together all the ingredients and turn into a greased 500 g/1 lb loaf tin. Bake in a preheated moderate oven (180 C/350 F, Gas Mark 4) for 40 minutes.
Variations: Canned mackerel or herrings may be used instead of tuna fish.

Avocado with Salmon
Serves 4

2 ripe avocados
juice of ½ lemon
1 small onion, grated
3 tablespoons mayonnaise
salt
pepper
200 g/7 oz canned pink
  salmon, drained and
  flaked
pinch of paprika

Halve the avocados lengthways and remove the stones. Scoop out the flesh, being careful not to damage the skins. Chop the flesh. Mix together the lemon juice, onion, mayonnaise, salt and pepper, then fold in the avocado flesh and salmon. Spoon into the avocado skin shells and sprinkle with the paprika. Chill before serving.

11

Brackenhurst Iced Prawn Curry
Serves 6

25 g/1 oz butter
1 onion, chopped
226 g/8 oz canned
  tomatoes
1 teaspoon flour
1 teaspoon sugar
2 tablespoons cream
dash of Tabasco sauce
2 tablespoons curry
  powder
1 tablespoon chutney
juice of ½ lemon
salt
150 ml/¼ pint mayonnaise
225 g/8 oz long-grain
  rice, boiled and cooled

Garnish
1 hard-boiled egg, sliced
225 g/8 oz shelled
  shrimps
parsley

Melt the butter in a saucepan and fry the onion until softened. Add the tomatoes, then blend in the flour. Stir in the sugar, cream, Tabasco sauce, curry powder, chutney, lemon juice and salt. Sieve or blend to a purée and mix with the mayonnaise.

Spread the rice on a serving plate and pour over the sauce. Garnish with egg slices, shrimps and parsley and serve chilled.

Pork and Egg Pâté
Serves 6

450 g/1 lb belly pork
225 to 350 g/8 to 12 oz
  pig's liver
1 small onion
2 eggs, beaten
50 g/2 oz fresh
  breadcrumbs
salt
pepper
1 tablespoon brandy
  (optional)
4 hard-boiled eggs

Mince together the pork, liver and onion (for a smoother pâté, mince the pork on its own first, then again with the other ingredients). Add the eggs, breadcrumbs, salt, pepper and brandy, if used, and beat well together.

Line a 1 kg/2 lb loaf tin with foil and grease well. Spread half the pork mixture on the bottom of the tin, then place the eggs on top. Cover with the rest of the pork mixture, pressing down carefully between each egg. Cover the tin with more greased foil and place in a roasting tin of hot water. Bake in a preheated moderately hot oven (190°C/375°F, Gas Mark 5) for 1 hour. Cool in the tin before turning out.

Cucumber Creams

Serves 6

1 lime jelly
1 teaspoon salt
175 ml/6 fl oz boiling
water
2 tablespoons white
vinegar
1 teaspoon grated onion
pepper
175 ml/6 fl oz soured
cream
75 ml/3 fl oz mayonnaise
1 large cucumber, minced
and drained
lettuce leaves to serve

Dissolve the jelly and salt in the boiling water. Stir in the vinegar, onion and pepper, then chill until thick. Mix in the soured cream and mayonnaise, then fold in the cucumber. Turn into individual moulds and chill until set.

To serve, line individual serving plates with lettuce leaves and turn out the moulded creams.

Orange and Tomato Salad

Serves 4

2 medium oranges
4 tomatoes, skinned and
sliced
1 small onion, thinly
sliced into rings
3 tablespoons French
dressing

Garnish
black grapes, halved and
pipped
chopped chives

Peel the rind from the oranges, not taking any of the white pith. Cut the rind into thin matchsticks. Remove the pith from the oranges and slice them.

Arrange overlapping slices of orange and tomato on a serving plate and scatter over the orange rind sticks and onion rings. Pour over the dressing and chill.

Garnish with grapes and chives before serving.

Prawn and Mushroom Cocktail

Serves 4

50 g/2 oz long-grain rice
100 g/4 oz frozen mixed
vegetables
100 g/4 oz shelled prawns
225 g/8 oz button
mushrooms, wiped clean
2 tablespoons mayonnaise
lettuce to serve

Cook the rice in boiling salted water until it is tender. Drain, if necessary, and cool. Cook the vegetables according to the directions on the packet, then drain and cool. Mix together the rice and vegetables and chill.

Add the prawns and mushrooms to the rice mixture, then fold the mayonnaise through the rice. Serve on a bed of lettuce.

Marinated Kipper Fillets

Serves 4–6

8 kipper fillets, halved
    lengthways
1 onion, thinly sliced into
    rings
1 bay leaf
pepper
watercress to garnish
lemon wedges to serve
Marinade
1 tablespoon lemon juice
    or wine vinegar
1 teaspoon sugar
150 ml/¼ pint olive oil

Lay the fillets in a shallow china or glass dish. Scatter the onion rings over them and add the bay leaf. Mix together the ingredients for the marinade and pour over the fillets. Cover and place on the lowest shelf in the refrigerator. Leave to marinate for about 24 hours.

Sprinkle with freshly ground black pepper and garnish with watercress. Serve with lemon wedges, and brown bread and butter.

Variations: Other vegetables or prawns, button mushrooms, cauliflower florets, cooked French or green beans, tomatoes, onion rings, lightly cooked celery or leeks, may be marinated in the same way. Add a dash of tomato ketchup to the marinade for celery or leeks.

Canapés Diane

Serves 4

2 tablespoons oil
4 chicken livers
4 streaky bacon rashers,
    rinded and fat removed
4 slices of French bread,
    toasted

Heat the oil in a frying pan and fry the chicken livers until tender and cooked through. Remove them from the pan and keep hot.

Add the bacon to the pan and fry until golden brown on both sides. Drain well, then wrap a rasher around each chicken liver. Serve on the toast.

Brochettes

pieces of smoked salmon
squares of rollmop
    herring
smoked oysters
squares of canned
    pimento
cocktail onions
folded lettuce leaves
Cos lettuce
French dressing to serve

Thread a piece of salmon, square of rollmop, an oyster, a square of pimento, an onion and a folded lettuce leaf onto a skewer and repeat twice. Prepare a skewer like this for each person and serve them on a bed of Cos lettuce leaves, with French dressing.

Prawn Cocktail

600 ml/1 pint shelled
* shrimps or prawns*
2 tablespoons thick
* mayonnaise*
3 tablespoons whipped
* cream*
1 tablespoon tomato
* ketchup or purée*
1 tablespoon
* Worcestershire sauce*
1 tablespoon lemon juice
1 teaspoon finely chopped
* onion*
1 teaspoon finely chopped
* celery, or $\frac{1}{4}$ teaspoon*
* celery salt*
salt
lettuce leaves to serve
chopped lettuce to
* garnish*

Mix together the shrimps or prawns, mayonnaise, cream, ketchup or purée, Worcestershire sauce, lemon juice, onion, celery or celery salt and salt. Serve on a lettuce leaf, garnished with chopped lettuce.

Herring Roes

175 g/6 oz soft herring
* roes*
4 bay leaves
300 ml/$\frac{1}{2}$ pint cider
4 peppercorns
salt
1 dill pickled cucumber,
* chopped*
1 teaspoon capers
little olive oil
buttered toast or
* crispbread*
cucumber slices to
* garnish*

Spread the roes flat in a baking dish and arrange the bay leaves on top. Put the cider, peppercorns and a pinch of salt in a saucepan and bring to the boil. Simmer for 2 minutes, then pour into the dish. Cover the dish and cook in a preheated moderately hot oven (200 C/400 F, Gas Mark 6) for 10 minutes. Cool.

Mix together the pickled cucumber, capers and oil and spread on toast or crispbread. Set one or two of the roes, carefully curled, on top and garnish with a twist of fresh cucumber.

Snails in Garlic Butter

Serves 3–4

*75 g/3 oz butter
1 tablespoon very finely
  chopped onion
2 garlic cloves, crushed
1 tablespoon chopped
  parsley
squeeze of lemon juice
salt
pepper
1 can escargots with
  shells (20 to 24 snails)*

Mash the butter with the onion, garlic, parsley, lemon juice, salt and pepper. Drain the snails and press one into each shell. Fill all the space in the shell with the garlic butter, pressing it well in. Arrange the shells in a baking dish, or snail dishes, so they will not fall over and bake in a preheated hot oven (220 C/425 F, Gas Mark 7) for 10 minutes. Serve hot with crusty bread.

Fish Cocktail

Serves 4

*1 small lettuce, shredded
225 g/8 oz smoked fish
  (cod or haddock),
  cooked and flaked
few pickled gherkins,
  chopped
French or other salad
  dressing*

Layer the lettuce, fish and gherkins in goblets, then pour over the dressing.

Cheese Pâté

Serves 4–6

*100 g/4 oz Lancashire
  cheese, grated
100 g/4 oz cream cheese
2 tablespoons milk
salt
pepper
2 teaspoons grated onion
1 teaspoon chopped
  capers
15 g/½ oz walnuts or
  hazelnuts, chopped
½ teaspoon made English
  mustard
paprika*

Mix together the grated cheese and cream cheese, then beat in the milk. Add the salt, pepper, onion, capers, nuts and mustard and mix well. Spoon into a dish and sprinkle with paprika. Chill well, then serve spread on biscuits. Alternatively, spread on toast and serve grilled.

Taramasalata

Serves 4–6

*3 slices of white bread,
  crusts removed
little milk
100 g/4 oz smoked cod
  roes, skinned
3 to 4 garlic cloves,
  crushed
juice of 1 lemon
4 tablespoons olive or
  corn oil
pepper*

Soak the bread in a little milk until well moistened, then squeeze out the excess milk. Blend all the ingredients together or pound in a mortar to a smooth consistency. Serve with warm pitta bread (see page 260) or toast.

Greek Eggs

Serves 4

*4 hard-boiled eggs
25 g/1 oz butter
pepper
3 teaspoons tomato
  ketchup
little lemon juice
75 g/3 oz cod roes,
  cooked, skinned and
  finely chopped
lettuce leaves
2 tablespoons mayonnaise
watercress to garnish*

Halve the eggs lengthways and scoop out the yolks. Mash the yolks with the butter, pepper, 1 teaspoon of the ketchup and the lemon juice. Mix in the cod roes. Stuff the egg white halves with this mixture.

Line a serving plate with lettuce leaves and arrange the egg halves on it.

Mix together the remaining ketchup and the mayonnaise and pour over the eggs. Garnish with watercress.

Terrine of Hare

Serves 8–10

*1 hare
1 onion
salt
pepper
pinch of grated nutmeg
200 ml/⅓ pint red wine
1 egg, beaten
6 streaky bacon rashers,
  rinded and stretched
flour and water paste*

Remove the hare meat from the bones and mince it with the onion. Add salt, pepper, the nutmeg, wine and egg and beat well.

Line an earthenware terrine with 4 of the bacon rashers. Spoon in the hare mixture and smooth the top, then cover with the remaining bacon rashers. Put the lid on the dish and seal with the flour and water paste.

Place the dish in a roasting tin of hot water and bake in a preheated moderate oven (180 C/350°F, Gas Mark 4) for 1½ hours. Leave to cool before unsealing.

Avocado Creams

Serves 4–5

2 ripe avocados, halved
  and stoned
75 g/3 oz soft cream
  cheese
1 garlic clove, crushed
  (optional)
1 tablespoon lemon juice
6 tablespoons single
  cream
salt
pepper
1 teaspoon gelatine
1 tablespoon hot water
chopped chives to garnish

Scoop out the avocado flesh and mash it, then beat in the cream cheese, garlic and lemon juice until smooth. Beat in the cream, salt and pepper. Dissolve the gelatine in the water and mix into the avocado mixture. Spoon into individual serving dishes, cover and chill for up to 2 hours. Sprinkle with chives and serve with oatcakes.

Ham Rolls

Serves 4

75 g/3 oz cream cheese
  or flavoured cheese
  spread
6 stuffed olives, chopped
2 tablespoons cream
1 teaspoon creamed
  horseradish
salt
pepper
225 g/8 oz cooked ham,
  thinly sliced

Mix together the cheese or cheese spread, olives, cream, horseradish, salt and pepper. Spread on the slices of ham, roll up and secure with cocktail sticks. Chill before serving.

Grape and Melon Coupe

Serves 6

175 g/6 oz grapes, halved
  and pipped
1 melon, peeled, seeded
  and diced
150 ml/¼ pint water
3 tablespoons honey
½ teaspoon ground ginger

Divide the grapes and melon between six glasses.
    Put the water and honey in a saucepan and bring to the boil. Simmer until syrupy, then remove from the heat and stir in the ginger. When cool, pour the syrup over the fruit.

Stuffed Tomatoes   *Serves 8*

8 large firm tomatoes
175 g/6 oz soft cream
 cheese
1 tablespoon chopped
 chives
salt
pinch of cayenne pepper
1½ tablespoons mayonnaise
walnut, cucumber or
 watercress to garnish

Cut the tops off the tomatoes. Scoops out the pulp and mix this with the cream cheese, chives, salt, cayenne and mayonnaise. Fill the tomatoes with the cheese mixture and garnish each with a piece of walnut or cucumber or a sprig of watercress.

Tomato Surprises   *Serves 4*

8 medium tomatoes
2 hard-boiled egg yolks
mayonnaise
salt
pepper
8 pickled walnut halves
lettuce to serve

Cut the tops off the tomatoes. Scoop out the pulp and mix this with the egg yolks, a little mayonnaise and salt and pepper.

Put a walnut half in each tomato and fill with the mayonnaise mixture. Replace the tops and serve on a bed of lettuce.

Devilled Avocado   *Serves 4*

2 avocados, halved and
 stoned
Worcestershire or
 Tabasco sauce
½ to 1 teaspoon curry
 powder
1 tablespoon mayonnaise
salt
pepper
2 tablespoons lemon juice
4 back bacon, rashers,
 rinded, cooked and
 crumbled
lemon slices to garnish

Scoop the avocado pulp out of the shells, keeping the shells intact. Mash the pulp until smooth, then beat in a few drops of Worcestershire or Tabasco sauce, the curry powder, mayonnaise, salt, pepper and lemon juice. Fold in the bacon.

Pile the mixture into the avocado shells and serve lightly chilled, garnished with lemon slices.

19

Soups

Cock-a-Leekie Soup
Serves 8

10 leeks, thinly sliced
1 × 1.5 kg/3 lb chicken,
  cleaned and trussed
2.25 litres/4 pints chicken
  stock
salt
pepper
10 prunes, soaked
  overnight

Blanch the leeks in boiling water for 2 minutes; drain and put into a large saucepan with the chicken, stock, salt and pepper. Bring to the boil, skim, cover and simmer for 2 hours.

Add the drained prunes and simmer for a further 30 minutes.

Remove the chicken from the pan. Untruss it and take the meat from the carcass. Put the meat in a warmed tureen, pour over the soup and serve.

Apple Soup
Serves 6

1 tablespoon cornflour
2 tablespoons cold water
450 ml/¾ pint apple purée
400 ml/14 fl oz berry
  juice (raspberry,
  loganberry or
  blackberry)
¼ teaspoon salt
2 teaspoons grated lemon
  rind
little honey (optional)
2 tablespoons lemon juice
150 ml/¼ pint white wine
grated nutmeg (optional)

Dissolve the cornflour in the water in a saucepan. Add the apple purée, berry juice, salt and lemon rind and stir well. Heat gently, stirring, until clear and thickened. Taste and add a little honey, if liked. Cool, then chill.

Stir in the lemon juice and wine before serving, sprinkled with nutmeg, if liked.

Berry Soup
Substitute 600 ml/1 pint stewed and sieved berries or currants for the berry juice above, and 150 ml/¼ pint single or soured cream for the wine.

20

Parsley and Potato Chowder   *Serves 4*

40 g/1½ oz butter or margarine
2 onions, finely chopped
40 g/1½ oz rice (brown or white)
350 g/12 oz potatoes, peeled and diced
600 ml/1 pint vegetable stock
75 g/3 oz bunch of parsley
salt
pepper
dash of Tabasco sauce
300 ml/½ pint milk
chopped salted peanuts to garnish

Melt the fat in a saucepan and fry the onions until softened. Stir in the rice and continue cooking for 2 minutes. Stir in the potatoes and stock.

Remove the stalks from the parsley, tie into a bunch with string and add to the pan. Bring to the boil and add salt, pepper and the Tabasco. Cover and simmer gently for 20 minutes or until the rice and potatoes are tender.

Finely chop the parsley tops. Discard the parsley stalks from the soup and stir in the chopped parsley and milk; Continue simmering for 5 to 10 minutes. Adjust the seasoning and serve sprinkled with the nuts, accompanied by hot granary bread and butter.

Watercress Soup   *Serves 6*

40 g/1½ oz butter
2 bunches of watercress
900 ml/1½ pints chicken stock
salt
pepper
2 tablespoons grated Parmesan cheese

Melt the butter in a saucepan and cook the watercress gently until it has softened, like spinach. Lift out the watercress, chop it finely and return to the pan. Stir in the stock and bring to the boil. Add salt, pepper and the cheese and serve.

Cream of Chicken Soup   *Serves 4*

25 g/1 oz butter
25 g/1 oz flour
600 ml/1 pint chicken stock
300 ml/½ pint milk
salt
pepper
1 egg yolk, beaten

Melt the butter in a saucepan and stir in the flour. Cook, stirring, for 2 minutes, then gradually stir in the stock and milk. Bring to the boil and simmer, still stirring, until thickened. Cool slightly, then strain the soup and return it to the cleaned pan. Add salt, pepper and the egg yolk and cook very gently, stirring, until the soup thickens.

Kidney and Beef Soup

Serves 4

*100 g/4 oz ox kidney, or
  2 sheep's kidneys
25 g/1 oz dripping
100 g/4 oz lean beef,
  diced or minced
1 small onion, sliced
600 ml/1 pint stock
¼ teaspoon celery seed
40 g/1½ oz long-grain rice
salt
pepper
croûtons to serve*

Soak the kidney in cold water for 15 minutes, then drain and remove the skin and core. Dice the kidney.

Melt the dripping in a saucepan and fry the kidney, beef and onion until the meat is browned. Stir in the stock, and the celery seed tied in muslin. Bring to the boil, skimming off the scum that rises to the surface. Add the rice. Cover and simmer gently for 2 hours, removing any scum as necessary.

Discard the celery seed. Pound the meat in the pan to break down the fibres, then sieve the soup, rubbing the meat and vegetable through the sieve. Reheat the soup, add salt and pepper and serve with croûtons.

Note: Sheep's kidney cooks more quickly than ox kidney.

Tomato Soup

Serves 5–6

*25 g/1 oz margarine
1 small carrot, diced
2 celery stalks, diced
1 onion, chopped
450 g/1 lb tomatoes,
  quartered
1 bouquet garni
salt
pepper
1 teaspoon sugar
2 cloves
600 ml/1 pint boiling
  water or stock
25 g/1 oz flour
2 tablespoons cold milk
chopped parsley to
  garnish*

Melt the margarine in a saucepan and fry the carrot, celery and onion until softened. Add the tomatoes, bouquet garni, salt, pepper, sugar, cloves and water or stock and bring to the boil. Cover and simmer for 20 minutes or until all the vegetables are tender.

Sieve the soup and return it to the pan. Dissolve the flour in the milk and add to the soup. Bring to the boil, stirring, and simmer for 15 minutes, stirring frequently. Serve sprinkled with parsley.

Green Tomato Soup   *Serves 6*

25 g/1 oz butter or
margarine
450 g/1 lb green
tomatoes, sliced
225 g/8 oz potatoes,
peeled and sliced
1 onion, chopped
1.2 litres/2 pints stock or
water
¼ teaspoon dried sage
salt
pepper
300 ml/½ pint creamy milk
chopped parsley to
garnish

Melt the fat in a saucepan and fry the tomatoes, potatoes and onion until softened. Add the stock or water, sage, salt and pepper and bring to the boil. Simmer for 30 minutes or until the vegetables are tender.

Sieve the soup and return to the pan. Stir in the milk and reheat. Serve hot or cold, garnished with parsley.

Lentil Soup   *Serves 6*

1.2 litres/2 pints bacon or
ham stock
225 g/8 oz lentils
1 onion, chopped
1 large carrot, grated
1 teaspoon chopped
parsley
snippets of fried bread to
serve

Remove all the fat from the stock, then bring it to the boil in a saucepan. Add the lentils and onion and simmer for 1 hour 10 minutes. Add the carrot and parsley and stir well. Simmer for a further 20 minutes or until the lentils are very tender and cooked down. Serve hot with fried bread snippets.

Leek and Potato Soup   *Serves 6*

50 g/2 oz mutton
dripping
1.2 litres/2 pints water
2 leeks, finely chopped
450 g/1 lb potatoes,
peeled and diced
salt
pepper
5 tablespoons milk or
single cream

Melt the dripping in a saucepan and stir in the water. Add the vegetables and salt and pepper and bring to the boil. Simmer gently for 2 hours.

Stir in the milk or cream before serving.

Vegetable Soup I

Serves 6

2 tablespoons olive oil
1 large onion, chopped
1 small swede, diced
1 slice of pumpkin or
  marrow, peeled, seeded
  and diced
½ small cabbage or 4
  Brussels sprouts,
  chopped
100 g/4 oz shelled peas
  or green beans, halved
4 to 6 tomatoes, skinned
  and chopped
few cauliflower florets
1 garlic clove, crushed
  (optional)
¼ teaspoon dried mixed
  herbs
salt
pepper
1.2 litres/2 pints water
grated cheese to serve

Heat the oil in a saucepan and add the vegetables, garlic, herbs, salt, pepper and water. Bring to the boil, then cover tightly and simmer for 1½ to 2 hours. Serve with grated cheese.
Note: Other vegetables in season may be used, but avoid turnip and potato.

Swiss Soup

Serves 4

25 g/1 oz margarine
2 tablespoons rolled oats
2 medium onions,
  chopped
2 carrots, chopped
2 potatoes, peeled and
  chopped
900 ml/1½ pints stock or
  water
salt
pepper
little milk (optional)
chopped parsley to
  garnish

Melt the margarine in a saucepan and fry the oats until lightly browned. Add the vegetables, water, salt and pepper and bring to the boil. Simmer gently for 30 minutes or until the vegetables are tender.

Sieve the soup and return to the pan. Stir in a little milk, if liked, and reheat. Serve garnished with parsley.

Vegetable Soup II
Serves 6

*100 g/4 oz carrots,
  shredded*
3 celery stalks, shredded
*100 g/4 oz spinach or
  watercress, shredded*
1 large onion, chopped
1.2 litres/2 pints water
*1 tablespoon chopped
  parsley*
salt
pepper
*4 tomatoes, skinned and
  chopped*
pinch of sugar
*1 green pepper, cored,
  seeded, and chopped
  (optional)*

Put the carrots, celery, spinach or watercress, onion, water, parsley, salt and pepper in a saucepan and bring to the boil. Simmer for 25 minutes.

Add the tomatoes, sugar and green pepper, if used, and simmer for a further 10 minutes or until all the vegetables are tender.

Cream of Vegetable Soup

Dissolve 1 tablespoon flour in 120 ml/4 fl oz milk and mix with 300 ml/½ pint of the soup before stirring into the rest of the soup. Bring to the boil, stirring, before serving.

Spanish Soup
Serves 6

*1.75 litres/3 pints chicken
  stock*
*175 g/6 oz cooked
  chicken, minced*
*75 g/3 oz cooked ham,
  minced*
*3 tablespoons sherry
  (optional)*
salt
pepper
6 eggs
*chopped parsley to
  garnish*

Bring the stock to the boil, then add the chicken and ham. Mix well, then stir in the sherry, if used, and salt and pepper. Heat through gently.

Break an egg into each of six warmed soup bowls and pour on the hot soup. Sprinkle with parsley and serve immediately.

Game Soup
Serves 4

game carcasses
6 white peppercorns
1 tablespoon salt
1 carrot, sliced
1 celery stalk, halved
1 onion, quartered
2 bay leaves
1 parsley sprig
150 ml/¼ pint port wine
225 g/8 oz cooked breast
   of game, chopped
hot toast to serve

Put the game carcasses on a baking sheet and place in a preheated hot oven (220 C/425 F, Gas Mark 7). Brown for 15 minutes, then tip the carcasses into a stock pot. Cover with cold water and bring to the boil, skimming off the scum. Add the peppercorns, salt, vegetables and herbs and simmer for 4 to 5 hours. Strain and cool.

When the stock is cold, remove any fat from the surface. Measure the stock and pour 1.2 litres/2 pints into a saucepan. Add the port and game and bring to the boil. Adjust the seasoning and serve hot with crisp hot dry toast.

Cream of Onion Soup
Serves 4

25 g/1 oz butter
2 small onions, finely
   chopped
300 ml/½ pint water
salt
pepper
300 ml/½ pint creamy milk
50 g/2 oz cheese, grated

Melt the butter in a saucepan and fry the onions until softened but not brown. Add the water, salt and pepper and bring to the boil. Simmer for 15 minutes.

Allow to cool slightly, then stir in the milk and reheat. Remove from the heat and stir in the cheese. Keep warm, but not over direct heat, for 5 minutes and serve.

Iced Cucumber and Yogurt Soup
Serves 4

1 large cucumber, grated
275 g/10 oz natural
   yogurt
1 tablespoon tarragon
   vinegar
2 tablespoons chopped
   chives
salt
pepper
1 tablespoon finely
   chopped gherkin
50 g/2 oz shelled prawns

Mix together the cucumber, yogurt, vinegar, chives, salt and pepper. Chill well. Stir in the gherkin and prawns just before serving.

White Foam Soup
Serves 4

40 g/1½ oz butter
25 g/1 oz flour
600 ml/1 pint milk
300 ml/½ pint stock
1 onion, finely chopped
1 small leek, finely chopped
1 celery stalk, finely chopped
pinch of ground mace
salt
pepper
2 eggs, separated
50 g/2 oz cheese, grated
chopped parsley to garnish

Melt the butter in a saucepan and add the flour. Cook, stirring, for 2 minutes, then gradually stir in the milk and stock. Bring to the boil, stirring. Add the vegetables, mace, salt and pepper and stir well. Cover and simmer gently for 30 minutes.

Beat the egg yolks slightly and mix in a little of the hot soup. Stir this into the rest of the soup with the cheese and heat gently, stirring, until the cheese has melted.

Whisk the egg whites until stiff. Fold half into the soup and divide the remainder between soup bowls or a tureen. Pour over the soup and sprinkle with parsley.

Cream of Chestnut Soup with Mornay Toast
Serves 6

450 g/1 lb chestnuts
40 g/1½ oz butter
2 carrots, thinly sliced
2 onions, chopped
1 small head of celery with leaves, chopped
3 parsley sprigs, chopped
1.2 litres/2 pints water
salt
pepper
2 tablespoons single cream or top of milk

Blanch the chestnuts in boiling water for 5 minutes. Remove them one by one and take off the skin and peel.

Melt the butter in a saucepan and gently stew the carrots, onions, celery and parsley until softened. Add the water, salt and pepper and bring to the boil. Simmer gently for 1 hour, then strain the stock and reserve.

Use half the stock to cook the chestnuts until they are quite soft. Sieve or blend to a purée and return to the pan. Stir in the remaining stock and adjust the seasoning. Reheat and stir in the cream before serving with Mornay toast.

Mornay Toast

Lay fingers of thinly sliced bread on a baking sheet and sprinkle thickly with grated cheese. Bake in a preheated moderately hot oven (200 C/400 F, Gas Mark 6) until brown and crisp. Serve hot.

Peasant Soup

Serves 6

25 g/1 oz butter
2 tablespoons oil
100 g/4 oz streaky bacon
  rashers, rinded and
  diced
450 g/1 lb leeks, chopped
5 celery stalks, thinly
  sliced
350 g/12 oz carrots,
  thinly sliced
350 g/12 oz courgettes,
  thinly sliced
1 large Spanish onion,
  chopped
1 garlic clove, crushed
1.75 litres/3 pints chicken
  stock
salt
pepper
1½ tablespoons tomato
  purée
4 tablespoons chopped
  parsley

Melt the butter with the oil in a saucepan. Add the bacon and fry for 3 minutes, then stir in the vegetables and garlic. Cover and cook gently for 20 minutes. Stir in the stock, salt and pepper and bring to the boil. Simmer gently for 2 hours.

Just before serving, stir in the tomato purée and parsley.

Note: Vegetables may be varied according to what is in season.

New England Clam Chowder

Serves 4

25 g/1 oz butter, or 2
  tablespoons oil
100 g/4 oz salt pork,
  diced
2 medium onions,
  chopped
2 medium potatoes,
  peeled and diced
600 ml/1 pint milk
salt
pepper
1 × 275 g/10 oz can clams
chopped parsley and
  butter to garnish

Melt the butter, or heat the oil, in a saucepan and fry the salt pork until it is crisp. Add the onions and continue cooking until they are softened. Add the potatoes and milk, stir well and cook until the potatoes are tender. Add salt, pepper and the clams with their liquor and heat through gently, stirring well. Serve hot, with each bowl garnished with parsley and a knob of butter.

Creamed Mixed Vegetable Soup
Serves 5–6

50 g/2 oz margarine or
 dripping
225 g/8 oz potatoes,
 peeled and diced
225 g/8 oz carrots,
 chopped
225 g/8 oz onions,
 chopped
225 g/8 oz tomatoes,
 halved
600 ml/1 pint stock
300 ml/½ pint milk
salt
pepper
grated cheese, croûtons,
 watercress or parsley
 to serve

Melt the margarine or dripping in a saucepan and add the vegetables. Cook gently until softened but not brown. Stir in the stock and bring to the boil. Simmer for 30 minutes or until the vegetables are tender.

Sieve the soup and return to the saucepan. Stir in the milk, salt and pepper and reheat. Serve with cheese, croûtons, watercress or parsley.

Note: Other vegetables in season may be used.

Bean and Bacon Chowder
Serves 4

25 g/1 oz butter or
 margarine
1 large onion, finely
 chopped
175 g/6 oz lean bacon
 rashers, rinded and
 diced
1 tablespoon flour
900 ml/1½ pints chicken
 stock
350 g/12 oz runner beans,
 thinly sliced
40 g/1½ oz long-grain rice
salt
pepper
Tabasco sauce
1 to 2 tablespoons
 chopped fresh herbs
croûtons to garnish

Melt the butter or margarine in a saucepan and fry the onion and bacon until golden brown. Stir in the flour, then gradually stir in the stock. Bring to the boil. Add the beans, rice, salt and pepper, cover the pan and simmer gently for 20 minutes.

Add a few drops of Tabasco sauce and the herbs. Serve garnished with croûtons.

Summer Tomato Soup

Serves 5–6

1 kg/2 lb ripe tomatoes
½ teaspoon lemon juice
* or vinegar*
½ teaspoon onion juice or
* finely grated onion*
¼ cucumber, peeled and
* diced*
1 tablespoon sugar
salt
pepper or Tabasco sauce
4 thin slices of cooked
* ham, finely diced*
2 tablespoons double
* cream*
parsley sprigs to garnish

Sieve the tomatoes, then chill well. Add the lemon juice or vinegar, onion juice or onion, cucumber, sugar, salt, pepper or Tabasco, ham and cream and mix together. Chill again. Serve in glasses, garnished with parsley.

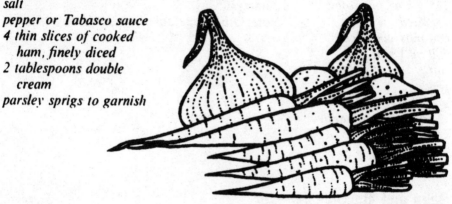

Carrot Soup

Serves 5

25 g/1 oz butter or
* margarine*
450 g/1 lb carrots,
* chopped*
1 medium potato, peeled
* and chopped*
1 onion, chopped
900 ml/1½ pints chicken
* stock*
salt
pepper
few bacon rinds
* (optional)*
pinch of dried tarragon
* or chopped chives and*
* top of milk to garnish*
* (optional)*

Melt the fat in a saucepan and add the vegetables. Cover and cook gently until the vegetables have absorbed the fat. Add the stock, salt, pepper and bacon rinds, if used, and bring to the boil. Simmer until the vegetables are soft.

Discard the bacon rinds and sieve or blend the soup to a smooth purée. Return to the saucepan and reheat. Adjust the seasoning and stir in the tarragon, if used. Alternatively, garnish with chopped chives and top of the milk.

Kidney Soup
Serves 4

225 g/8 oz ox kidney
25 g/1 oz dripping
1 small onion, thinly
sliced
1.2 litres/2 pints brown
stock
1 small carrot, chopped
1 small turnip, chopped
salt
pepper
1 bouquet garni
25 g/1 oz flour
4 tablespoons cold water

Soak the kidney in cold water for 15 minutes, then drain and remove the skin and core. Slice the kidney.

Melt the dripping in a saucepan and fry the onion until softened. Add the kidney and fry until browned. Stir in the stock, vegetables, salt, pepper and bouquet garni. Bring to the boil, then simmer for 1½ to 2 hours.

Strain the soup into a clean saucepan, reserving the kidney. Cut the kidney into dice and return to the soup. Dissolve the flour in the water and stir into the soup. Bring back to the boil, stirring, and simmer for 3 to 4 minutes before serving.

Cream of Mushroom Soup
Serves 4

50 g/2 oz butter or
margarine
225 g/8 oz mushrooms,
finely chopped
50 g/2 oz flour
600 ml/1 pint stock
450 ml/¾ pint milk
salt
pepper

Melt the fat in a saucepan. Add the mushrooms and fry, stirring, for 5 minutes. Add the flour and stir in well. Cook for a further 2 minutes. Gradually stir in the stock and milk and bring to the boil, stirring. Simmer until thickened. Add salt and pepper and serve.

Cream of Sweetcorn Soup
Serves 4-6

25 g/1 oz butter
1 teaspoon chopped onion
400 g/14 oz canned
sweetcorn, drained
1 bay leaf
2 peppercorns
600 ml/1 pint stock
1 tablespoon cornflour
300 ml/½ pint milk
salt
pepper

Melt the butter in a saucepan and add the onion, sweetcorn, bay leaf and peppercorns. Cook gently for 5 minutes, then stir in the stock. Bring to the boil, cover and simmer for 25 minutes.

Remove the bay leaf and peppercorns and sieve the soup. Return it to the saucepan. Dissolve the cornflour in the milk and add to the pan with salt and pepper. Bring to the boil, stirring, and simmer for 8 to 12 minutes.

31

Beanpot Chowder
Serves 4–6

2 tablespoons oil
1 large onion, finely
  chopped
1 leek, chopped
1 garlic clove, crushed
4 streaky bacon rashers,
  rinded and chopped
2 tablespoons flour
600 ml/1 pint chicken
  stock
100 to 175 g/4 to 6 oz
  dried butter beans,
  soaked overnight
425 g/15 oz canned
  tomatoes
salt
pepper
1 bay leaf
chopped fresh herbs to
  garnish

Heat the oil in a saucepan and fry the onion until softened. Stir in the leek, garlic and bacon and fry gently for 5 minutes. Add the flour and stir well, then gradually stir in the stock. Bring to the boil. Drain the beans and add to the pan with the tomatoes, salt, pepper and bay leaf. Return to the boil, cover and simmer gently for about 1 hour or until the beans are tender.

Discard the bay leaf and serve sprinkled with fresh herbs.

Onion Soup
Serves 4

50 g/2 oz bacon fat
6 medium onions, thinly
  sliced
stale white bread slices,
  crusts removed
75 to 100 g/3 to 4 oz
  cheese, grated
salt
pepper
600 ml/1 pint chicken
  stock or water
chopped parsley to
  garnish

Melt the fat in a frying pan and fry the onions gently until they are softened. Remove from the heat.

Line a casserole with bread slices. Cover with a layer of onions, then a layer of grated cheese and then a layer of bread fingers. Continue making layers in this way to fill the casserole, ending with cheese. Add salt and pepper.

Pour the stock into the frying pan and bring to the boil. Pour into the casserole, then bake in a preheated moderate oven (180°C/350°F, Gas Mark 4) for 30 minutes. Serve hot, garnished with parsley.

Herby Onion Soup

Serves 6–8

300 ml/½ pint milk
1 bay leaf
1 rosemary sprig
1 clove
1 parsley sprig
1 thyme sprig
25 g/1 oz butter
3 large onions, chopped
25 g/1 oz flour
900 ml/1½ pints stock
salt
pepper

Put the milk, bay leaf, rosemary, clove, parsley and thyme in a saucepan and heat until bubbles form around the edge. Remove from the heat, cover the pan and leave to infuse for 15 minutes.

Meanwhile, melt the butter in another saucepan and add the onions. Cover the pan and cook gently until the onions are very soft but not brown. Stir in the flour and cook for 3 to 4 minutes, stirring well. Gradually stir in the stock and bring to the boil, stirring. Strain the milk and add to the pan with salt and pepper. Serve hot.

Tripe Soup

Serves 6–8

1 kg/2 lb tripe, cut into small pieces
2.25 litres/4 pints white stock
2 onions, minced
2 potatoes, chopped
25 g/1 oz butter
25 g/1 oz flour
300 ml/½ pint milk
chopped parsley
salt
pepper

Put the tripe into a saucepan with the stock, onions and potatoes. Bring to the boil, then simmer for 1 hour.

Blend the butter and flour to a paste and add to the pan in small pieces, stirring. Simmer until thickened. Add the milk, parsley, salt and pepper and heat through.

Mock Kidney Soup

Serves 7–8

225 g/8 oz liver
2.25 litres/4 pints water
piece of turnip, chopped
1 large carrot, chopped
1 onion, chopped
salt
pepper
pinch of ground cloves
1 tablespoon flour

Put the liver in a saucepan with the water and vegetables. Bring to the boil and simmer for 1 hour. Grate or mince the liver and return it to the pan with salt, pepper and the cloves. Mix the flour with a little water and add to the pan. Simmer, stirring, for 5 minutes

Scotch Broth
Serves 6

25 g/1 oz pearl barley
225 g/8 oz boiling beef
1.2 litres/2 pints water
225 g/8 oz carrots, diced
450 g/1 lb swede, diced
75 g/3 oz onion or leek,
  sliced
salt
pepper
50 g/2 oz cabbage, sliced
1 tablespoon chopped
  parsley

Pour boiling water over the barley, leave for 1 minute, then drain. Put the barley into a saucepan with the beef and water and bring to the boil, skimming off any scum from the surface. Simmer for 1 hour.

Add the carrots, swede, onion or leek, salt and pepper and continue simmering for 1½ to 2 hours. Add the cabbage 15 minutes before the cooking time is up.

Stir in the parsley and serve.

Crab and Potato Soup
Serves 4-5

450 g/1 lb potatoes,
  peeled and chopped
600 ml/1 pint stock
225 g/8 oz fresh or
  canned crabmeat,
  flaked
1 garlic clove, crushed
1 tablespoon chopped
  fresh chives
salt
pepper
150 ml/¼ pint milk

Put the potatoes and stock in a saucepan and bring to the boil. Simmer until the potatoes are tender. Sieve or blend to a purée, then return to the pan. Add the crabmeat, garlic, chives, salt and pepper and simmer gently for 5 minutes. Stir in the milk and heat through.

Avgolemono (Greek Lemon Soup)   *Serves 6*

*1.2 litres/2 pints chicken
    stock
50 g/2 oz rice
2 egg yolks
juice of 1 lemon
2 tablespoons top of milk
lemon slices and chopped
    parsley to garnish*

Bring the stock to the boil in a saucepan. Add the rice and cook until it is tender. Beat the egg yolks and lemon juice together in a small bowl. Mix in a little of the hot stock, then add this mixture to the rest of the stock. Heat through very gently, then serve in bowls swirled with the top of the milk and garnished with lemon slices and parsley.

Mediterranean Soup   *Serves 6–8*

*25 g/1 oz butter
2 onions, chopped
4 tomatoes, skinned and
    sliced
900 ml/1½ pints stock or
    water
4 potatoes, peeled and
    quartered
100 g/4 oz green beans,
    sliced
salt
pepper*

Pistou
*4 basil leaves
3 garlic cloves
1 tablespoon olive oil
1 tablespoon grated
    Parmesan cheese*

Melt the butter in a saucepan and fry the onions until softened. Add the tomatoes, stock or water, potatoes, beans, salt and pepper and bring to the boil. Cover and simmer for 40 minutes.

Meanwhile, for the pistou, crush the basil and garlic with the oil in a mortar and pestle. Pound in the cheese.

Add the pistou to the soup just before serving.

Quick Cheese Soup

Serves 4

25 g/1 oz butter
1 small onion, finely
  chopped
25 g/1 oz flour
600 ml/1 pint milk
300 ml/½ pint water
2 tablespoons tomato
  purée (optional)
salt
pepper
100 g/4 oz Cheddar
  cheese, grated
croûtons to serve

Melt the butter in a saucepan and fry the onion until softened. Add the flour and cook, stirring, for 2 minutes. Gradually stir in the milk and water, followed by the tomato purée, if using, then bring to the boil, still stirring. Add salt and pepper and simmer for 10 minutes.

Stir in the grated cheese until melted and serve hot, with croûtons.

Fish Chowder

Serves 4–5

40 g/1½ oz butter
1 onion, finely chopped
40 g/1½ oz flour
600 ml/1 pint milk
150 ml/¼ pint white wine
grated rind of ½ lemon
225 g/8 oz white fish
  fillets, cooked and
  flaked
salt
pepper
150 ml/¼ pint double
  cream
2 tablespoons chopped
  parsley
thin lemon slices to
  garnish

Melt the butter in a saucepan and fry the onion until softened. Stir in the flour and cook for 2 minutes, then gradually stir in the milk and wine. Bring to the boil, stirring. Add the lemon rind, fish, salt and pepper and simmer for 15 minutes.

Stir in the cream and parsley and heat through gently. Serve garnished with lemon slices.

Fish

Shrimpers
Serves 4

225 g/8 oz cod fillets,
*   skinned and flaked*
1 tablespoon oil
2 teaspoons tomato purée
lemon juice
salt
pepper
100 g/4 oz shelled
*   shrimps*
self-raising flour
oil for deep frying
tartare sauce to serve

Mix the cod with the oil, tomato purée, and lemon juice, salt and pepper to taste. Mix in the shrimps, then bind with flour. Shape into walnut-sized balls and deep fry until golden brown. Drain on paper towels and serve hot with tartare sauce.

Kedgeree
Serves 4

350 g/12 oz smoked
*   haddock or cod*
1 teaspoon salt
saffron powder (optional)
175 g/6 oz long-grain rice
100 g/4 oz butter or
*   margarine*
4 hard-boiled eggs,
*   chopped*

Poach the fish in a little water until it will flake easily. Remove the fish from the pan with a slotted spoon and set aside.

Add more water to the pan with the salt and a pinch of saffron, if used, and bring to the boil. Sprinkle in the rice and cook until it is tender. Drain the rice, if necessary, and dry it in a warm place.

Meanwhile, flake the fish, removing all skin and large bones.

Melt the fat in another saucepan and add the fish, rice, eggs and another pinch of saffron, if liked. Heat through gently, stirring well, and serve hot.

37

Cider Cod Pie
Serves 4

*350 g/12 oz cod fillet,
skinned and cut into
2.5 cm/1 inch cubes
300 ml/½ pint medium
sweet cider
450 g/1 lb potatoes,
peeled, cooked and
mashed
25 g/1 oz margarine
25 g/1 oz flour
salt
50 g/2 oz cheese, grated
2 tomatoes, sliced*

Put the cod cubes in a baking dish and pour over the cider. Cover with a sheet of greased greaseproof paper and bake in a preheated moderate oven (180 C/350°F, Gas Mark 4) for about 30 minutes or until the fish will flake easily. Drain the cider from the dish and reserve. Keep the fish hot.

Melt the margarine in a saucepan and add the flour. Cook, stirring, for 2 minutes, then gradually stir in the reserved cider. Bring to the boil and simmer, still stirring, until thickened. Season with a little salt.

Spoon or pipe the mashed potato around the edge of a flameproof serving dish and put the fish in the centre. Pour over the sauce. Sprinkle with the cheese and garnish with the tomato slices. Brown in a preheated moderately hot oven (190 C/375 F, Gas Mark 5) for 15 minutes or under the grill.

Plaice Marengo
Serves 2

*450 g/1 lb plaice, filleted
and skinned
juice of 1 lemon
298 g/10½ oz canned
condensed tomato soup
chopped parsley, lemon
butterflies and red
pepper rings to garnish*
Stuffing
*50 g/2 oz margarine
½ small onion, chopped
6 tablespoons fresh
breadcrumbs
salt
pepper
1 tablespoon chopped
parsley
pinch of paprika*

First make the stuffing. Melt the margarine in a frying pan and fry the onion until softened. Remove from the heat and stir in the remaining stuffing ingredients.

Sprinkle the plaice fillets with lemon juice and put them in a baking dish, alternating with stuffing. Pour the soup around the fish and cover the dish. Bake in a preheated moderately hot oven (190 C/375 F, Gas Mark 5) for 45 minutes. Garnish with parsley, lemon butterflies and red pepper rings.

Stuffed Fillets of Plaice   *Serves 2*

4 plaice fillets
2 tablespoons chopped
  shallots
1 lemon slice
1 teaspoon capers
4 button mushrooms
salt
pepper
300 ml/½ pint mixed white
  wine and tomato juice

Roll the fillets loosely, tail first, skin side inside, and arrange them in a buttered baking dish. Open them slightly so there is a cavity in the centre of each roll.

Mince together the shallots and lemon and mix with the capers. Fill the cavities in the fish rolls with this mixture and stopper each with a mushroom. Sprinkle with salt and pepper and pour around the wine and tomato juice. Cover the dish and bake in a preheated moderate oven (180 C/350 F, Gas Mark 4) for 20 minutes or until the fish will flake easily.

Baked Fish with Mornay Sauce   *Serves 2*

1 whole cod or haddock,
  cleaned, or 450 g/1 lb
  middle steak of cod
½ teaspoon chopped
  parsley
½ teaspoon chopped fresh
  thyme
½ teaspoon chopped fresh
  sage
½ teaspoon chopped fresh
  rosemary
1 small shallot, chopped
1 tomato, cut into eighths
salt
paprika
25 g/1 oz butter

Mornay Sauce
300 ml/½ pint white sauce
1 egg yolk
25 g/1 oz Parmesan
  cheese, grated
25 g/1 oz Gruyère cheese,
  grated
salt
cayenne pepper

Cut deep slits into the flesh of the fish. Mix together the herbs and shallot and insert in the slits in the fish with the tomato segments. Place the fish in a baking dish and sprinkle over a little salt and paprika.

Put the butter in the dish, cover and bake in a preheated moderate oven (180°C/350°F, Gas Mark 4) for 30 minutes or until the fish flakes easily.

Meanwhile, make the sauce. If necessary, heat the white sauce, then beat in the egg yolk. Add the cheese, salt and cayenne and stir until the sauce is smooth.

Serve the fish with the mornay sauce.

Haddock Espagñol

Serves 3–4

50 g/2 oz long-grain rice
25 g/1 oz butter
1 small onion, finely
  chopped
225 g/8 oz tomatoes,
  skinned and chopped
225 g/8 oz smoked
  haddock, cooked,
  skinned, boned and
  flaked
salt
pepper
chopped parsley to
  garnish

Cook the rice in boiling salted water until tender.

Meanwhile, melt the butter in a saucepan and fry the onion until softened. Stir in the tomatoes, fish, salt and pepper and heat through gently.

Pile the fish mixture in the centre of a warmed serving dish and arrange the rice around it. Garnish with parsley.

Fish Soufflé

Serves 4

25 g/1 oz butter
25 g/1 oz flour
150 ml/¼ pint milk
100 g/4 oz Cheddar
  cheese, grated
225 g/8 oz cooked cod or
  haddock, skinned,
  boned and flaked
2 eggs, separated
salt
pepper
squeeze of lemon juice
½ teaspoon dry mustard
  powder

Melt the butter in a saucepan and add the flour. Cook, stirring, for 1 minute, then gradually stir in the milk and the grated cheese. Cook, stirring, until thick. Remove from the heat and add the fish. Pound together, then beat in the egg yolks, salt, pepper, lemon juice and mustard powder.

Whisk the egg whites until stiff and fold into the fish mixture. Spoon into a greased mould. Cook in a moderately hot oven (190°–200°C/ 375°–400°F, Gas Mark 5–6) for 30 minutes. Serve at once.

Halibut Bake

Serves 2

2 × 225 g/8 oz halibut
  steaks
150 ml/¼ pint dry cider
¼ teaspoon ground mace
1 teaspoon finely chopped
  fresh herbs

Arrange the halibut steaks in a buttered baking dish. Mix together the cider, mace and herbs and pour over the fish. Cover the dish and bake in a preheated moderately hot oven (200°C/400°F, Gas Mark 6) for 15 to 20 minutes or until the fish will flake easily.

Fillets of Sole Cardinal

Serves 4

4 sole fillets
150 ml/¼ pint white wine
salt
pepper
hot mashed potatoes
150 ml/¼ pint hot white
  sauce
4 slices of lobster back,
  or 100 g/4 oz shelled
  prawns, warmed
  through

Fold the fillets in half and arrange in a buttered baking dish. Pour over the wine and sprinkle with salt and pepper. Leave for 10 minutes, then bake in a preheated moderately hot oven (200 C/400 F, Gas Mark 6) for 10 minutes or until cooked.

Pile the mashed potatoes in the centre of a warmed serving dish. Arrange the fillets on the potatoes, overlapping each other. Coat the fillets with the sauce and garnish with the lobster or prawns. Serve hot.

Plaice with Béchamel Sauce

Serves 4

4 tablespoons chopped
  mushrooms
1 tablespoon chopped
  parsley
1 tablespoon finely
chopped onion
salt
pepper
4 plaice fillets, skinned
paprika
parsley sprigs and lemon
  wedges to garnish

Béchamel Sauce

300 ml/½ pint milk
1 slice of onion
1 slice of turnip
1 piece of celery or celery
  salt
1 bouquet garni
1 mace blade
3 peppercorns
2 cloves
25 g/1 oz butter or
  margarine
25 g/1 oz flour

Mix together the mushrooms, parsley, onion, salt and pepper. Divide between the plaice fillets and fold in half. Arrange in a greased baking dish and cover. Bake in a preheated moderate oven (180 C/350 F, Gas Mark 4) for 20 minutes.

Meanwhile, for the sauce, put the milk, onion, turnip, celery, bouquet garni, mace, peppercorns and cloves in a saucepan and heat until bubbles form around the edges. Remove from the heat, cover and leave to infuse for 15 minutes.

Strain the milk. Melt the butter in a clean saucepan and add the flour. Cook, stirring, for 2 minutes, then gradually stir in the strained milk. Bring to the boil and simmer, still stirring, until thickened.

Pour the sauce over the fish, sprinkle with paprika and garnish with parsley and lemon wedges.

Koulibiac

Serves 4–6

350 g/12 oz puff pastry
beaten egg to glaze
Filling
350 g/12 oz white fish
fillets
150 ml/¼ pint milk
salt
pepper
1 bay leaf
25 g/1 oz butter
1 small onion, chopped
75 g/3 oz mushrooms,
sliced
1 tablespoon flour
1 tablespoon capers
2 hard-boiled eggs, sliced
25 g/1 oz rice, cooked

For the filling, put the fish, milk, salt, pepper and bay leaf in a saucepan and poach gently until the fish will flake easily. Drain off the milk and reserve 150 ml/¼ pint. Discard the bay leaf and flake the fish.

Melt the butter in a clean saucepan and fry the onion until softened. Add the mushrooms and fry for a further 3 minutes. Sprinkle over the flour and cook, stirring, for 1 minute. Gradually stir in the reserved milk and bring to the boil. Simmer, stirring, until thickened. Remove from the heat and stir in the fish and capers. Cool.

Roll out the dough and trim to a 30 cm/12 inch square. Spread half the fish mixture down the centre third of the dough square, leaving a 2.5 cm/1 inch margin at each end. Cover with the egg slices, then the rice and spread over the remaining fish mixture. Cut the outside two-thirds of the dough square into strips about 2.5 cm/1 inch wide, to within 4 cm/1½ inches of the filling.

Fold the ends of the dough square over the filling and brush with beaten egg. Take a strip from one side and fold it over the filling, then follow with a strip from the other side, plaiting down the length. Brush each strip with beaten egg as it is plaited. Transfer the koulibiac to a baking sheet.

Brush all over with beaten egg and bake in a preheated hot oven (220 C/425 F, Gas Mark 7) for 30 minutes. Reduce the heat to moderate (180°C/350°F, Gas Mark 4) and bake for a further 10 to 15 minutes. Cover with grease-proof paper if the koulibiac is browning too much. Serve hot or cold.

Sunset Fish Salad
Serves 6

*750 g/1½ lb cod or hake,
    cooked, skinned, boned
    and flaked*
25 g/1 oz butter
25 g/1 oz flour
300 ml/½ pint milk
salt
pepper
¼ teaspoon dry mustard
pinch of grated nutmeg
3 eggs, separated
*1 tablespoon white wine
    (elderflower is good)*
2 tablespoons cream
lettuce to serve

Sunset Dressing
1 egg yolk
1 tablespoon vinegar
½ teaspoon dry mustard
pinch of paprika
2½ teaspoons sugar
pinch of salt
120 ml/4 fl oz olive oil
*1 tablespoon boiling
    water*
1½ tablespoons lemon juice

Sieve the fish or blend to a smooth purée. Melt the butter in a saucepan and add the flour. Cook, stirring, for 2 minutes, then gradually stir in the milk. Bring to the boil and simmer, still stirring, until thickened. Add salt, pepper, the mustard and nutmeg and remove from the heat. Cool slightly. Beat the egg yolks with the wine, then gradually beat in the warm sauce. Mix in the fish and cream. Whisk the egg whites until stiff and fold in.

Spoon into a greased casserole and bake in a preheated moderate oven (180 C/350 F, Gas Mark 4) for 45 minutes. Cool, then chill.

Meanwhile, make the dressing. Put the egg yolk, vinegar and seasonings in the blender goblet and blend at high speed for 15 seconds. Add the oil in a thin steady stream. When the mixture begins to thicken, add the oil more quickly. When all the oil has been added, mix in the boiling water and lemon juice.

Line a serving plate with lettuce leaves and turn out the fish salad. Pour over the dressing and serve.

Golden Puff Grill
Serves 3

*3 halibut, cod or haddock
    fillets*
*1 tablespoon melted
    butter or oil*
1 egg white
25 g/1 oz cheese, grated
salt
pinch of cayenne pepper

Arrange the fish fillets on the grill rack and brush with the butter or oil. Cook under a preheated grill for 5 to 10 minutes, turning once, until the fish is cooked through.

Whisk the egg white until stiff and fold in the cheese, salt and cayenne. Spread this mixture over the fillets and grill until the top is golden and puffy. Serve with a crisp green salad and heated potato crisps.

Enveloped Herrings
Serves 4

40 g/1½ oz butter
salt
pepper
4 shallots, finely chopped
4 mushrooms, finely
  chopped
4 teaspoons chopped
  parsley
4 equal-sized herrings
4 slices of fried bread,
  cut to fit the herrings
finely grated lemon rind
  to garnish

Cut four ovals from greaseproof paper large enough to wrap the herrings. Grease the paper with half the butter and sprinkle with salt and pepper.

Melt the remaining butter in a frying pan and fry the shallots and mushrooms until softened. Stir in half the parsley and salt and pepper.

Split the herrings down the backbone and stuff with the mushroom mixture. Reshape the herrings and wrap individually in the paper ovals. Place in a baking dish and bake in a preheated moderate oven (180 C/350 F, Gas Mark 4) for 30 to 40 minutes or until the fish will flake easily.

Unwrap the fish and place on the fried bread. Garnish with the remaining parsley and the lemon rind.

Fish Flan
Serves 4

175 g/6 oz shortcrust
  pastry
25 g/1 oz butter
1 small onion, thinly
  sliced
150 ml/¼ pint single
  cream or top of milk
salt
pepper
grated nutmeg
2 eggs, beaten
3 large ripe tomatoes,
  skinned, sliced and
  seeded
100 g/4 oz fresh or
  smoked haddock,
  kipper, salmon, etc.,
  cooked, skinned, boned
  and flaked
25 g/1 oz cheese, grated

Roll out the dough and use to line an 18 cm/7 inch flan tin. Bake blind in a preheated moderately hot oven (190 C/375 F, Gas Mark 5) for 10 to 15 minutes or until just set.

Meanwhile, melt the butter in a saucepan and fry the onion until softened. Remove from the heat and stir in the cream, salt, pepper, nutmeg and eggs.

Arrange the tomato slices and fish in the flan case and pour over the onion and egg mixture. Sprinkle with the cheese and bake in a preheated moderate oven (180 C/350 F, Gas Mark 4) for 25 minutes or until set and golden.

Devilled Cod
Serves 4

4 cod cutlets
15 g/½ oz butter
salt
pepper
4 small parsley sprigs
'Devil'
1 tablespoon
  Worcestershire sauce
6 tablespoons tomato
  ketchup
pinch of cayenne pepper
1 teaspoon anchovy
  essence
dash of Tabasco sauce

Arrange the cutlets in a buttered baking dish. Dot with the butter and sprinkle with salt and pepper. Cover and bake in a preheated moderately hot oven (190 C/375 F, Gas Mark 5) for 20 minutes or until the fish will flake easily.

Meanwhile, put all the ingredients for the 'devil' in a saucepan and heat through, stirring.

Transfer the fish to a warmed serving dish and pour over the 'devil'. Garnish with the parsley.

Trout à la Meunière
Serves 4

4 trout, cleaned
salt
pepper
flour for coating
65 g/2½ oz butter
1 teaspoon oil
Beurre Noisette
75 g/3 oz butter

Rub the trout with salt and pepper, then coat lightly with flour. Melt 65 g/2½ oz of butter with the oil in a frying pan. Slip in the trout and cook gently until brown on both sides and cooked through.

To make the beurre noisette, melt the butter and heat until light brown. Pour over the trout and serve hot.

Soused Mackerel
Serves 4

1 carrot, thinly sliced
1 onion, thinly sliced
4 parsley sprigs
4 dill sprigs
4 bay leaves
6 juniper berries
1 teaspoon salt
pepper
juice of 1 lemon
dry cider
4 mackerel, cleaned

Put the carrot, onion, parsley, dill, bay leaves, juniper berries, salt and pepper in a saucepan and add the lemon juice. Pour over enough cider to cover and bring to the boil. Simmer until the vegetables are soft.

Arrange the mackerel in a baking dish and pour over the cider mixture. Cover the dish and bake in a preheated cool oven (150 C/300 F, Gas Mark 2) for 1½ hours.

Serve hot, with the strained liquid, or cold with a cucumber salad.

Fish Cakes
Serves 4

225 g/8 oz instant
  mashed potato
knob of butter
1 egg, beaten
225 g/8 oz cod, hake or
  fresh haddock fillets,
  cooked, skinned and
  flaked
salt
pepper
pinch of grated nutmeg
oil and butter for shallow
  frying

Make up the potato as directed on the packet, using a little less water so that the mixture is firm. Add the butter and egg and beat well. Fold in the fish and add salt, pepper and the nutmeg. On a floured board form into round flat cakes.

Shallow fry the fish cakes in oil and butter and serve hot.

Variations: Add finely chopped parsley, dill or fennel leaves or a few capers. Use canned salmon instead of the fresh fish.

Woodcock of the Sea

1 slice of fennel, diced
1 mullet per person,
  cleaned and scaled
white wine
olive oil
stoned black olives

Scatter the fennel dice over the bottom of a buttered baking dish. Arrange the mullet on top and cover with a mixture of equal parts wine and olive oil. Bake uncovered in a pre-heated moderate oven (180 C/350 F, Gas Mark 4) for 15 minutes.

Add some black olives and bake for a further 5 minutes or until the fish will flake easily. Serve hot.

Note: Woodcock of the sea is the country name for red or grey mullet, and implies that it should be cooked with its insides in. However, clean the fish if you prefer.

Fish au Gratin
Serves 4

450 g/1 lb white fish
  fillets, skinned
298 g/10½ oz canned
  condensed mushroom
  soup
2 tomatoes, sliced
50 g/2 oz cheese, grated
toast triangles to garnish

Arrange the fish fillets in a baking dish. Heat the soup and pour over the fish. Cover the dish and bake in a preheated moderately hot oven (190 C/375 F, Gas Mark 5) for 15 minutes.

Uncover the fish and top with the tomato slices and grated cheese. Return to the oven and bake for a further 5 minutes or until the cheese has melted. Serve hot, garnished with toast triangles.

Salmon or Tuna Mousse

Serves 3–4

1 teaspoon gelatine
150 ml/¼ pint hot water
150 ml/¼ pint stock
150 ml/¼ pint mayonnaise
2 tablespoons lemon juice
salt
pepper
½ teaspoon paprika
1 teaspoon
  Worcestershire sauce
1 teaspoon onion juice
  (from grated onion)
450 g/1 lb canned salmon
  or tuna fish, drained
  and flaked
150 ml/¼ pint double
  cream, whipped

Dissolve the gelatine in the hot water, then stir in the stock. Cool.

Mix together the mayonnaise, lemon juice, salt, pepper, paprika, Worcestershire sauce and onion juice. Mash the salmon or tuna and mix into the mayonnaise mixture. Stir in the gelatine mixture, then fold in the cream. Turn into a dampened 900 ml/1½ pint mould and chill until set.

Salmon with Watercress Cream

Serves 4

butter
salt
pepper
4 salmon cutlets
4 bay leaves

Watercress Cream
1 bunch of watercress
150 ml/¼ pint double
  cream
salt
pepper
1 tablespoon lemon juice

Cut out four squares of foil large enough to enclose a salmon cutlet. Grease them with butter and sprinkle with salt and pepper. Place a cutlet on each square and dot with more butter. Sprinkle with salt and pepper and place a bay leaf on top. Wrap the foil around the cutlets and poach for 15 minutes or until cooked through. Cool in the foil packets.

For the watercress cream, simmer the watercress in boiling water until it is tender. Drain well and sieve or blend to a purée. Mix with the remaining ingredients and chill slightly.

Remove the salmon cutlets from the foil packets and discard the cooking juices and bay leaves. Arrange the cutlets on a serving plate and serve with the watercress cream.

Oven-baked Fish Grenadier   *Serves 4*

6 small cod or hake
  fillets, skinned
150 ml/¼ pint milk
100 g/4 oz fresh
  breadcrumbs
2 tablespoons chopped
  parsley
2 tablespoons chopped
  fresh dill
coarsely grated rind of 1
  lemon
salt
pepper
50 g/2 oz butter, melted
paprika
lemon wedges to serve

Dip the fish in the milk. Mix together the breadcrumbs and herbs and use to coat the fish. Arrange them in a buttered baking dish. Sprinkle over the lemon rind, salt and pepper, then pour on the melted butter. Bake in a hot oven (230 C/450 F, Gas Mark 8) for 15 minutes.

Sprinkle with a little paprika and serve with lemon wedges.

Baked Whiting with French Mustard Sauce   *Serves 4*

4 whiting, cleaned and
  filleted
salt
pepper
2 tablespoons finely
  chopped onion or
  spring onion
4 tablespoons dry white
  wine or cider
1 tablespoon French
  mustard
1 tablespoon grated
  lemon rind
juice of ½ lemon
1 tablespoon chopped
  parsley
25 g/1 oz butter
2 tablespoons cream
  (optional)
chopped parsley to
  garnish

Lay the fillets in a buttered baking dish. Sprinkle with salt, pepper and the onion or spring onion. Mix together the wine or cider, mustard and lemon rind and juice and pour over the fish. Cover the dish and bake in a preheated moderate oven (180°C/350°F, Gas Mark 4) for about 30 minutes or until tender.

Strain the cooking liquor into a saucepan and simmer for 2 to 3 minutes. Stir in the parsley, butter and cream, if used, and heat through gently.

Arrange the fish fillets on a warmed serving dish and pour over the sauce. Garnish with parsley.

Tweed Salmon

1 salmon
salt
mayonnaise to serve

Weigh the salmon, then cut down the back and open out. Clean and wash thoroughly. Cut into 4cm/1½ inch slices through the joint of the bones. bones.

Place the salmon slices in a fish kettle or saucepan of boiling salted water and bring back to the boil. Boil rapidly for 1 minute for every 450 g/1 lb of salmon. Drain, cool and serve with mayonnaise.

Note: Small pieces of salmon may be cooked in the same way, after ascertaining the total weight of the fish

Mackerel with Herb Stuffing   *Serves 3*

3 mackerel, cleaned
2 slices of brown bread,
  crumbled
1 egg, beaten
chopped fresh herbs
melted butter or oil

Blanch the fish in a bowl of hot water for 1 minute. Drain.

Mix together the breadcrumbs, egg and herbs and use to stuff the fish. Grill, basting with melted butter or oil, or fry in butter or oil, or bake in a preheated moderate oven (180 C/350 F, Gas Mark 4) for 20 minutes or until the fish will flake easily.

Fish in Cider   *Serves 4*

4 white fish fillets
2 tomatoes, sliced
50 g/2 oz mushrooms,
  sliced
salt
pepper
pinch of cayenne pepper
juice of ½ lemon
300 ml/½ pint dry cider
25 g/1 oz butter
25 g/1 oz flour
chopped parsley to
  garnish

Put the fish in a baking dish and arrange the tomatoes and mushrooms on top. Sprinkle with salt, pepper, the cayenne and lemon juice and pour in the cider. Cover the dish and bake in a preheated moderately hot oven (190 C/375 F, Gas Mark 5) for 25 minutes.

Drain the liquid from the fish and reserve. Keep the fish hot.

Melt the butter in a saucepan and add the flour. Cook, stirring, for 2 minutes, then gradually stir in the reserved cooking liquid. Bring to the boil and simmer, stirring, until thickened.

Garnish the fish with parsley and serve with the sauce.

Fish Pie

Serves 3-4

450 g/1 lb white fish
   fillets, cooked, skinned
   and flaked
750 g/1½ lb potatoes,
   peeled, cooked and
   mashed
65 g/2½ oz butter
300 ml/½ pint hot milk
1 tablespoon chopped
   parsley
1 tablespoon chopped
   fresh fennel leaves
50 g/2 oz shelled shrimps
3 hard-boiled eggs, sliced
salt
pepper
pinch of grated nutmeg
4 tablespoons browned
   breadcrumbs
2 tomatoes, skinned
   and sliced

Mix together the fish, potatoes, butter, milk and herbs, beating well to combine. Fold in the shrimps, eggs, salt pepper and nutmeg. Turn into a buttered baking dish and smooth the top. Sprinkle with the breadcrumbs and make a diagonal line on top with the tomato slices. Bake in a preheated moderate oven (160 C/ 325 F, Gas Mark 3) for 45 minutes.

Curried Prawns

Serves 4

50 g/2 oz lard
2 small onions, sliced
1 large tomato, skinned
   and sliced
1 garlic clove, crushed
   (optional)
salt
pepper
350 g/12 oz shelled
   prawns
2 tablespoons desiccated
   coconut soaked in
   150 ml/¼ pint water
½ to 1 tablespoon curry
   powder
2 tablespoons flour
squeeze of lemon juice

Melt the lard in a saucepan and fry the onions until golden brown. Remove them with a slotted spoon.

Add the tomato, garlic, salt, pepper and prawns to the pan and cook gently for 3 minutes. Squeeze a little of the liquid from the coconut and mix with the curry powder and flour to form a paste. Add to the pan with the rest of the coconut mixture and the onions. Bring to the boil, stirring, then simmer very gently for 20 minutes.

Stir in the lemon juice and serve with boiled rice.

Note: This is a dry curry and the prawns should not float in liquid; however, if the mixture seems to be drying out too much during cooking, add a little hot stock or water.

Haddock Rolls

Makes 8–10

75 g/3 oz smoked
   haddock, cooked,
   skinned and flaked
75 g/3 oz mashed potato
25 g/1 oz cheese, grated
½ egg, beaten
salt
pepper
175 g/6 oz flaky or rough
   puff pastry
beaten egg to glaze

Mix together the fish, potato, cheese, egg, salt and pepper. Roll out the dough thinly and cut into 5 × 10 cm/2 × 4 inch oblongs. Divide the fish mixture between the oblongs and roll up like sausage rolls. Place on a baking sheet and brush with beaten egg. Bake in a preheated hot oven (220 C/425 F, Gas Mark 7) for 15 minutes or until golden brown.

Cod with Nut Dressing

Serves 4

flour for coating
salt
pepper
4 individual frozen cod
   steaks or 3 frozen fish
   fingers per person
50 g/2 oz margarine
hot creamed potatoes to
   serve
25 g/1 oz unsalted
   peanuts or blanched
   almonds
juice of 1 lemon

Garnish
tomato slices
chopped parsley

Mix the flour with salt and pepper and use to coat the cod steaks. (Do not coat fish fingers.) Melt the margarine in a frying pan and fry the fish for 7 to 10 minutes or until it is golden brown on both sides and cooked through.

Put the creamed potatoes down the centre of a warmed serving platter. Arrange the fish on the potatoes and keep hot.

Add the nuts to the fat in the frying pan and stir in the lemon juice. Fry until lightly browned, then pour over the fish. Garnish with tomato slices and chopped parsley.

Curried Plaice Fillets

Serves 4

4 plaice fillets, halved
   lengthways
300 ml/½ pint milk
1 teaspoon curry powder
1 teaspoon chutney

Roll up the fillet strips. Put the milk in a saucepan, stir in the curry powder and chutney and bring to the boil. Place the fish rolls in the pan and return to the boil. Simmer very gently for 5 minutes or until the fish will flake easily. Serve with boiled rice.

Herrings in Tomato Rolls

Makes 4

150 g/6 oz canned herrings in tomato
Pastry
100 g/4 oz plain flour
salt
pepper
50 g/2 oz margarine
50 g/2 oz cheese, grated
egg, milk or water to mix
milk or beaten egg to glaze

For the pastry, sift the flour into a bowl with salt and pepper. Rub in the margarine, then mix in. the cheese. Bind to a dough with egg, milk or water.

Roll out the dough thinly and cut into oblongs, about 8 × 10 cm/3 × 4 inch. Divide the herrings in tomato between the oblongs, then roll up like sausage rolls. Place on a greased baking sheet and brush with milk or beaten egg. Bake in a preheated moderately hot oven (190°C/375°F, Gas Mark 5) for 20 to 25 minutes or until golden brown.

Haddock Custard

Serves 4

225 g/8 oz smoked haddock, cooked, skinned and flaked
300 ml/½ pint hot milk
2 eggs, beaten
salt
pepper
175 g/6 oz Cheddar cheese, grated
15 g/½ oz butter

Put the fish in a buttered baking dish. Beat together the milk, eggs, salt, pepper and cheese until the cheese has melted. Pour over the fish and dot the top with the butter. Bake in a preheated cool oven (150°C/300°F, Gas Mark 2) for 45 to 60 minutes or until set.

Nutty Herrings

Serves 4

4 herrings, cleaned and boned
salt
coarse oatmeal for coating
25 g/1 oz butter
Mustard Sauce
1 onion
25 g/1 oz butter
15 g/½ oz flour
1 teaspoon dry mustard
150 ml/¼ pint vinegar
150 ml/¼ pint water

Rub the herrings with salt, then coat with oatmeal, pressing it on well with a knife. Melt the butter in a frying pan and fry the herrings for about 15 minutes or until golden brown on both sides and cooked through.

To make the mustard sauce, chop the onion finely and fry in the butter until light brown. Add all the other ingredients and then bring gently and slowly to the boil, stirring all the time. Simmer gently without a lid for 15 minutes.

Pour the mustard sauce over the fish and serve hot.

Rainbow Trout with Horseradish Sauce

Serves 4

flour for coating
salt
pepper
4 rainbow trout, cleaned
. and scaled
75 g/3 oz butter
1 tablespoon oil
100 g/4 oz flaked
almonds

Sauce
25 g/1 oz fresh
horseradish root,
cleaned and grated
wine vinegar
salt
cream

Garnish
lemon slices
tarragon sprig

Mix the flour with salt and pepper and use to coat the trout. Melt 25 g/1 oz of the butter with the oil in a frying pan. Add the almonds and fry until they are golden brown. Remove them from the pan and keep warm.

Add the remaining butter to the pan. When it has melted, add the trout and fry for about 10 minutes on each side or until golden brown and cooked through.

Meanwhile, for the sauce, mix the horseradish with a few drops of vinegar and salt and put in a small dish. Cover with cream.

Arrange the trout on a warmed serving dish and sprinkle them with the almonds. Garnish with lemon slices and a tarragon sprig and serve with the horseradish sauce.

Prawn Créole

Serves 4

25 g/1 oz butter
1 onion, chopped
1 small green pepper,
cored, seeded and
chopped
25 g/1 oz flour
400 g/14 oz canned
tomatoes
1 teaspoon dried oregano,
basil or mixed herbs
1 teaspoon sugar
salt
pepper
150 ml/¼ pint dry white
wine
225 g/8 oz shelled prawns
boiled rice to serve

Melt the butter in a saucepan and fry the onion and green pepper until the onion is softened. Stir in the flour and cook for 2 minutes, then add the tomatoes, herbs, sugar, salt and pepper and mix well. Simmer gently for 15 minutes.

Stir in the wine and prawns and cook for a further 10 minutes. Serve with boiled rice.

Dorada en Sal
Serves 4–6

*approx. 1 kg/2 lb table
  salt*
*1 × 1 kg/2 lb tail piece of
  cod, cleaned*

Garlic Mayonnaise
6 tablespoons mayonnaise
1 garlic clove, crushed
little lemon juice

Garlic Dressing
4 tablespoons lemon juice
*2 tablespoons white wine
  vinegar*
4 tablespoons oil
salt
pepper
4 garlic cloves, crushed
*2 tablespoons chopped
  parsley*
caster sugar to taste

Put a layer of salt in a roasting tin or baking dish just large enough to hold the fish. Cover the cut surface of the fish with foil and place it in the dish, foil downward. Pour salt all over the fish so that it is completely enclosed. Bake in a preheated moderate oven (180 C/350 F, Gas Mark 4) for 1 to 1¼ hours.

Meanwhile, mix together the ingredients for the mayonnaise and dressing, and place in separate bowls or jugs.

To serve, lift the fish out of the tin in its crust of salt, then break the crust and remove it carefully, taking the skin of the fish at the same time. Serve with the mayonnaise and dressing.

Sole Véronique
Serves 4

*175 g/6 oz white or black
  grapes, peeled and
  pipped*
*8 small sole fillets,
  skinned*
salt
white pepper
*300 ml/½ pint white wine,
  or 150 ml/¼ pint white
  wine and 150 ml/¼ pint
  milk*
25 g/1 oz butter
25 g/1 oz flour
2 egg yolks, beaten
2 tablespoons cream

Scatter half of the grapes on the fillets and fold them in half. Place in a buttered baking dish and sprinkle with salt and pepper. Pour in the wine, or wine and milk, and bake in a preheated moderate oven (180 C/350 F, Gas Mark 4) for 15 minutes.

Lift the fish carefully from the liquid and arrange on a warmed serving dish. Keep hot. Strain the liquid.

Melt the butter in a saucepan and add the flour. Cook, stirring, for 2 minutes, then gradually stir in the reserved liquid. Bring to the boil and simmer, stirring, until thickened. Add the egg yolks, cream, salt and pepper and heat through gently without boiling. Stir in the remaining grapes and pour over the fish.

Fish Plaki
Serves 3

50 g/2 oz butter
250 ml/8 fl oz white wine
2 tablespoons chopped parsley
1 tablespoon chopped fresh basil
1 tablespoon chopped fresh chervil
1 tablespoon chopped fresh lovage (if available)
1 bay leaf
salt
4 peppercorns
100 g/4 oz mushrooms, sliced
1 egg, beaten
3 mackerel, cleaned and boned

Melt the butter in a saucepan and stir in half the wine, the herbs, salt, peppercorns and mushrooms. Simmer for 5 minutes. Stir in the rest of the wine and the egg and remove from the heat.

Arrange the mackerel in a baking dish and pour over the wine mixture. Cover with foil. Bake in a preheated moderately hot oven (190 °C/375 F, Gas Mark 5) for 20 minutes or until the fish will flake easily. Serve hot with celery, spinach, rice and green peppers.

Fish and Bacon Casserole
Serves 5-6

15 g/$\frac{1}{2}$ oz butter
100 g/4 oz streaky bacon, rinded and diced
3 onions, chopped
750 g/1$\frac{1}{2}$ lb white fish fillets
salt
cayenne pepper
1 teaspoon Worcestershire sauce
150 ml/$\frac{1}{4}$ pint tomato ketchup
150 ml/$\frac{1}{4}$ pint water

Melt the butter in a frying pan and fry the bacon and onion until the onion is softened.

Make alternate layers of fish and the bacon mixture in a baking dish, sprinkling each layer with salt and cayenne. Mix together the remaining ingredients and pour over the top. Cover the dish and bake in a preheated moderate oven (180 C/350 F, Gas Mark 4) for 45 minutes.

Baked Fish

Serves 6–8

*1 × 1.5 kg/3 lb white fish,
 such as cod, cleaned*
salt
pepper
juice of 1 lemon
3 tablespoons oil
1 onion, chopped
*½ green pepper, cored,
 seeded and chopped*
*226 g/8 oz canned
 tomatoes, drained*
½ teaspoon dried thyme

Rub the fish with salt, pepper and the lemon juice and place in a greased baking tin.

Heat the oil in a saucepan and fry the onion and green pepper until softened. Stir in the tomatoes and thyme and cook gently for 15 minutes.

Pour the vegetable mixture over the fish and bake in a preheated moderate oven (160°C/ 325 'F, Gas Mark 3) for 25 to 30 minutes or until the fish will flake easily.

Swedish Herring

Serves 4

*4 large potatoes, peeled,
 cooked and sliced*
3 onions, thinly sliced
8 small herrings, filleted
*8 anchovy fillets
 (optional)*
6 large tomatoes, sliced
*50 g/2 oz fresh
 breadcrumbs*
15 g/½ oz butter

Cover the bottom of a buttered baking dish with the potato slices. Place the onion slices on top. Roll up the herrings, skin side out, with an anchovy in each, if used. Place the rolled herrings on the onions. Cover with the tomato slices, then sprinkle over the breadcrumbs. Dot with the butter.

Bake in a preheated moderate oven (180 C/350 F, Gas Mark 4) for 30 to 40 minutes.

Serve hot with a green salad.

Trout with Almonds and Cream

Serves 4

flour for coating
salt
pepper
4 trout, cleaned
175 g/6 oz butter
*50 g/2 oz blanched
 almonds*
juice of ½ lemon
*150 ml/¼ pint single
 cream*
lemon wedges to garnish

Mix the flour with salt and pepper and use to coat the fish. Melt 100 g/4 oz of the butter in a frying pan. Slip in the trout and cook for 15 minutes or until golden brown on both sides and cooked through. Drain the trout and keep warm on a serving dish.

Clean the pan, then melt the remaining butter in it. Add the almonds and fry until they are lightly browned. Stir in the lemon juice.

Heat the cream gently in a separate pan and pour it over the fish. Sprinkle with the almonds and garnish with lemon wedges.

Cod Provençal

Serves 4

4 cod steaks or cutlets
salt
pepper
25 g/1 oz butter or
  margarine
2 tablespoons oil
1 onion, thinly sliced
1 garlic clove, crushed
100 g/4 oz mushrooms,
  sliced
250 ml/8 fl oz stock
4 tablespoons white wine
  or cider
2 to 3 tablespoons
  tomato paste
2 large tomatoes, skinned
  and chopped
1 bay leaf
parsley sprigs to garnish

Rub the cod with salt and pepper, then grill, fry or poach, using the butter or margarine.

Meanwhile, make the sauce. Heat the oil in a saucepan and fry the onion and garlic until softened. Add the mushrooms and fry for a further 3 minutes, then stir in the remaining sauce ingredients and bring to the boil. Simmer for 10 to 15 minutes.

Discard the bay leaf and spoon the sauce over the cooked fish. Garnish with parsley.

Tuna and Mixed Bean Salad

Serves 4

225 to 350 g/8 to 12 oz
  mixed dried beans
  (haricot, kidney,
  butter, flageolet, etc.),
  soaked overnight
salt
6 tablespoons garlicky
  French dressing
2 eating apples, cored
  and diced
1 tablespoon lemon juice
1 small onion, very thinly
  sliced
200 g/7 oz canned tuna
  fish, drained and flaked
lettuce to serve
watercress and lemon
  slices to garnish

Drain the beans and put in a saucepan. Cover with fresh cold water, add salt and bring to the boil. Simmer for about 1 hour or until tender. Drain well and place in a bowl. Add the dressing, toss thoroughly and cool.

Dip the apple dice in the lemon juice, then add to the beans with the onion and tuna. Mix well, then cover and leave for 20 minutes.

'Line a serving dish with lettuce leaves and spoon on the bean and tuna salad. Garnish with watercress and lemon slices.

Mackerel in the Normandy Manner   *Serves 4*

4 mackerel, cleaned
salt
2 tablespoons vinegar
1 bay leaf
Sauce
2 teaspoons French
  mustard
1 tablespoon chopped
  parsley
1 small onion, chopped
50 g/2 oz butter, melted ·
2 egg yolks

Put the mackerel in a flat pan and sprinkle with salt. Add the vinegar and bay leaf and cover with water. Bring to the boil, then cover and simmer gently for 20 to 30 minutes or until the fish are just tender. Cool slightly in the liquor.

Drain the mackerel and remove the skin and bones. Put the fillets on a serving plate and keep warm.

Mix together the sauce ingredients and pour over the fillets. Serve hot or cold.

Haddock and Orange Gougère   *Serves 4*

100 g/4 oz choux pastry
450 g/1 lb haddock fillet
300 ml/½ pint mixed milk
  and water
salt
pepper
40 g/1½ oz butter
1 onion, chopped
25 g/1 oz flour
grated rind and juice of 1
  orange
1 tablespoon chopped
  parsley
1 hard-boiled egg,
  chopped

Spread or pipe the choux dough in a 20 cm/ 8 inch ring on a greased baking sheet. Bake in a preheated hot oven (220 C/425 F, Gas Mark 7) for 30 to 40 minutes or until well risen, golden brown and firm.

Meanwhile, put the fish, milk and water, salt and pepper into a saucepan and poach gently until the fish is tender. Drain off the milk and make up to 300 ml/½ pint with more milk if necessary. Flake the fish.

Melt the butter in another saucepan and fry the onion until softened. Add the flour and cook, stirring, for 2 minutes. Gradually stir in the milk and orange rind and juice and bring to the boil, stirring well. Stir in the parsley, egg and fish.

Cut the choux ring in half and scoop out any uncooked dough. Fill with the fish mixture, then replace the top and bake for a further 5 minutes to heat through.

Meats

Lamb Chops with Honey
Serves 4

4 loin or chump lamb
  chops
salt
pepper
15 g/½ oz butter or
  margarine
2 teaspoons dried mint
3 tablespoons thick honey
½ teaspoon grated lemon
  rind (optional)

Rub the chops with salt and pepper and arrange on the grill rack. Dot with half the butter or margarine and grill for 8 to 10 minutes or until well browned. Turn over, dot with the rest of the fat and continue cooking for 3 to 4 minutes.

Mix together the mint, honey and lemon rind, if used, and spread over the chops. Continue cooking for about 5 minutes or until the chops are cooked through. Serve with the pan juices spooned over.

Workman's Goose
Serves 2–3

100 g/4 oz fresh
  breadcrumbs
2 medium onions,
  parboiled and chopped
1 tablespoon chopped
  fresh sage
salt
pepper
1 small egg, beaten, or a
  little cream
1 large breast of mutton
  or lamb, boned

Mix together the breadcrumbs, onions, sage, salt and pepper and bind with the egg or cream. Shape into a firm roll. Lay the meat flat, fat side down, and place the roll of stuffing in the centre. Roll up the meat and secure the flap. Wrap in foil or place in a roasting tin and cover. Cook in a preheated moderate oven (180°C/ 350 F, Gas Mark 4) for 2 hours.

Twenty minutes before the cooking time is finished, unwrap the meat or uncover it so that it can brown. Baste several times with the fat in the tin. Serve with a thick gravy.

59

Lamb with Apple
Serves 6

1 tablespoon oil
750 g to 1 kg/1½ to 2 lb
middle neck of lamb,
trimmed of excess fat
1 large onion, chopped
450 g/1 lb potatoes,
peeled and sliced
2 large cooking apples,
sliced
300 ml/½ pint beef stock
chopped parsley to
garnish

Heat the oil in a flameproof casserole. Add the lamb and onion and brown the meat on all sides. Remove the meat from the pot and the pot from the heat.

Arrange half the potato slices on the bottom of the casserole, then cover with the meat, onion and apples. Cover this with the rest of the potatoes and pour in the stock.

Cover the casserole and cook in a preheated moderate oven (180°C/350°F, Gas Mark 4) for 1½ to 2 hours or until the meat is tender. Serve garnished with parsley.

Variation: Replace the lamb with skinned and halved pork sausages, and the stock with dry cider.

Navarin of Lamb
Serves 4

50 g/2 oz fat
450 g/1 lb stewing lamb
(middle or best end of
neck) cut into small
pieces
1½ tablespoons flour
salt
pepper
pinch of sugar
450 ml/¾ pint stock or
water
1 garlic clove, crushed
(optional)
6 small onions
6 small carrots
450 g/1 lb new potatoes
1 small turnip, chopped
chopped parsley to
garnish

Melt 25 g/1 oz of the fat in a heavy-based saucepan and fry the meat until well browned. Drain off the fat and sprinkle over the flour, salt, pepper and sugar. Cook gently until the flour begins to brown, then stir in the stock or water. Bring to the boil. Add the garlic, if using, and simmer gently for 1 hour.

Meanwhile, melt the remaining fat in a frying pan. Add the onions and fry until browned on all sides. Drain well. Add the onions to the lamb with the carrots, potatoes and turnip 45 minutes before the lamb is ready.

Serve sprinkled with parsley.

Spicy Lamb Chops

Serves 2

2 loin lamb chops
salt
pepper
40 g/1½ oz butter
2 streaky bacon rashers,
  rinded and cut into
  1 cm/½ inch strips
1 small onion, chopped
50 g/2 oz mushrooms,
  sliced
2 small tomatoes,
  skinned, sliced and
  seeded
150 ml/¼ pint stock
1 teaspoon
  Worcestershire sauce

Rub the chops with salt and pepper. Melt the butter in a frying pan, add the chops and brown lightly on both sides. Transfer the chops to a casserole.

Add the bacon, onion and mushrooms to the pan and fry until the onion is softened. Stir in the remaining ingredients and bring to the boil. Pour over the chops in the casserole.

Cover and cook in a preheated moderate oven (180 C/350 F, Gas Mark 4) for 25 to 30 minutes.

Barbecued Lamb

Serves 2–3

1 breast of lamb, boned
  and trimmed of excess
  fat
100 g/4 oz forcemeat
  stuffing
225 g/8 oz carrots, sliced
225 g/8 oz potatoes,
  peeled and sliced

Sauce
1 small onion, chopped
1 garlic clove, crushed
5 tablespoons vinegar
5 tablespoons water
few drops of Tabasco
  sauce
1 tablespoon
  Worcestershire sauce
1 tablespoon tomato
  purée
salt
pepper

Cut the lamb into 7.5 cm/3 inch wide strips. Spread each strip with stuffing and roll them up. Secure with wooden cocktail sticks. Arrange in a baking dish and bake in a preheated hot oven (220°C/425°F, Gas Mark 7) for 30 minutes or until well browned.

Drain off all the fat and surround the meat with the carrots and potatoes. Mix together all the ingredients for the sauce and pour over the meat and vegetables. Cover and bake for a further 2 hours in a moderate oven (180°C/ 350 F, Gas Mark 4) or until the meat is tender.

China-China
Serves 6–8

*50 to 75 g/2 to 3 oz
clarified butter
1 kg/2 lb mutton or
lamb, minced
1 small onion, chopped
1 lettuce, shredded
350 g/12 oz shelled fresh
peas
1 cucumber, chopped
4 tablespoons stock
salt
pepper
boiled rice to serve*

Heat the butter in a stew pan and add the mutton or lamb, onion, lettuce, peas, cucumber, stock, salt and pepper. Cover tightly and simmer gently for 2 hours. Serve with boiled rice, as for curry.

Note: This dish, pronounced Chinner-Chinner, comes from Lady Buchanan's great-grandmother's recipe book.

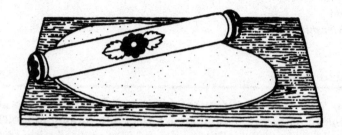

Lamb Pasties
Makes 4

*225 g/8 oz rich shortcrust
pastry
175 to 225 g/6 to 8 oz
lean cooked lamb,
diced or coarsely
minced
2 teaspoons chopped
fresh mint
1 tablespoon grated onion
salt
pepper
50 g/2 oz peas, cooked
2 to 3 tablespoons
cream
beaten egg to glaze*

Roll out the dough and cut into four 18 cm/7 inch rounds. Mix together all the remaining ingredients except the beaten egg and divide between the dough rounds. Dampen the edges, bring them together and press firmly to seal. Crimp. Place on a greased baking sheet and brush with beaten egg.

Bake in a preheated hot oven (220 C/425 F, Gas Mark 7) for about 25 minutes or until golden brown. Cool on a wire rack.

Roast Rolled Mutton   *Serves 6*

*1.5 kg/3 lb breast of
mutton or lamb, boned
225 g/8 oz white bread,
cut into cubes
milk, water or stock to
bind
2 tablespoons chopped
parsley
1 teaspoon chopped fresh
thyme
salt
pepper
grated rind of 1 lemon
(optional)*

Lay the meat flat on a working surface, then beat it flat with a rolling pin.

Soak the bread cubes in milk, water or stock until soft, then squeeze out the excess moisture. Mix the bread cubes with the parsley, thyme, salt, pepper and lemon rind, if used. Add any extra milk, water or stock to bind the mixture, then spread it on the meat, on the side from which the bones have been removed. Roll up loosely and tie into shape. Place in a roasting tin.

Bake in a preheated moderate oven (180 C/350 F, Gas Mark 4) for about $1\frac{3}{4}$ hours, basting frequently with the fat in the tin.

Variation: 3 or 4 cooked, stoned and chopped prunes may be added to the stuffing, in which case omit the thyme.

Stuffed Breast of Lamb   *Serves 4*

*200 g/7 oz canned
pineapple chunks,
drained (syrup
reserved) and
chopped
1 tomato, skinned and
chopped
2 tablespoons sultanas
2 tablespoons fresh white
breadcrumbs
salt
pepper
1 breast of lamb, boned*

Mix together the pineapple, tomato, sultanas, breadcrumbs, salt and pepper. Spread the mixture on the meat, on the side from which the bones were taken, then roll up and tie into shape. Wrap in foil, including some of the pineapple can syrup, or use a roasting bag. Roast in a preheated cool oven (150°C/300°F, Gas Mark 2) for about 2 hours.

If using foil, unwrap about 20 minutes before the cooking time is completed to allow the meat to brown.

Crispy Lamb Cutlets

Serves

8 lamb cutlets or 4 loin
lamb chops
salt
pepper
flour for coating
50 g/2 oz walnuts or
salted peanuts, finely
chopped
40 g/1½ oz cornflakes
beaten egg
oil for shallow frying

Rub the cutlets or chops with salt and peppei then coat lightly with flour. Mix together th nuts and cornflakes. Dip the cutlets in th beaten egg, then coat with the cornflake mix ture, pressing it on well.

Shallow fry for 5 to 8 minutes on each side o until well browned and cooked through.

Lancashire Hot Pot

Serves ʼ

1.5 kg/3 lb best end neck
of mutton or lamb, cut
into chops
4 mutton or lamb
kidneys, cored, skinned
and sliced
4 onions, each cut into 3
slices
1.5 kg/3 lb potatoes,
peeled and sliced
salt
pepper
curry powder
300 ml/½ pint stock

Make a layer of chops in a brown earthenwar₍ stew pot. Add a layer of sliced kidneys, on₍ sliced onion and 225 g/8 oz of the potato slices Sprinkle with salt, pepper and 1 teaspoon curr₎ powder. Continue making layers in this wa₎ until the pot is full, ending with potatoes. Pou₁ in the stock.

Bake in a preheated moderate over (180 C/350 F, Gas Mark 4) for 1¼ hours o₁ until the chops and vegetables are tender. Serv₍ with a napkin pinned around the pot.

Note: The top layer of potatoes may be brushec with melted butter to encourage browning.

Neck of Lamb aux Herbes

Serves 4

1 kg/2 lb best end of
neck of lamb
1 garlic clove, halved
salt
pepper
dried thyme
dried rosemary
1 bay leaf, crushed
olive oil

Open out the joint and rub it with the garlic salt and pepper. Mix together the herbs anc sprinkle over the meat. Roll it up and tie intc shape. Rub salt, pepper and olive oil over the rolled meat and place in a roasting tin.

Roast in a preheated moderate over₁ (180°C/350°F, Gas Mark 4) for 1 hour (or 3C minutes to each 450 g/1 lb of meat). Bast₍ occasionally with the meat juices in the tin.

Moussaka
Serves 4–6

approx. 120 ml/4 fl oz oil
450 g/1 lb minced beef or
lamb
1 large onion, finely
chopped
salt
pepper
2 tablespoons tomato
purée
4 tablespoons water
4 medium aubergines,
peeled and sliced
300 ml/½ pint cheese
sauce, made with
175 g/6 oz cheese

Heat 2 tablespoons of the oil in a frying pan and fry the meat and onion until browned. Stir in salt, pepper, the tomato purée and water. Cover and cook gently for 40 minutes.

Meanwhile, heat 2 tablespoons of the remaining oil in another frying pan. Add one-third of the aubergine slices and brown on all sides. Brown the rest of the aubergine slices in the same way, using the remaining oil.

Make alternate layers of the meat mixture and aubergine slices in a baking dish, finishing with aubergine. Pour over the sauce. Bake in a preheated moderately hot oven (190°C/375°F, Gas Mark 5) for 40 minutes or until the top is golden brown.

Braised Beef
Serves 6–8

1.5 kg/3 lb topside of
beef
25 g/1 oz butter or 3
tablespoons oil
150 ml/¼ pint stock
4 tablespoons flour
300 ml/½ pint cream
salt
pepper
Marinade
150 ml/¼ pint red wine
1 tablespoon wine vinegar
1 carrot, sliced
1 onion, sliced
4 whole cloves
2 bay leaves
2 thyme sprigs
1 teaspoon dry mustard
salt

Mix together the ingredients for the marinade in a deep bowl. Add the meat and leave to marinate for 48 hours, turning occasionally.

Drain the meat, reserving the marinade. Melt the butter or heat the oil in a flameproof casserole and brown the meat on all sides. Pour in the reserved marinade and the stock and bring to the boil. Cover the casserole and transfer to a preheated cool oven (150°C/300°F, Gas Mark 2). Cook for 3 hours or until the meat is tender.

Remove the meat, slice it and arrange on a warmed serving platter. Keep hot. Strain the cooking liquid, then thicken it with the flour. Stir in the cream, salt and pepper and heat through gently. Pour the sauce over the meat and serve.

Meat Balls in Sweet and Sour Sauce   *Serves 4*

450 g/1 lb minced beef
1 small onion, chopped
1 tablespoon chopped
  parsley
salt
pepper
1 egg, beaten
3 to 4 tablespoons oil
Sauce
2 tablespoons vinegar
2 tablespoons soy sauce
2 tablespoons tomato
  ketchup
300 ml/½ pint water
15 g/½ oz cornflour
2 tablespoons light brown
  sugar

Mix together the beef, onion, parsley, salt and pepper and bind with the egg. Divide into 12 or 16 portions and shape into small balls. Heat the oil in a frying pan and add the meat balls. Cook gently, turning occasionally, until they are browned on all sides and cooked through.

Meanwhile, mix together all the sauce ingredients in a saucepan. Bring to the boil, stirring, and simmer until clear and thickened.

Drain the meat balls and turn them into a warmed serving dish. Pour over the sauce and serve with creamed potatoes, boiled rice or noodles.

Guinness Stew   *Serves 4*

25 g/1 oz lard
2 onions, sliced
2 garlic cloves, crushed
½ green pepper, cored,
  seeded and chopped
450 g/1 lb stewing steak,
  cubed
100 g/4 oz mushrooms,
  sliced
300 ml/½ pint canned
  Guinness
1 teaspoon dried
  rosemary
1 teaspoon chopped
  parsley
1 teaspoon garam masala
salt
pepper

Melt the lard in a flameproof casserole. Add the onions, garlic and green pepper and fry until softened. Add the steak cubes and brown on all sides. Stir in the remaining ingredients and bring to the boil. Cover the casserole. Transfer to a preheated moderate oven (180°C/350°F, Gas Mark 4) and cook for 1½ hours or until the meat is tender.

Goulash
Serves 6

3 tablespoons oil
2 large onions, chopped
1 garlic clove, crushed
750 g/1½ lb chuck or
  stewing steak, cut into
  4 cm/1½ inch cubes
1 tablespoon flour
1 tablespoon paprika
300 ml/½ pint stock
salt
pepper
400 g/14 oz canned
  tomatoes
1 green pepper, cored,
  seeded and chopped
150 g/5 oz soured cream

Dumplings
100 g/4 oz self-raising
  flour
salt
pepper
1 teaspoon dried mixed
  herbs (optional)
50 g/2 oz chopped suet

Heat the oil in a saucepan and fry the onions and garlic until softened. Add the steak cubes and brown on all sides. Sprinkle over the flour, paprika, salt and pepper and stir in well, then add the tomatoes and the stock. Bring to the boil, cover and simmer gently for 1 hour.

Meanwhile, make the dumplings. Sift the flour, salt and pepper into a bowl and mix in the herbs, if using, and suet. Bind to a dough with cold water. Divide into 8 or 12 portions and shape into balls with floured hands.

Add the green pepper to the goulash and continue simmering for 10 minutes.

Add the dumplings to the goulash and continuing simmering, still covered, for 20 minutes or until the meat is tender and the dumplings are cooked through. Stir in the soured cream, heat through gently and serve.

Crofter's Savoury Roll
Serves 4

225 to 350 g/8 to 12 oz
  cooked meat (brisket
  of beef and/or poultry
  are very good)
1 bacon rasher, rinded
1 small onion
pinch of dried mixed
  herbs
salt
pepper
100 g/4 oz fresh
  breadcrumbs
stock or gravy to bind

Mince the meat, bacon and onion and mix together with the herbs, salt, pepper and breadcrumbs. Bind with stock or gravy. Shape into a roll and wrap in greased greaseproof paper. Place on a baking sheet and bake in a preheated moderate oven (180 C/350 F, Gas Mark 4) for 30 minutes.

Serve hot or cold, in slices.

Note: This is a good way to use up leftovers as the quantities can be easily varied.

Steakburgers

Serves 4–5

2 tablespoons oil
450 g/1 lb frying steak
  (preferably rump or
  fillet), cut into short
  thin strips
2 celery stalks, thinly
  sliced
1 small carrot, thinly
  sliced
1 spinach or green
  cabbage leaf, shredded
2 spring onions, finely
  chopped
1 tablespoon soy sauce
1 teaspoon curry powder
salt
pepper
200 ml/⅓ pint water

Heat the oil in a heavy-based frying pan. Add the steak strips and brown quickly. Add the remaining ingredients and stir-fry until the vegetables are just tender. Serve with boiled or fried rice.

Beef Olives

Serves 4

1 tablespoon shredded
  suet
2 tablespoons fresh
  breadcrumbs
1 teaspoon chopped
  parsley
¼ teaspoon dried mixed
  herbs
salt
pepper
1 egg yolk, beaten
450 g/1 lb steak, thinly
  sliced and beaten
1 tablespoon dripping
1 tablespoon flour
600 ml/1 pint stock
mashed potatoes and
  cooked peas to garnish

Sprinkle the suet with the breadcrumbs and chop very finely. Add the parsley, herbs, salt and pepper and bind with the egg yolk.

Cut the steak into strips 7.5 cm/3 inches long and 5 cm/2 inches wide. Spread each strip with the suet mixture and roll them up. Secure with string.

Melt the dripping in a frying pan and fry the steak rolls until well browned on all sides. Remove them from the pan. Add the flour to the pan and cook, stirring, until it is browned. Gradually stir in the stock and bring to the boil. Return the steak rolls to the pan and simmer gently for 1½ hours.

Arrange the beef olives on a heated serving dish and garnish with piped rosettes of mashed potatoes. Strain over the cooking liquor and add the peas in neat groups.

Beef Stroganoff

Serves 4

25 g/1 oz butter
3 tomatoes, skinned and
 quartered
50 g/2 oz mushrooms,
 sliced
2 potatoes, peeled,
 cooked and sliced
225 g/8 oz rump steak,
 cut into thin strips
150 g/5 oz natural yogurt
 or soured cream
1 teaspoon French
 mustard
pinch of dried mixed
 herbs
1 bay leaf
salt
pepper

Melt the butter in a frying pan and add the tomatoes, mushrooms and potatoes. Cook gently for 5 minutes. Push the vegetables to the side of the pan and add the steak. Fry until it is browned and tender.

Mix together the yogurt or soured cream, mustard, herbs, bay leaf, salt and pepper and add to the pan. Heat through gently, stirring well to mix all the ingredients together. Serve with boiled rice or noodles.

Beef and Parsnip Pie

Serves 4

1 tablespoon dripping
1 large onion, chopped
1 garlic clove, crushed
450 g/1 lb minced beef
1 tablespoon flour
226 g/8 oz canned
 tomatoes
150 ml/¼ pint stock
salt
pepper
1 teaspoon dried basil or
 marjoram
225 g/8 oz potatoes,
 peeled, cooked and
 mashed
450 g/1 lb parsnips,
 cooked and mashed
50 g/2 oz butter

Melt the dripping in a saucepan and fry the onion and garlic until softened. Add the beef and fry for 10 minutes or until browned. Stir in the flour, then add the tomatoes, stock, salt, pepper and herbs. Bring to the boil, cover and simmer for 15 to 20 minutes.

Turn the beef mixture into a baking dish. Mix together the mashed potatoes and parsnips and add the butter, salt and pepper. Beat well, then spread or pipe over the top of the beef mixture. Bake in a preheated moderately hot oven (200°C/400°F, Gas Mark 6) for 25 to 30 minutes or until the top is beginning to brown.

Dolmades

Serves 4–6

350 g /12 oz canned vine
leaves, drained
2 tablespoons oil
2 onions, thinly sliced
450 g/1 lb cooked beef,
lamb or pork, minced
40 g/1½ oz cooked long-
grain rice
1 tablespoon chopped
parsley
4 tablespoons tomato
ketchup or sauce
juice of 1 lemon
salt
pepper
150 ml/¼ pint stock

Blanch the vine leaves in boiling water for 2 minutes, then drain well.

Heat the oil in a frying pan and fry the onions until softened. Stir in the meat, rice, parsley, 2 tablespoons of the ketchup, 1 tablespoon of the lemon juice, salt and pepper and heat through.

Divide the meat mixture between the vine leaves and roll them up. If necessary, secure them with wooden cocktail sticks. Place the rolls in a baking dish.

Heat together the stock, remaining ketchup and lemon juice, salt and pepper and pour over the dolmades. Cover and bake in a preheated moderate oven (180 C/350 F, Gas Mark 4) for 30 minutes.

Serve hot or cold.

Variation: Blanched cabbage leaves or fresh vine leaves may be used instead of canned vine leaves.

Steak Diane

Serves 4

50 g/2 oz butter
1 tablespoon oil
4 pieces of rump steak,
beaten and nicked
round
2 shallots, or 1 onion,
chopped
2 tomatoes, diced
dash of Worcestershire
sauce
salt
pepper
1 tablespoon brandy
chopped parsley to
garnish

Melt the butter with the oil in a frying pan and fry the steak on both sides until it is done to your liking. Remove from the pan and keep hot.

Add the shallots or onion and tomatoes to the pan with the Worcestershire sauce, salt and pepper and cook until softened. Stir in the brandy, then set it alight. When the flames have died down, spoon the tomato mixture over the steaks and sprinkle with parsley.

Meat Balls

450 g/1 lb minced beef
75 g/3 oz minced pork or
 bacon fat or streaky
 bacon
1 small onion, chopped
100 g/4 oz fresh white
 breadcrumbs
1 tablespoon chopped
 parsley
salt
pepper
approx. 150 ml/¼ pint
 milk
flour for coating
50 g/2 oz butter
sliced black olives to
 garnish

Sauce

15 g/½ oz butter
15 g/½ oz flour
600 ml/1 pint sieved
 canned tomatoes
1 bay leaf
salt
pepper
2 tablespoons natural
 yogurt (optional)

Mix together the beef, pork, onion, bread-crumbs, parsley, salt and pepper and bind with the milk. Shape into walnut-sized balls and coat lightly with flour. Melt the butter in a frying pan and brown the balls on all sides. Transfer them to a baking dish.

To make the sauce, melt the butter in a saucepan and stir in the flour. Cook for 2 minutes, then gradually stir in the sieved to-matoes. Add the bay leaf, salt and pepper and bring to the boil, stirring well. Pour this sauce over the meat balls and bake in a preheated moderate oven (180°C/350°F, Gas Mark 4) for 40 minutes.

Stir the yogurt gently into the sauce and cook for a further 5 minutes. Serve garnished with olive slices.

Meat Rolls

225 g/8 oz streaky bacon
 rashers, rinded
750 g/1½ lb thinly cut
 steak, cut into small
 oblongs
chopped parsley
salt and pepper
lard for frying
2 onions, sliced
300 ml/½ pint stock
1 tablespoon vinegar

Lay a rasher of bacon on each steak oblong, then sprinkle with parsley, salt and pepper. Roll up the meat and tie with string. Melt lard in a frying pan and fry the rolls until browned on all sides. Add the onion and continue frying until softened, then stir in the stock and vinegar. Bring to the boil and simmer for 1 hour.

Remove the strings and serve the rolls with the cooking liquor, slightly thickened if you like.

Beef Bourguignonne
Serves 4

1 tablespoon fat
450 g/1 lb stewing beef,
    cut into 8 pieces
1 large onion, finely
    chopped
1 garlic clove, crushed
2 tablespoons flour
300 ml/½ pint water
salt
pepper
½ bay leaf
pinch of dried thyme or
    mixed herbs
½ teaspoon chopped
    parsley
150 ml/¼ pint red wine

Melt the fat in a saucepan and brown the pieces of beef on all sides. Remove them from the pan. Add the onion and garlic to the pan and fry until browned. Sprinkle over the flour and fry, stirring well, until brown. Gradually stir in the water, then add salt, pepper and the herbs and bring to the boil. Return the meat to the pan and simmer gently for about 1½ hours or until the meat is tender.

Fifteen minutes before the meat is ready, stir in the wine.

Savoury Cottage Pie
Serves 4

2 tablespoons oil
1 large onion, finely
    chopped
450 g/1 lb minced raw or
    cooked beef
salt
pepper
1 tablespoon curry
    powder
226 g/8 oz canned
    tomatoes
750 g/1½ lb potatoes,
    peeled
2 tablespoons milk
knob of butter
melted butter or grated
    cheese to finish

Heat the oil in a frying pan and fry the onion until softened. Add the beef and fry until it is browned. (If using cooked beef, just heat it.) Add salt, pepper, the curry powder and tomatoes and bring to the boil. Simmer for 30 minutes.

Meanwhile, cook the potatoes in boiling water until tender. Drain well, then mash with the milk, butter, salt and pepper.

Turn the beef mixture into a flameproof serving dish and cover with the mashed potato. Make a criss-cross pattern on top with a fork and brush with melted butter or sprinkle with grated cheese. Brown under a hot grill.

Gypsy Casserole
Serves 5-6

750 g/1½ lb stewing steak, cut into cubes, or 1 rabbit, jointed
600 ml/1 pint stout
50 g/2 oz fat or dripping
40 g/1½ oz flour
½ teaspoon dried mixed herbs
350 g/12 oz carrots, sliced
1 tablespoon Worcestershire sauce
salt
pepper
100 g/4 oz button mushrooms

Put the steak or rabbit into a bowl and pour over half the stout. Leave to marinate for 1 to 2 hours.

Melt the fat or dripping in a flameproof casserole and add the flour. Cook, stirring, for 2 minutes, then gradually stir in the remaining stout. Bring to the boil, stirring. Tip in the meat and liquid and add the herbs, carrots, Worcestershire sauce, salt and pepper. Mix well and cover.

Transfer to a preheated cool oven (150°C/300°F, Gas Mark 2) and cook for 1½ to 2 hours or until tender.

Stir in the mushrooms, cover again and cook for a further 25 minutes.

Beef and Mushroom Casserole
Serves 4-5

25 g/1 oz cornflour
salt
pepper
450 g/1 lb stewing steak, cut into cubes
2 tablespoons oil
2 onions, sliced
1 garlic clove, finely chopped
600 ml/1 pint beef stock
2 carrots, sliced
1 small green pepper, cored, seeded and diced
50 g/2 oz mushrooms, sliced

Mix the cornflour with salt and pepper and use to coat the steak cubes. Heat the oil in a flameproof casserole and add the onions and garlic. Fry until softened. Add the steak cubes and brown on all sides. Stir in the stock and bring to the boil. Add the carrots.

Cover the casserole and transfer to a preheated moderate oven (160°C/325°F, Gas Mark 3). Cook for 1½ to 2 hours.

Add the green pepper and the mushrooms. Cover again and cook for a further 30 minutes.

Minced Beef Patties
Serves 4

25 g/1 oz fat
2 onions, chopped
1 carrot, chopped
450 g/1 lb minced beef
1 tablespoon tomato
  purée
salt
pepper
25 g/1 oz flour
200 ml/⅓ pint stock
flour for coating
fat for shallow frying

Melt the fat in a frying pan. Add the onions and carrot and fry until softened. Add the beef and continue frying until browned. Stir in the tomato purée, salt, pepper and flour and cook, stirring, for 3 minutes. Gradually stir in the stock and bring to the boil. Simmer, stirring, until thickened.

Allow to cool, then divide into 8 portions and shape into flat cakes. Coat in flour and shallow fry until golden brown on both sides. Drain on paper towels and serve with creamed potatoes and fried onion rings.

Boiled Pressed Brisket of Beef
Serves 24

3.5 kg/8 lb good quality
  pickled brisket of beef
6 onions
6 carrots
1 turnip
little celery if in season

Put the brisket in a saucepan of boiling water with the vegetables and simmer gently for 3 to 4 hours. Leave to cool in the liquid.

When still just warm, drain the brisket, discard all the bones and place the meat in a dish. Press with a board and weight and leave for 12 hours.

Stuffed Skirt of Beef
Serves 6–7

1 kg/2 lb skirt of beef
salt
pepper
50 g/2 oz fresh
  breadcrumbs
1 onion, chopped
1 teaspoon chopped
  parsley
25 g/1 oz chopped suet
1 egg, beaten
little stock

Remove the skin from the meat. Rub the meat with salt and pepper. Mix together the breadcrumbs, onion, parsley, suet, salt and pepper and bind with the egg. Spread this mixture over the meat and roll up. Tie into shape and place in a baking dish. Add a little stock to the dish, cover and bake in a preheated moderate oven (180°C/350°F, Gas Mark 4) for 2 to 2½ hours or until tender. Baste frequently with the stock in the dish.

Fifteen minutes before the meat has finished cooking, uncover it to allow it to brown. Serve with gravy.

Beef with Rosemary
Serves 6

1.25 to 1.5 kg/2½ to 3 lb shin of beef, cubed
175 g/6 oz bacon, rinded and chopped
4 tomatoes, skinned
3 garlic cloves, crushed
½ teaspoon chopped fresh rosemary
150 ml/¼ pint red wine
2 tablespoons tomato purée
salt
pepper

Put the meat into a casserole and add the remaining ingredients. Cover and cook in a preheated cool oven (150°C/300°F, Gas Mark 2) for 4 to 5 hours or until the meat is tender.

Gingered Forehock
Serves 8–10

1.75 kg/4 lb boned, rolled forehock, soaked for 4 to 6 hours
1 tablespoon dried rosemary
1 small bottle of ginger ale
100 g/4 oz demerara sugar
1 teaspoon dry mustard
50 g/2 oz blanched almonds, chopped
1 teaspoon chopped stem ginger
Garnish
cream cheese
ground ginger
tomato slices

Drain the forehock and put into a saucepan with the rosemary. Cover with fresh water and bring to the boil. Simmer gently for half the total cooking time (allow 25 minutes per 450 g/1 lb plus 25 minutes over). Drain the forehock and place on a sheet of foil in a baking tin. Pour over all but 2 tablespoons of the ginger ale, then wrap the foil around the bacon to seal well. Bake in a preheated moderately hot oven (200°C/400°F, Gas Mark 6) for the remaining cooking time. Baste twice during the cooking period with the ginger ale in the foil.

Drain off the remaining ginger ale and remove the rind from the bacon. Mix the sugar, mustard, almonds and ginger with the reserved ginger ale and spread over the bacon. Return to the oven, uncovered, and bake for a further 15 minutes.

Meanwhile, for the garnish, mix cream cheese with a little ginger and spread over tomato slices. Grill until the cheese is lightly brown.

Transfer the bacon to a serving dish and surround with the tomatoes.

Pork and Apples

Serves 6

6 *slices of belly pork*
4 *medium cooking apples,*
peeled, cored and
quartered
2 *tablespoons flour*
300 ml/½ pint milk or
cider
salt
pepper

Fry the pork in a frying pan until crisp on both sides. Remove from the pan with tongs and arrange in a baking dish. Surround with the apple quarters.

Pour off all but 2 tablespoons of the fat from the frying pan. Add the flour and cook, stirring, for 2 minutes. Gradually stir in the milk or cider and bring to the boil. Add salt and pepper, then pour this sauce over the pork and apples. Bake in a preheated moderate oven (180 C/350 F, Gas Mark 4) for 35 to 45 minutes. Serve with creamed potatoes.

Nasi Goreng

Serves 4

2 *tablespoons oil*
1 *onion, sliced*
1 *garlic clove, crushed*
(optional)
½ *teaspoon chilli powder*
1 *teaspoon curry powder*
¼ *teaspoon ground*
coriander
½ *teaspoon caraway seeds*
(optional)
1 *to 2 tablespoons soy*
sauce
salt
pepper
350 to 450 g/12 oz to 1
lb cooked lean pork,
diced
175 g/6 oz long-grain
rice, cooked
225 g/8 oz peas, cooked
1 *egg, beaten*
1 *tablespoon water*
15 g/½ oz butter or
margarine
2 *tomatoes, quartered*

Heat the oil in a frying pan and fry the onion and garlic, if used, until golden brown. Stir in the spices, soy sauce, salt and pepper and cook gently for 2 to 3 minutes. Add the pork and rice and heat through, stirring frequently. Add the peas and continue cooking gently.

Meanwhile, beat the egg with the water, salt and pepper. Melt the butter in a small frying pan and pour in the egg mixture. Cook gently, undisturbed, until set. Turn out of the pan and cut into thin strips.

Turn the meat mixture into a warmed serving dish and garnish with the egg strips and tomato quarters.

Pork Chops Dijon
Serves 4

4 pork chops
salt
pepper
25 g/1 oz butter
1 tablespoon wine vinegar
   or orange juice
3 tablespoons stock or
   water
1 tablespoon French
   mustard
150 ml/¼ pint single
   cream or top of milk

Rub the chops with salt and pepper. Melt the butter in a frying pan and fry the chops until they are browned on both sides and cooked through. Transfer them to a warmed serving plate and keep hot.

Pour off all but 2 tablespoons of the juices from the pan. Stir in the vinegar or orange juice and stock or water and bring to the boil. Simmer until reduced slightly, then remove from the heat and stir in the mustard followed by the cream. Pour over the chops and serve.

Sweet and Sour Pork Balls
Serves 4

450 g/1 lb lean minced
   pork
1 garlic clove, crushed
25 g/1 oz fresh
   breadcrumbs
salt
pepper
1 teaspoon dried mixed
   herbs
1 egg, beaten
flour for coating
fat for shallow frying
1 large red pepper, cored,
   seeded and sliced
200 g/7 oz canned
   crushed pineapple
75 g/3 oz brown sugar
4 tablespoons cider
   vinegar
2 tablespoons soy sauce
300 ml/½ pint stock
1 tablespoon cornflour

Mix together the pork, garlic, breadcrumbs, salt, pepper and herbs and bind with the egg. Shape into 16 balls and coat lightly with flour. Shallow fry for 5 minutes until golden brown on all sides. Drain well and place in a baking dish.

Put the red pepper, pineapple, sugar, vinegar, soy sauce, stock, salt and pepper in a saucepan and bring to the boil. Dissolve the cornflour in a little water and add to the pan. Simmer, stirring, until thickened. Pour this sauce over the pork balls, then cover the dish and bake in a preheated moderate oven (180°C/350°F, Gas Mark 4) for 45 minutes. Serve hot with boiled rice.

Pork with Orange Sauce

Serves 4–5

flour for coating
salt
pepper
575 g/1¼ lb boneless
pork, cut into 2.5 cm/1
inch cubes
25 g/1 oz butter
1 small onion, chopped
1 green pepper, cored,
seeded and chopped
juice of 2 oranges
½ teaspoon grated orange
rind
1 tablespoon
Worcestershire sauce
150 ml/¼ pint stock
orange segments to
garnish

Mix the flour with the salt and pepper and use to coat the cubes of pork. Melt the butter in a frying pan and add the onion and green pepper. Fry until softened. Add the pork and continue frying until the cubes are lightly browned on all sides. Stir in the orange juice and rind, Worcestershire sauce and stock and bring to the boil. Simmer for 30 minutes, stirring occasionally.

Garnish with the orange segments and serve with a green salad.

Apple Cider Pork

Serves 4

4 pork chops or belly of
pork slices
1 tablespoon vinegar
cider
1 bay leaf
juice of ½ lemon
1 bouquet garni
salt
pepper
lemon slices to garnish

Sauce
50 g/2 oz butter
75 g/3 oz sugar
1 kg/2 lb cooking apples,
peeled, cored and
quartered
300 ml/½ pint cider

Put the pork chops or slices in a baking dish. Add the vinegar and enough cider to come halfway up the sides of the meat. Add the bay leaf, lemon juice, bouquet garni, salt and pepper. Cook in a preheated moderately hot oven (190°C/375°F, Gas Mark 5) for 45 minutes.

Meanwhile, make the sauce. Melt the butter in a heavy-based saucepan. Stir in the sugar and cook until golden. Add the apples and cider, cover the pan and cook gently until soft. Sieve the sauce and keep hot.

Transfer the chops or slices to a warmed serving dish. Garnish with lemon slices and serve with the sauce.

Barbecued Spare Ribs
Serves 4–5

2 teaspoons ground
  ginger
2 teaspoons demerara
  sugar
2 teaspoons dry mustard
salt
pepper
750 g to 1 kg/1½ to 2 lb
  spare ribs or belly of
  pork slices
3 tablespoons oil
1 onion, chopped
1 to 2 garlic cloves,
  crushed
grated rind and juice of 1
  lemon
3 tablespoons
  Worcestershire sauce
3 tablespoons soy sauce
3 tablespoons tomato
  ketchup

Mix together the ginger, sugar, mustard, salt and pepper and use to coat the spare ribs. Heat the oil in a frying pan and fry the spare ribs until they are lightly browned. Transfer them to a baking dish.

Add the onion and garlic to the pan and fry until softened, then stir in the remaining ingredients. Bring to the boil. Pour the mixture over the spare ribs. Cover the dish and bake in a preheated moderately hot oven (190°C/375°F, Gas Mark 5) for 25 to 30 minutes or until the spare ribs are tender.

Devilled Pork Chops with Baked Apples
Serves 2

15 g/½ oz dripping
2 loin pork chops,
  trimmed of fat
1 small onion, sliced
15 g/½ oz flour
300 ml/½ pint stock
2 whole cloves
1 teaspoon
  Worcestershire sauce
1½ teaspoons tomato
  ketchup
salt
pepper
1 teaspoon dry mustard
2 hot small baked apples
100 g/4 oz hot mashed
  potato

Melt the dripping in a frying pan. Add the chops and brown on both sides. Transfer the chops to a baking dish.

Add the onion to the pan and fry until softened. Stir in the flour and cook for 2 minutes, then gradually stir in the stock. Add the cloves, Worcestershire sauce, ketchup, salt, pepper and mustard and bring to the boil. Pour over the chops and bake in a preheated moderate oven (160°C/325°F, Gas Mark 3) for 1 hour.

Add the baked apples to the dish and pipe the potato around the apples before serving.

Honeyed Pork
Serves 4

6 tablespoons oil
450 g/1 lb boneless lean
  pork, diced
1 garlic clove, crushed
1 green pepper, cored,
  seeded and chopped
225 g/8 oz canned
  pineapple chunks
100 g/4 oz mushrooms,
  sliced
3 tomatoes, quartered
1 chicken stock cube
2 tablespoons honey
1 tablespoon soy sauce
2 tablespoons cornflour

Heat the oil in a frying pan and fry the pork, garlic, and green pepper until the pork is lightly browned. Reduce the heat and continue cooking for about 45 minutes or until the pork is tender.

Drain the pineapple chunks, reserving the can syrup, and add the pineapple to the pan with the mushrooms and tomatoes.

Make the pineapple syrup up to 300 ml/ $\frac{1}{2}$ pint with water. Crumble in the stock cube and stir well to dissolve, then add the honey and soy sauce. Dissolve the cornflour in a little water and add to the honey mixture.

Stir the liquid into the pork mixture and bring to the boil, stirring well. Simmer until thickened. Serve with boiled rice.

Pork with Red Beans and Coriander
Serves 4

1 tablespoon oil
350 g/12 oz lean belly of
  pork, skinned, boned
  and cut into narrow
  strips
2 onions, sliced
2 carrots, sliced
2 teaspoons coriander
  seeds, crushed
225 g/8 oz dried red
  kidney beans, soaked
  overnight and drained
600 ml/1 pint boiling
  stock
salt
pepper
chopped parsley to
  garnish

Heat the oil in a frying pan and brown the pork strips on both sides. Transfer them to a casserole.

Add the onions to the pan and fry until golden brown. Drain off all the fat, then add the onions to the casserole with the carrots, coriander, beans, stock, salt and pepper. Cover and cook in a preheated moderate oven (160°C/325°F, Gas Mark 3) for 1½ to 2 hours or until the meat and beans are very tender.

Spoon off any excess fat and serve garnished with parsley.

Curried Pork Loaf
Serves 4

350 g/12 oz lean minced pork
2 teaspoons curry powder
2 tablespoons mango chutney
1 onion, finely chopped
50 g/2 oz fresh breadcrumbs
salt
pepper
2 eggs, beaten
300 ml/½ pint white sauce flavoured with curry powder

Mix together the pork, curry powder, chutney, onion, breadcrumbs, salt and pepper and bind with the eggs. Press into a greased 500 g/1 lb loaf tin and smooth the surface. Place the tin in a roasting tin of water and bake in a moderate oven (160°C/325 F, Gas Mark 3) for about 1¼ hours.

Turn out the loaf onto a warmed serving dish and serve with the sauce. To serve cold, cool in the tin and chill before turning out and slicing.

Pickled Pig's Trotters
Serves 2–3

6 pigs' trotters, soaked for 6 to 8 hours
600 ml/1 pint malt vinegar
6 whole cloves
1 bay leaf
2 mace blades

Drain the trotters and split and crack them in several places. Put into a saucepan and cover with some fresh water. Bring to the boil and simmer gently until tender. Drain and place in a heatproof dish.

Put the remaining ingredients in a saucepan and bring to the boil. Boil for a few minutes, then pour over the trotters. Leave to cool, then keep in a cool place for 24 hours.

Melton Mowbray Pork Pies
Makes 6 or 7

3.5 kg/8 lb boneless pork, minced or finely chopped
50 g/2 oz salt
25 g/1 oz pepper
little water
hot water crust pastry, made with 2.5 kg/5lb flour, 25 g/1 oz salt, 1.25 kg/2½ lb lard and 750 ml/1½ pints water (see page 125)

Mix the meat with the salt, pepper and a little water. Raise and shape six or seven pies (see page 82) and fill with the meat. Wrap the pies round with greaseproof paper to keep them in good shape and place on a baking sheet. Bake in a preheated moderate oven (180°C/350°F, Gas Mark 4) for 1¼ hours or until golden brown.

Raised Pork Pie

Serves 6

1 pig's trotter
750 g/1½ lb lean pork
  (blade bone or hand),
  finely chopped
salt
pepper
dried sage
1 large onion
450 g/1 lb hot water
  crust pastry, made with
  1 lb flour, 1 level
  teaspoon salt and 6 oz
  lard (see page 125)
beaten egg to glaze

Cut open the trotter and take out as much lean meat as possible. Finely chop the meat and mix with the pork, salt, pepper and sage. Put the remains of the trotter and any trimmings into a saucepan with the onion, salt and pepper. Cover with water, bring to the boil and simmer for 3 hours.

Meanwhile, roll out three-quarters of the dough to a strip about 12.5 cm/5 inches wide. Keep it very even at the edges and an equal thickness all over. Dampen one side and one end, then bring the two ends together to form a ring, overlapping them. Press well together. Gather the dampened side together to form a bottom for the pie. Stand it up and make into a good shape.

Fill with the meat mixture, but not too tightly. Level the top. There should be just a small rim of dough standing above the meat filling. Roll out the rest of the dough thinly and cut out a round to cover the top of the pie. Press the dampened edges together to seal, then trim neatly with scissors to leave a ridge 1 cm/½ inch high standing straight up around the pie. Snip this ridge, making the cuts 1 cm/½ inch apart. Make a small hole in the centre of the lid, then brush all over with beaten egg.

Pin a band of doubled greaseproof paper almost the same depth around the pie. Place the pie on a greased baking sheet and bake in a preheated moderate oven (180 C/350 F, Gas Mark 4) for 1 hour. Reduce the heat to cool (150 C/300 F, Gas Mark 2) and continue baking for 2 hours, covering the top of the pie with greaseproof paper halfway through this period.

Remove the paper from the sides of the pie and brush with beaten egg. Continue baking for 30 minutes.

Strain the stock, then using a funnel pour it into the hot pie through the hole in the lid.

Pork and Bacon Loaf

Serves 6–8

450 g/1 lb lean belly
  pork, minced, or
  minced beef
225 g/8 oz unsmoked
  back bacon, rinded and
  minced, or finely
  chopped
175 to 225 g/6 to 8 oz
  fresh breadcrumbs
1 onion, finely chopped
½ teaspoon dried mixed
  herbs or mint
salt
pepper
1 egg, beaten
150 ml/¼ pint cider

Mix together the pork or beef, bacon, breadcrumbs, onion, mixed herbs or mint, salt and
pepper and bind with the egg and cider. Press
into a greased 1 kg/2 lb loaf tin and smooth the
top. Cover with greased greaseproof paper or
foil.

Bake in a preheated moderate oven
(180°C/350°F, Gas Mark 4) for about 1½ hours.
Turn out and serve hot with a parsley or onion
sauce, or cold with salads.

Pork with Cider

Serves 4

2 tablespoons flour
salt
pepper
4 boneless pork steaks or
  slices
40 g/1½ oz butter
100 g/4 oz mushrooms,
  sliced
300 ml/½ pint dry cider
good dash of
  Worcestershire sauce
150 ml/¼ pint single
  cream
1 tablespoon chopped
  parsley
1 tablespoon chopped
  chives or spring onions

Mix the flour with salt and pepper and use half
to coat the pork. Melt the butter in a deep
frying pan and brown the pork slices on both
sides. Remove them from the pan.

Add the mushrooms to the pan and fry for
2 to 3 minutes, then stir in the remaining
seasoning flour. Cook for 1 minute. Gradually
stir in the cider and bring to the boil. Add the
Worcestershire sauce, salt and pepper and
replace the pork in the pan. Cover and simmer
gently for 10 minutes or until tender.

Stir in the cream, parsley and chives or
spring onions and heat through gently without
boiling. Serve with noodles or creamed
potatoes.

Gammon Casserole
Serves 2

50 g/2 oz butter
3 tablespoons flour
300 ml/½ pint stock
6 very thin lemon slices
75 g/3 oz mixed dried
  fruit or sliced
  pineapple
¼ teaspoon mixed spice
75 ml/2 fl oz sherry
2 thick gammon slices,
  cut into serving pieces

Melt the butter in a saucepan and stir in the flour. Cook for 2 minutes, then gradually stir in the stock. Bring to the boil. Add the lemon slices, fruit, spice and sherry and stir well.

Put the gammon pieces in a buttered casserole and pour over the sauce. Bake in a preheated moderate oven (160°C/325°F, Gas Mark 3) for 1 hour.

Hampshire Bacon Pudding
Serves 4

225 g/8 oz flour
½ teaspoon baking powder
½ teaspoon salt
75 to 100 g/3 to 4 oz
  shredded suet
2 onions, chopped
6 bacon rashers, rinded
½ teaspoon dried sage

Sift the flour, baking powder and salt into a bowl. Mix in the suet, then bind with water. Roll out the dough into an oblong. Cover with the onions and bacon, leaving a margin clear around the edge. Sprinkle with the sage, salt and pepper. Dampen the edges and roll up. Tie in a cloth and boil for 2 hours, or steam wrapped in greaseproof paper for 3 hours.

Pineapple Glazed Ham

1 piece of ham, soaked
  overnight
whole cloves
175 g/6 oz canned
  crushed pineapple
175 g/6 oz brown sugar
pineapple rings to garnish

Drain the ham and put into a saucepan. Cover with fresh water and bring to the boil. Simmer, allowing 15 minutes per 450 g/1 lb plus 15 minutes over.

Drain the ham and remove the brown skin. Score the surface of the fat and stud with cloves. Put the ham in a baking tin. Mix together the crushed pineapple and sugar and spread over the ham. Bake in a preheated moderate oven (170°C/325°F, Gas Mark 4) for 45 minutes, basting frequently with the glaze.

Serve hot or cold, garnished with pineapple.

Bacon Provençal

*2.75 kg/6 lb prime collar
    bacon, boned, rolled
    and soaked overnight*
*300 ml/½ pint white wine
    or dry cider*
*350 g/12 oz button
    onions*
*400 g/14 oz canned
    tomatoes*
*1 teaspoon dried oregano
    or marjoram*
pepper
*4 large garlic cloves,
    each cut into 4 slivers
    (optional)*

Drain the bacon and put into a saucepan. Add half the wine or cider and enough cold water to cover. Bring to the boil and simmer for half the total cooking time (allow 25 minutes per 450g/1 lb plus 25 minutes over).

Meanwhile, blanch the onions in boiling water for 15 minutes. Drain.

Drain the bacon and remove the rind. Stand the bacon in a baking dish and surround with the onions and tomatoes. Sprinkle with the herbs and pepper. Pour over the rest of the wine or cider. If using the garlic, stick the slivers into the bacon fat.

Cover and cook in a preheated moderately hot oven (190°C/375°F, Gas Mark 5) for the remaining cooking time, removing the lid for the last 15 minutes.

Serve hot in slices with the vegetable mixture. Any leftover bacon is delicious served cold.

Brawn

½ pig's head
225 g/8 oz piece fat ham
1 pig's trotter
2 onions
salt
pepper
15 g/½ oz gelatine

Put the pig's head into a saucepan with the ham, trotter, onions, salt and pepper. Cover with water and bring to the boil, skimming off the scum that rises to the surface. Simmer until the meat is nearly coming off the bones.

Remove the pig's head from the pan and take the meat from the bones, discarding any gristle. Chop the meat coarsely. Chop the ham and meat from the trotter and mix with the meat from the head.

Strain the stock, then skim off any fat. Dissolve the gelatine in 150 ml/¼ pint of the stock. Adjust the seasoning, then mix in the meat. Turn into a pudding basin, cover with a plate and place a 1 kg/2 lb weight on top. Leave for 24 hours before turning out to serve.

Viking Special

Serves 4

4 tomatoes, sliced
4 carrots, cooked and sliced
4 potatoes, peeled, cooked and sliced
1 apple, cored and chopped
juice of ½ lemon
2 celery stalks, chopped
2 tablespoons salad cream
1 bacon hock, cooked, skinned and minced or finely chopped

French Dressing

2 tablespoons oil
1 tablespoon wine vinegar
salt
pepper

Put the tomatoes, carrots and potatoes in a bowl. Mix together the ingredients for the dressing and pour into the bowl. Fold together gently.

Mix the apple with the lemon juice, then stir in the celery and salad cream. Add the bacon and mix well. Spoon this meat mixture on top of the tomato mixture, and serve with coleslaw or a green salad.

Fidget Pie

Serves 4 6

450 g/1 lb potatoes, peeled and sliced
approx. 225 g/8 oz cooked bacon or ham, diced
450 g/1 lb apples, peeled, cored and sliced
sugar (optional)
stock
salt
pepper
approx. 100 g/4 oz shortcrust pastry

Make a layer of potato slices in a pie dish, then cover with some of the bacon or ham. If the apples are very sour, dip the slices in sugar and make a layer on top of the bacon or ham. Repeat the layers until all the ingredients are used and the dish is full. Pour in a little stock and add salt and pepper. Roll out the dough and use to cover the dish.

Bake in a preheated moderately hot oven (190 C/375 F, Gas Mark 5) for about 1 hour or until the pastry is golden brown.

Note: If you prefer, the bacon or ham may be cut into 5 mm/¼ inch thick slices.

Variation: Instead of the bacon or ham, use chops cut from the scrag end of a neck of mutton.

Hubble Bubble

Serves 4

450 g/1 lb potatoes,
  peeled, cooked and
  sliced
4 streaky bacon rashers,
  rinded and chopped
1 onion, finely chopped
225 g/8 oz pork sausages,
  skinned and quartered
2 eggs
150 ml/¼ pint milk
salt
pepper

Line the bottom of a greased baking dish with half the potato slices. Mix together the bacon, onion and sausage pieces and place on top of the potato layer. Lightly beat the eggs with the milk, salt and pepper and pour into the dish. Cover the top with the remaining potato slices.

Bake in a preheated moderate oven (180°C/350°F, Gas Mark 4) for about 45 minutes or until the eggs are set.

Veal Casserole

Serves 4–5

750 g/1½ lb boned
  shoulder of veal, cut
  into cubes
2 onions, quartered
2 large carrots, quartered
3 bay leaves
1 parsley sprig
1 tablespoon lemon juice
salt
pepper
1 litre/1¾ pints water
175 g/6 oz mushrooms,
  sliced
40 g/1½ oz butter
40 g/1½ oz flour
450 ml/¾ pint single
  cream
1 egg yolk

Put the veal cubes in a saucepan and cover with cold water. Bring to the boil, then drain. Return the veal to the cleaned-out saucepan and add the onions, carrots, bay leaves, parsley, lemon juice, salt, pepper and water. Bring to the boil, then cover and simmer for 1 hour.

Add the mushrooms and continue simmering for 30 minutes or until the veal is tender.

Drain the veal and vegetables, reserving the cooking liquor, and arrange on a warmed serving dish. Keep hot.

Return the cooking liquor to the pan and boil until reduced to 600 ml/1 pint.

Melt the butter in another saucepan. Add the flour and cook, stirring, for 2 minutes. Gradually stir in the cooking liquor and bring to the boil. Simmer, stirring, until thickened.

Mix together the cream and egg yolk in a bowl. Add a little of the hot sauce, then stir this into the rest of the sauce in the pan. Heat through gently without boiling. Pour the sauce over the veal and vegetables and serve.

Fricadelles

Serves 4–5

450 g/1 lb pie veal
100 g/4 oz fat veal or salt pork, minced
1 small onion, finely chopped
2 or 3 parsley sprigs
2 lemon thyme or lemon balm sprigs, or grated rind of ½ lemon
150 g/5 oz stale white bread soaked in a little cold milk
salt
pepper
2 teaspoons paprika
approx. 150 ml/¼ pint water
flour for coating
butter or oil for frying
lemon wedges to garnish

Sauce

25 g/1 oz fat or margarine
2 tablespoons flour
300 ml/½ pint stock or consommé
2 to 3 tablespoons soured cream or natural yogurt (optional)

Mince the veal twice. Add the fat veal or salt pork, onion, parsley and lemon thyme or balm or lemon rind. Squeeze the bread of excess milk, then add to the veal mixture. Put all through the mincer. Mix in salt, pepper and paprika, then gradually work in the water as if making bread. Do not add the water too quickly or the mixture will become sloppy instead of firm and light.

Roll the mixture into marble-sized balls and coat with flour. Fry quickly in butter or oil until browned on all sides.

For the sauce, melt the fat or margarine in a saucepan. Stir in the flour and cook for 2 minutes, then gradually stir in the stock or consommé. Bring to the boil and simmer, stirring, until thickened.

Drain the veal balls and arrange them in a baking dish. Pour over the sauce. Cook in a preheated cool oven (150°C/300°F, Gas Mark 2) for 15 to 20 minutes.

Stir in the soured cream or yogurt and serve garnished with lemon wedges.

Veal and Bean Sauté

Serves 6

40 g/1½ oz butter or
  margarine
1 kg/2 lb veal fillet, cut
  into 1 cm/½ inch wide
  strips
750 g/1½ lb runner beans,
  sliced
2 large onions, thinly
  sliced
250 ml/8 fl oz dry white
  wine
2 teaspoons Dijon or
  French mustard
1 tablespoon chopped
  fresh parsley
2 teaspoons chopped
  fresh sage
salt
pepper

Melt the butter in a saucepan and fry the veal strips until they are browned all over. Add the beans and onions and continue cooking until the onions are softened. Stir in the remaining ingredients and bring to the boil. Cover and cook gently for 30 minutes or until tender. Serve with boiled rice or potatoes.

Puffy Lemon Veal Pie

Serves 4

25 g/1 oz butter or
  margarine
1 tablespoon oil
1 large onion, sliced
450 g/1 lb lean pie veal,
  cubed
1 tablespoon flour
1 tablespoon paprika
450 ml/¾ pint chicken
  stock
grated rind and juice of 1
  small lemon
salt and pepper

Pastry
100 g/4 oz flour
75 g/3 oz semi-frozen
  margarine
beaten egg or milk to
  glaze

Melt the butter or margarine with the oil in a frying pan. Add the onion and fry until softened. Add the veal and brown on all sides, then stir in the flour and paprika. Add the stock, lemon rind and juice, salt and pepper and bring to the boil. Cover and simmer gently for 1 hour or until the veal is tender.

Meanwhile, make the pastry. Sift the flour into a bowl, then grate in the margarine and mix to a firm but lumpy dough with cold water.

Cool the veal mixture slightly, then pour into a pie dish. Roll out the dough and use to cover the pie. Crimp the edges and decorate with the dough trimmings. Brush with beaten egg or milk and bake in a preheated moderately hot oven (200°C/400°F, Gas Mark 6) for 25 to 30 minutes or until puffy and well browned.

Cromwell's Choice
Serves 6

1 leg or shoulder of veal
salt
pepper
4 fat bacon rashers
little stock
orange slices to garnish
Glaze
4 oranges
2 tablespoons brown
  sugar
2 teaspoons cornflour
pepper
100 ml/3 fl oz Curaçao
  or white wine

Rub the veal with salt and pepper and place in a greased roasting tin. Cover with the bacon. Roast in a preheated hot oven (220°C/425°F, Gas Mark 7) for 25 minutes per 450 g/1 lb plus 25 minutes over. Baste frequently with stock.

Meanwhile make the glaze. Peel the oranges thinly, not taking any of the white pith, and cut the peel into thin shreds. Put the shreds into a saucepan, cover with water and bring to the boil. Boil for 3 minutes, then drain. Squeeze the oranges and strain the juice into another saucepan. Add the brown sugar and cook, stirring frequently, until syrupy. Dissolve the cornflour in a little water and add to the pan with a little pepper. Cook, stirring, until thickened, then add the orange shreds and Curaçao or wine.

Discard the bacon from the veal and pour off any juices in the tin. Pour the glaze over the meat and return to the oven. Turn off the heat and leave in the oven for 5 minutes. Serve garnished with orange slices.

Liver and Bacon Rolls
Serves 4

8 streaky bacon rashers,
  rinded
made mustard
100 g/4 oz lamb's liver,
  cut into eight 5 × 1 cm/
  2 × ½ inch pieces
salt
pepper
dried sage or 8 sage
  leaves
50 g/2 oz butter or 4
  tablespoons oil
mashed potatoes and peas
  to serve

Spread the bacon rashers on one side with mustard. Rub the liver pieces with salt and pepper and place one on each bacon rasher. Sprinkle with sage or add a sage leaf and roll up. Secure with wooden cocktail sticks.

Melt the butter or heat the oil in a frying pan. Add the liver and bacon rolls and fry for about 7 minutes or until golden brown and cooked through.

Line a warmed serving dish with a piped border of mashed potato, then add a border of peas. Remove the cocktail sticks from the liver and bacon rolls and pile them in the centre. If you like, make a brown sauce with the pan juices.

Kidneys au Vin Blanc

40 g/1½ oz butter
1 small onion, chopped
1 garlic clove, crushed
6 sheep's kidneys,
  skinned and thickly
  sliced
25 g/1 oz flour
salt
pepper
50 g/2 oz mushrooms,
  sliced
1 teaspoon chopped fresh
  herbs
150 ml/¼ pint white wine
150 ml/¼ pint stock
3 large tomatoes,
  skinned, quartered and
  seeded
croûtons to garnish

Melt the butter in a frying pan and fry the onion and garlic until softened. Add the kidneys and fry until lightly browned.

Remove the pan from the heat and stir in the flour, salt, pepper, mushrooms, herbs, wine and stock. Bring to the boil and simmer for 10 minutes.

Add the tomatoes and cook for a further 2 to 3 minutes. Serve garnished with croûtons.

Liver Paprika

15 g/½ oz butter
225 g/8 oz lamb's liver,
  sliced
salt
pepper
150 g/5 oz soured cream
1 teaspoon paprika
paprika to garnish

Melt the butter in a frying pan. Rub the liver slices with salt and pepper and add to the pan. Fry until lightly browned on both sides and cooked through. Transfer the liver slices to a flameproof serving dish and keep hot.

Mix the soured cream with the paprika and pour over the liver. Grill for 1 to 2 minutes, then sprinkle with a little more paprika and serve with noodles or creamed potatoes and watercress.

Sausage and Kidney Casserole   Serves 4

25 g/1 oz butter or
  margarine
225 g/8 oz chipolata
  sausages, halved
8 lambs' kidneys,
  skinned, halved and
  cored
1 large onion, sliced
15 g/½ oz flour
300 ml/½ pint beef stock
6 tablespoons white wine
salt
pepper
½ teaspoon dried dill
100 g/4 oz mushrooms,
  sliced
750 g/1½ lb potatoes,
  peeled, cooked and
  mashed
beaten egg or melted
  butter to glaze
chopped parsley to
  garnish

Melt the fat in a frying pan and fry the sausages until they are lightly browned on all sides. Transfer them to a casserole. Add the kidneys to the pan and fry until well sealed. Add them to the casserole.

Put the onion in the pan and fry until softened. Stir in the flour, then add the stock, wine, salt, pepper and dill. Bring to the boil, stirring. Stir in the mushrooms and pour into the casserole. Cover the casserole and cook in a preheated moderate oven (180°C/350°F, Gas Mark 4) for 30 to 40 minutes or until the sausages and kidneys are tender.

Meanwhile, pipe the potato around the edge of a shallow flameproof serving dish. Brush the potato with beaten egg or melted butter and brown under a hot grill.

Spoon the sausage and kidney mixture into the dish and garnish with parsley.

Kidneys in Baked Potatoes   Serves 4

4 large potatoes
4 kidneys, skinned
4 bacon rashers, rinded
salt
pepper

Bake the potatoes in a preheated moderately hot oven (200°C/400°F, Gas Mark 6) for 1 hour.

Cut a slice from the wide part of each potato and hollow out. Wrap each kidney in a bacon rasher and place in the potatoes. Add salt and pepper, then replace the 'tops'. Wrap the potatoes individually in foil and bake for a further 1 hour.

Devilled Kidneys

Serves 2

4 sheep's kidneys
1 tablespoon butter
1 teaspoon made mustard
salt
pepper

Split the kidneys, open out flat and remove the cores, skin and fat. Make little gashes in the cut surfaces. Mix half the butter with the mustard, salt and pepper to a paste and rub this into the gashes in the kidneys. Skewer them to keep them opened flat and arrange in the grill pan. Dot with the rest of the butter and grill for 7 to 8 minutes, turning once. Serve with the pan juices poured over.

Chipstead Churdles

Makes 4–5

25 g/1 oz bacon fat
1 large onion, sliced
225 g/8 oz lamb's liver,
* sliced*
225 g/8 oz bacon pieces,
* rinded*
50 g/2 oz mushrooms,
* chopped*
1 medium cooking apple,
* peeled, cored and*
* chopped*
1 tablespoon chopped
* parsley*
1 teaspoon dried
* rosemary*
salt
pepper
225 g/8 oz shortcrust
* pastry*
1 tablespoon browned
* breadcrumbs*
1 tablespoon grated
* cheese*
beaten egg to glaze

Melt the bacon fat in a frying pan and fry the onion and liver until lightly browned. Mince together the onion, liver and bacon pieces, then add the mushrooms, apple, parsley, rosemary and salt and pepper. Mix well.

Roll out the dough and cut out 15 cm/6 inch rounds. Divide the liver mixture between the rounds, then shape the dough up around it to form a Bishop's hat, leaving the mixture exposed in the centre. Mix together the breadcrumbs and cheese and sprinkle over the exposed centres.

Place the churdles on a baking sheet and brush with beaten egg. Bake in a preheated moderate oven (180°C/350°F, Gas Mark 4) for 30 minutes or until the pastry is golden. Serve with redcurrant jelly, if you like.

California Ox Tongue
Serves 6-8

1 ox tongue
4 tablespoons oil
2 onions, chopped
1 garlic clove, crushed
175 g/6 oz seedless raisins
300 g/11 oz canned tomatoes
50 g/2 oz stuffed olives, sliced
1 green pepper, cored, seeded and chopped
salt

Put the tongue in a saucepan and cover with water. Bring to the boil and simmer, allowing 30 minutes per 450 g/1 lb and 30 minutes over. Cool in the water, then drain and remove the skin. Put the tongue in a roasting tin.

Heat the oil in a saucepan and fry the onions and garlic until golden brown. Stir in the raisins, then add the remaining ingredients and bring to the boil, stirring well.

Pour the sauce over the tongue and bake in a preheated moderate oven (180 C/350°F, Gas Mark 4) for 1 hour.

Oxtail Stew
Serves 4

1 onion stuck with 3 cloves
6 peppercorns
salt
pepper
1 oxtail, jointed
225 g/8 oz carrots, chopped or sliced
225 g/8 oz turnips, chopped or sliced
225 g/8 oz onions, chopped
25 g/1 oz butter
1 tablespoon flour
gravy browning (optional)

Put the onion, peppercorns, salt, pepper and oxtail pieces in a saucepan and cover with water. Bring to the boil and simmer gently for $2\frac{1}{2}$-3 hours.

Skim any fat from the surface, then add the carrots, turnips and chopped onions. Continue simmering until the vegetables are tender.

Mix together the butter and flour to make a paste and divide into three or four portions. Add these, one at a time, to the stew, stirring well. Simmer for a further 10 minutes. Add a drop or two of gravy browning to improve the colour, if you like.

Braised Ox Tongue

Serves 6–8

1 ox tongue
salt
pepper
2 or 3 onions
2 or 3 carrots
little flour
2 or 3 tablespoons red
  wine (optional)

Put the tongue in a saucepan with the vegetables and add salt and pepper. Cover with water, bring to the boil and simmer, allowing 30 minutes per 450 g/1 lb and 30 minutes over. Drain the tongue, reserving the liquid and vegetables, and remove the skin. Cut the tongue into slices about 3 mm/$\frac{1}{8}$ inch thick and arrange on a warmed serving platter. Keep hot.

Sieve the vegetables to make a purée, then stir in as much of the liquid as you like to make a sauce. Thicken with a little flour and stir in the wine, if using. Pour this sauce over the tongue and serve.

Fried Sweetbreads

Serves 4

2 pairs calf or lamb
  sweetbreads, soaked
  for 3 hours
50 g/2 oz butter
squeeze of lemon juice
chicken stock or water
flour for coating
salt
pepper
1 egg, beaten

Drain the sweetbreads and put into a saucepan. Cover with fresh water, bring to the boil and drain. Cover with fresh water, bring to the boil again and drain. Rinse in cold water and remove the black veins.

Return the sweetbreads to the pan and add 15 g/$\frac{1}{2}$ oz of the butter, the lemon juice and enough stock or water to cover. Bring to the boil and simmer for 20 minutes. Cool in the liquid.

Drain the sweetbreads and cut into thick slices. Mix the flour with salt and pepper and use to coat the slices. Dip them in the beaten egg. Melt the remaining butter in a frying pan and fry the sweetbread slices until they are golden brown.

Brains au Beurre   *Serves 4*

*450 g/1 lb calves' or
    sheep's brains
2 tablespoons vinegar
salt
pepper
75 g/3 oz butter
2 tablespoons capers
juice of ½ lemon*

Soak the brains in cold water for 3 or 4 hours, changing the water several times. Drain and remove the skin and any particles of blood. Put the brains into a saucepan with the vinegar, salt and pepper and cover with fresh water. Bring to the boil and simmer gently for 15 minutes. Press between two plates until quite firm. Cut the brains into small pieces.

Melt the butter in a frying pan and gently fry the pieces until they are lightly browned. Transfer the brain pieces to a warmed serving dish and keep hot. Stir the capers and lemon juice in to the butter in the pan, heat through and pour over the brains.

Baked Stuffed Hearts   *Serves 4–5*

*2 sheep's hearts, veins
    and gristle removed
little stock*
Stuffing
*1 streaky bacon rasher,
    rinded and diced
1 small onion, chopped
4 tablespoons fresh
    breadcrumbs
1 tablespoon chopped
    suet
1 teaspoon chopped
    parsley
grated rind of ½ lemon
1 egg, beaten*

Fry the bacon and onion together until softened, then stir in the remaining stuffing ingredients. Fill the cavity in the hearts and sew up. Put the hearts in a baking tin with a little stock and bake in a preheated moderate oven (180°C/350°F, Gas Mark 4) for 2 hours. Baste occasionally with the stock.

Serve with gravy and redcurrant jelly.

Faggots
Serves 4

450 g/1 lb pig's fry
3 small onions, chopped
75 g/3 oz fresh
  breadcrumbs
½ teaspoon chopped fresh
  sage
½ teaspoon chopped fresh
  thyme
salt
pepper
1 pig's caul or veil,
  soaked in warm water

Put the pigs' fry and onions in a saucepan, cover with water and bring to the boil. Simmer for 45 minutes. Drain off the liquid, reserving a little to moisten the breadcrumbs. Mince the pigs' fry and onions, then mix in the moistened breadcrumbs, herbs, salt and pepper.

Drain the caul and cut into 2.5 or 5 cm/1 or 2 inch squares. Divide the mixture between the squares and shape into balls. Pack the balls closely into a greased roasting tin. Bake in a preheated moderately hot oven (190°C/375°F, Gas Mark 5) for 45 minutes or until well browned. Serve with a good gravy and creamed potatoes.

Fried Tripe
Serves 3

450 g/1 lb tripe, cut into
  finger-sized pieces
600 ml/1 pint milk
salt
pepper
oil for deep frying
tartare sauce to serve
Batter
100 g/4 oz flour
1 egg
300 ml/½ pint milk

Put the tripe into a saucepan with the milk, salt and pepper. Simmer gently for about 45 minutes or until tender. Drain well, reserving the milk to make the batter, if you like.

Sift the flour into a bowl and make a well in the centre. Add the egg and half the milk and beat in the flour, then gradually beat in the rest of the milk.

Dip the pieces of tripe in the batter and deep fry until golden brown. Drain on paper towels and serve with tartare sauce.

Sausage Meat Flan
Serves 4

100 g/4 oz shortcrust
  pastry
225 g/8 oz sausage meat
1 onion, chopped
½ teaspoon dried sage
2 to 3 tomatoes, sliced

Roll out the dough and use to line a 18 cm/7 inch pie dish. Mix together the sausage meat, onion and sage and put into the pastry case. Smooth the top and cover with the tomato slices.

Bake in a preheated moderately hot oven (200°C/400°F, Gas Mark 6) for 20 to 30 minutes.

97

Poultry & Game

Chicken Maryland
Serves 4

*1 × 1.5 kg/3 lb chicken,
   cut into joints
salt and pepper
flour
1 egg, beaten with 2
   tablespoons cold water
fresh breadcrumbs
75 g/3 oz bacon fat or
   butter*

Rub the chicken joints with salt and pepper,
then coat with flour. Dip in the egg, then coat
with breadcrumbs. Melt the fat or butter in a
frying pan and fry the chicken joints until
golden brown. Add a little water to the pan,
cover and cook gently until the chicken is
tender. Serve with sweetcorn fritters and
halved bananas fried in butter.

French Roast Chicken

*bunch of parsley or
   tarragon
knob of butter
1 chicken
stock
melted dripping or fat, or
   bacon rashers
1 bouquet garni
2 tablespoons lemon juice
   or red wine*

Put the parsley or tarragon and butter inside
the chicken and truss. Put in a roasting tin and
brush with melted dripping or fat, or cover with
bacon rashers. Pour enough stock into the tin
to make a 2.5 cm/1 inch layer and add the
bouquet garni and lemon juice or wine. Cover
the tin with foil and roast in a preheated cool
oven (150 C/300 F, Gas Mark 2) for roughly
twice as long as for ordinary roast chicken, i.e.
40 minutes per 450 g/1 lb, plus 40 minutes. Baste
from time to time with the liquid in the tin.
   Serve with gravy and a watercress salad.

Chicken Sunshine Salad

Serves 4

*350 g/12 oz canned
    pineapple cubes
1 green pepper, cored,
    seeded, chopped and
    blanched
4 to 6 spring onions,
    chopped
1 × 5 cm/2 inch piece
    cucumber, diced
175 g/6 oz long-grain
    rice, cooked
2 tablespoons French
    dressing
salt
pepper
75 to 100 g/3 to 4 oz
    salami, sliced
225 to 350 g/8 to 12 oz
    cooked chicken meat,
    cut into strips
2 tablespoons mayonnaise
4 tablespoons whipped
    cream
2 tablespoons chutney
Worcestershire sauce
cucumber slices to
    garnish*

Drain the pineapple, reserving 2 tablespoons of the can syrup. Put the pineapple in a bowl with the green pepper, spring onions, cucumber and rice. Add the reserved pineapple syrup, the dressing and salt and pepper and toss well.

Reserve some salami slices for the garnish and dice the remainder. Mix together the chicken, diced salami mayonnaise, cream, chutney, a good dash of Worcestershire sauce and salt and pepper.

Arrange the rice mixture on a serving dish and spoon the chicken mixture on top, down the centre. Chill for at least 2 hours before serving, garnished with the cucumber and salami slices.

Bread Sauce

Serves 5–6

*1 onion stuck with 4
    cloves
300 ml/½ pint milk
4 heaped tablespoons
    fresh white
    breadcrumbs
knob of butter
little single cream or top
    of milk
salt
pinch of cayenne pepper*

Put the onion and milk in a saucepan and leave to soak for 15 minutes. Bring gently to the boil, then stir in the breadcrumbs. Simmer for 10 minutes. Add the butter, cream, salt and cayenne and reheat gently. Discard the onion and serve.

Farmhouse Favourite

Serves 4–6

450 g/1 lb potatoes,
  peeled, cooked and
  mashed
25 g/1 oz butter
1 egg, beaten
salt
pepper
Filling
½ boiling fowl, cooked,
  skinned, boned and
  diced
100 g/4 oz mushrooms,
  sliced
1 hard-boiled egg,
  quartered
1 tablespoon chopped
  chives
300 ml/½ pint cheese sauce
Garnish
bacon rolls
1 hard-boiled egg, sliced
1 tomato, skinned and
  sliced
chopped parsley
watercress

Beat the mashed potatoes with the butter, egg, salt and pepper. Use to line a greased deep baking dish. Bake in a preheated moderate oven (180°C/350°F, Gas Mark 4) for 10 to 15 minutes. (The potato case should not brown.)

Place the chicken, mushrooms, egg and chives in the potato case and pour over the sauce. Bake for a further 20 minutes. Garnish and serve hot.

Chicken Cayenne

Serves 4

25 g/1 oz butter or 2
  tablespoons oil
4 chicken pieces
2 Spanish onions, sliced
1 green pepper, cored,
  seeded and thinly sliced
225 g/8 oz runner beans,
  thinly sliced
225 g/8 oz mushrooms,
  sliced
salt
pepper
cayenne pepper

Melt the butter or heat the oil in a saucepan. Add the chicken pieces and brown on all sides. Remove from the pan.

Add the onions, green pepper, beans, mushrooms and seasonings to the pan and stir well. Place the chicken on top of the vegetables, cover the pan tightly and cook for about 30 minutes or until the chicken is very tender.

Pan Fried Chicken with Mushrooms   *Serves 4*

4 large chicken quarters
salt
pepper
2 tablespoons wine
  vinegar
6 tablespoons orange
  juice
25 g/1 oz butter
1 tablespoon oil
1 onion, finely chopped
150 ml/¼ pint chicken
  stock
1 tablespoon orange
  marmalade
175 g/6 oz button
  mushrooms, halved
4 tablespoons double
  cream
chopped parsley and
  orange slices to garnish

Cut the chicken quarters in half, removing excess bone where possible. Rub the pieces with salt and pepper, then arrange in a shallow dish. Sprinkle with the vinegar and orange juice and leave to marinate for at least 2 hours.

Drain the chicken pieces, reserving the marinade. Melt the butter with the oil in a frying pan. Add the chicken pieces and onion and fry until the chicken pieces are browned on all sides. Add the reserved marinade, the stock and marmalade and bring to the boil, stirring well. Cover and simmer gently for about 20 minutes or until the chicken is tender.

Add the mushrooms and cook for a further 4 minutes. Stir in the cream, adjust the seasoning and serve, garnished with parsley and orange slices.

Grilled Chicken Parmesan

flour
salt
pepper
1 boiling fowl, cooked
  and cut into serving
  pieces
beaten egg
breadcrumbs
grated Parmesan cheese
grilled tomatoes to
  garnish
cheese sauce to serve

Mix flour with salt and pepper and use to coat the chicken pieces. Dip them in egg, then in a mixture of one part breadcrumbs to three parts cheese. Brown under a preheated hot grill, then arrange in a baking dish. Heat through in a preheated moderate oven (180 C/350 F, Gas Mark 4). Garnish with grilled tomatoes and serve with cheese sauce.

Note: The same cheese and breadcrumb coating can be used when frying a young uncooked chicken, cut into pieces. Brown in hot fat, then add a little stock or water to the pan, cover and cook until tender.

Chicken Casserole
Serves 4

2 tablespoons flour
salt
pepper
4 chicken portions,
  skinned
50 g/2 oz butter
2 tablespoons oil
1 onion, chopped
1 red pepper, cored
  seeded and sliced
50 g/2 oz mushrooms,
  chopped
pinch of paprika
1 teaspoon tomato paste
300 ml/½ pint stock
1 bouquet garni
100 ml/3 fl oz wine

Mix the flour with salt and pepper and use to coat the chicken portions. Melt the butter with the oil in a frying pan and brown the chicken portions on all sides. Transfer them to a casserole.

Add the onion, red pepper and mushrooms to the pan and fry until the onion is softened. Add the paprika plus any leftover seasoned flour, then stir in the tomato paste and stock. Bring to the boil and simmer, stirring, until thickened. Add the bouquet garni and wine, then pour this mixture over the chicken in the casserole.

Cover and cook in a preheated moderate oven (180 C/350 F, Gas Mark 4) for 1 to 1½ hours or until the chicken is tender. Serve with creamed potatoes or boiled rice.

Chicken and Rice Salad
Serves 6

225 g/8 oz rice
salt
6 tablespoons olive oil
pepper
grated nutmeg
2 tablespoons lemon juice
  or white wine vinegar
100 g/4 oz mushrooms,
  sliced
1 red or green pepper,
  cored, seeded and
  sliced
½ garlic clove, crushed
  (optional)
1 boiling fowl, cooked,
  skinned, boned and
  sliced
2 celery stalks, cut into
  strips

Cook the rice in boiling salted water until it is tender. Drain if necessary, then mix in 4 tablespoons of the oil, salt, pepper and nutmeg to taste, and 1 tablespoon of the lemon juice or vinegar. Leave for at least 8 hours.

Meanwhile, mix together the mushrooms, red or green pepper, garlic and remaining oil and lemon juice or vinegar. Leave to soak for at least 8 hours.

About 2 hours before serving, mix together the rice and mushroom mixtures and fold in the chicken and celery.

Add a little more oil if the mixture seems too dry. Serve in a flat dish.
Note: This dish can be prepared the day before

Roast Chicken

1 chicken
forcemeat or herb stuffing
knob of dripping
bacon rashers (optional)
flour

Stuff the chicken with forcemeat or herb stuffing and truss. Melt the dripping in a roasting tin in a preheated hot oven (220°C/425°F, Gas Mark 7). Put the chicken in the tin and baste with the dripping. If you like, cover the breast with bacon rashers. Roast for 15 minutes, then lower the temperature to moderately hot (190°C/375°F, Gas Mark 5). Continue roasting until the chicken is cooked: test by piercing the thigh with a skewer – the juices that run out should be clear.

Fifteen minutes before the chicken is cooked, remove the bacon rashers if used. Lightly dredge the bird with flour and baste with the fat in the tin. Continue roasting to brown the breast.

Accompany with gravy, bread sauce and rolls of grilled or fried bacon.

Fowl Pie

Serves 5–6

1 boiling fowl
2 onions, chopped
1 celery stalk
pinch of ground mace
$\frac{1}{4}$ teaspoon dried thyme
3 tablespoons chopped
   parsley
salt
4 peppercorns
3 hard-boiled eggs, sliced
225 g/8 oz cooked ham,
   diced
pepper
175 g/6 oz rough puff or
   shortcrust pastry

Put the fowl in a saucepan with the onions, celery, mace, thyme, 1 tablespoon of the parsley, salt and the peppercorns. Cover with water and bring to the boil. Simmer until the bird is tender – the cooking time will depend on the age of the bird. Strain off the liquid and reserve. Skin the bird and remove the meat from the carcass. Cut the meat into neat pieces.

Make a layer of some of the fowl in a pie dish and moisten with a little of the cooking liquid. Add a layer of eggs sprinkled with some of the remaining parsley and salt and pepper, then follow with a layer of ham. Continue making layers until all the ingredients are used. Add a little more of the cooking liquid.

Roll out the pastry and use to cover the dish. Bake in a preheated moderately hot oven (200°C/400°F, Gas Mark 6) for 20 minutes or until the pastry is nicely browned. Serve hot or cold.

103

Chicken Sicilian

Serves 4

4 chicken pieces
25 g/1 oz margarine
1 onion, chopped
50 g/2 oz mushrooms,
  chopped
150 g/5 oz natural yogurt
2 eggs, beaten
300 ml/½ pint milk
½ teaspoon ground ginger
½ teaspoon grated
  nutmeg
boiled rice to serve
50 g/2 oz flaked almonds
  to garnish (optional)

Cook the chicken pieces until tender, then remove the meat from the bone.

Melt the margarine in a saucepan and fry the onion and mushrooms until the onion is softened. Add the chicken meat. Mix together the yogurt, eggs, milk and spices and stir into the chicken mixture. Bring to the boil, stirring well.

Serve on a bed of rice, sprinkled with almonds.

Curried Chicken

Serves 5–6

1 × 1.5 kg/3 lb chicken,
  cut into joints
salt
25 g/1 oz butter
2 onions, sliced
1 tablespoon curry
  powder
1 tablespoon flour
600 ml/1 pint chicken
  stock
1 tablespoon vinegar
1 tablespoon sugar
1 tablespoon chutney or
  apricot jam
1 tablespoon sultanas

Put the chicken joints in a saucepan, cover with warm water, add salt and bring to the boil. Simmer until the chicken is tender. Drain the chicken and keep warm.

Melt the butter in another pan and fry the onions until they are golden brown. Stir in the curry powder and flour, then gradually stir in the stock. Add the vinegar, sugar, chutney or jam and sultanas and bring to the boil, stirring well. Pour this sauce over the chicken joints in the other pan, cover and simmer for 15 minutes.

Serve with rice, accompanied by sliced bananas, cubes of tomato and desiccated coconut.

Chicken Italienne

Serves 4

4 tablespoons olive oil
1 large onion, chopped
1 × 1.5 kg/3½ lb chicken,
  cut into joints
flour
salt
pepper
450 g/1 lb tomatoes,
  chopped
2 green peppers, cored,
  seeded and chopped

Heat 2 tablespoons of the oil in a frying pan and fry the onion until softened. Remove the onion with a slotted spoon and reserve.

Add the remaining oil to the pan and heat it. Rub the chicken joints with salt and pepper, then coat with flour. Add to the pan and fry until browned on all sides. Return the onions to the pan with the tomatoes and green peppers, cover and cook for 50 minutes, or until the chicken is tender. Add a little stock or water to the pan if the mixture seems too dry.

Chicken with Sherry Sauce

Serves 4 5

flour
salt
pepper
1 × 1.5 kg/3 lb roasting
  chicken, cut into pieces
75 g/3 oz butter
1 onion, minced
200 ml/⅓ pint dry white
  wine
300 ml/½ pint chicken
  stock
mushroom liquor (see
  note – optional)
½ shallot, chopped
1 bouquet garni
fried mushrooms to
  garnish

Sauce

15 g/½ oz butter
scant 1 tablespoon flour
175 ml/6 fl oz double
  cream
1 tablespoon sherry
1 teaspoon brandy

Mix flour with salt and pepper and use to coat the chicken pieces. Melt the butter in a frying pan and add the chicken pieces and onion. Cover and cook gently for 20 minutes, not letting the chicken brown. Add the wine, stock, mushroom liquor, shallot and bouquet garni and continue cooking until the chicken is tender.

Transfer the chicken pieces on to a serving platter and keep hot.

Blend together the butter and flour to a paste and add a little of the hot cooking liquid. Stir this into the remaining liquid in the pan and simmer, stirring, until thickened. Stir in the cream, sherry and brandy and heat through gently. Strain the sauce over the chicken pieces and garnish with mushrooms.

Note: Mushroom liquor is made by stewing a few mushrooms in a very little water with a few drops of lemon juice for 3 or 4 minutes.

Boiled Fowl

1 boiling fowl
slice of lemon
salt
1 onion, quartered
1 carrot, chopped
1 bouquet garni
6 peppercorns

Rub the breast of the fowl with the lemon to whiten it and place the fowl in a saucepan of warm water. Add salt, the onion, carrot, bouquet garni and peppercorns. Bring to the boil and simmer very gently until tender – the cooking time varies according to the age of the bird. Skim off any scum that rises to the surface.

Drain the fowl and serve with parsley, lemon or cream sauce and grilled bacon rolls.

Canje   *Serves 4*

1 bowling fowl, cut into
* joints*
2 tomatoes, sliced
1 onion, sliced
1 carrot, sliced
3 tablespoons rice
salt
pepper
1 tablespoon chopped
* parsley*

Put all the ingredients in a saucepan and just cover with water. Bring to the boil, then simmer for 3 to 4 hours or until the chicken is tender – the cooking time will vary according to the age of the bird. Serve hot or cold.

Fowl Pudding   *Serves 4–5*

1 boiling fowl
225 g/8 oz suet pastry
1 onion, chopped
1 garlic clove, chopped
* (optional)*
salt
pepper
chopped parsley
1 bay leaf
stock or water

Remove the skin from the fowl, then take the meat from the carcass. Use it all for the pudding, or save the breast to cook separately and serve with a salad.

Line a pudding basin with three-quarters of the suet pastry dough, then make alternate layers of fowl, onion, garlic, if used, salt, pepper and parsley in the basin. Put the bay leaf in the centre and pour in enough stock or water to peep through the meat. Cover with the remaining suet pastry dough.

Cover the basin with greased paper or a cloth and boil for 2½ to 3 hours, or steam for 4 hours.

Chicken Royale

Serves 4-5

50 g/2 oz butter
4 small onions
100 g/4 oz bacon rashers,
  rinded and diced
1 × 1.5 kg/3 lb chicken,
  cut into joints
150 ml/¼ pint chicken
  stock
100 g/4 oz mushrooms,
  sliced
1 bouquet garni
salt
pepper
300 ml/½ pint red wine
1 tablespoon flour
fried bread triangles to
  garnish

Melt 25 g/1 oz of the butter in a saucepan and fry the onions until golden brown. Add the bacon and chicken joints and fry until the chicken is browned on all sides. Add the stock, mushrooms, bouquet garni, salt and pepper and bring to the boil. Cover and simmer gently until the chicken is tender.

Transfer the chicken and mushrooms to a warmed serving dish and keep hot. Skim any fat from the cooking liquid and discard the bouquet garni. Stir in the wine.

Melt the remaining butter in another saucepan and stir in the flour. Gradually stir in the cooking liquid and bring to the boil. Simmer, stirring, until the sauce has thickened. Pour the sauce over the chicken and mushrooms and garnish with fried bread triangles.

Chicken Casserole

Serves 4

4 chicken pieces
2 carrots, chopped
2 garlic cloves, crushed
2 teaspoons chopped
  parsley
1½ teaspoons salt
900 ml/1½ pints water
Sauce
25 g/1 oz butter or 2
  tablespoons oil
100 g/4 oz mushrooms,
  sliced
1 teaspoon chopped
  parsley
50 g/2 oz flour
100 ml/3 fl oz white wine
2 tablespoons soured
  cream
1 tablespoon milk

Put the chicken in a saucepan with the carrots, garlic, parsley and salt. Pour over the water and bring to the boil. Simmer until the chicken is tender. Remove the chicken from the pan. Discard the skin and bones and keep the meat warm. Strain the stock and reserve.

To make the sauce, melt the butter or heat the oil in another saucepan and fry the mushrooms with the parsley for 3 minutes. Stir in the flour and cook for 2 minutes, then gradually stir in the wine and reserved stock. Bring to the boil, stirring, and simmer for 20 minutes.

Add the soured cream and milk and stir well. Put the chicken meat into the sauce and reheat. Serve with rice or noodles.

Watermelon Chicken

Serves 4-5

1 × 1.5 kg/3 lb chicken,
 cut into joints
300 ml/½ pint water
2 tablespoons sherry
salt
1 watermelon

Put the chicken joints in a saucepan and pour over the water and sherry. Add salt and bring to the boil. Simmer for 30 minutes.

Remove a 'lid' from the watermelon and scoop out enough of the flesh to make room for the chicken joints and cooking liquid. Put in the chicken and liquid and add more salt. Replace the 'lid' and secure it with skewers.

Put the melon in a large pot and steam or simmer gently for 1½ hours, or until the skin of the melon turns yellow. Try not to break the melon when serving as it is all delicious.

Spatchcock Chicken

Serves 4-5

poussins or small roasting
 chickens
salt
pepper
lemon juice
melted butter
fine breadcrumbs
lemon wedges and
 watercress to garnish

Split the birds in half using poultry shears. Open them out and flatten them on a board. Skewer the legs in position. Sprinkle with salt, pepper and lemon juice and leave for 30 minutes.

Arrange the spatchcocked birds on the grill rack and brush with melted butter. Cook under a preheated grill for 3 to 4 minutes on each side or until golden brown and cooked through. Brush with more melted butter from time to time.

Sprinkle over the crumbs and more melted butter and continue grilling until the crumbs are crisp. Serve garnished with lemon wedges and watercress.

Curry from the United Provinces

Serves 5-6

100 g/4 oz butter
450 g/1 lb onions, sliced
1 × 1.5 kg/3 lb chicken,
 cut into joints
1 tablespoon curry
 powder
300 ml/½ pint natural
 yogurt

Melt the butter in a frying pan and fry the onions until softened. Add the chicken joints and fry until they are browned on all sides. Stir in the curry powder, then mix in the yogurt. Cover and cook very gently until the chicken is tender. Add a little water if necessary, but not too much as this is a thick curry. Serve with rice.

Chicken Mandarin

Serves 4

cornflour for coating
salt
pepper
4 chicken joints, skinned
2 tablespoons corn oil
200 g/7 oz canned
  mandarin oranges
300 ml/½ pint white sauce
¼ teaspoon dried tarragon
2 tablespoons Curaçao
75 g/3 oz unsalted
  peanuts, chopped

Mix the cornflour with salt and pepper and use to coat the chicken joints. Heat the oil in a frying pan and brown the chicken joints on all sides. Transfer them to a casserole.

Drain the mandarin oranges and add the can syrup to the white sauce with the tarragon and Curaçao. Pour the sauce over the chicken. Cover the casserole and cook in a preheated moderate oven (180 C/350 F, Gas Mark 4) for 40 to 45 minutes or until the chicken is tender.

Stir the mandarin oranges into the casserole and sprinkle the peanuts on top. Cook, uncovered, for a further 10 minutes.

Chicken Marengo

Serves 4

4 chicken quarters
2 tablespoons olive oil
3 medium onions, sliced
200 ml/⅓ pint tomato
  juice
300 ml/½ pint chicken
  stock
1 bay leaf
salt
pepper
gravy browning

Boil the fowl in the usual way. Twenty minutes before it is ready, make the sauce. Heat the oil in a saucepan and fry the onions until softened. Add the tomato juice, stock, bay leaf, salt and pepper and bring to the boil. Simmer for 15 minutes without a lid, then add enough gravy browning to make the sauce a rich, dark tomato colour.

Drain the chicken and cut into serving pieces. Add to the sauce and reheat gently if necessary.

Chicken with Soured Cream

Serves 5–6

flour
salt
pepper
1 × 1.5 kg/3 lb chicken,
  cut into joints
50 g/2 oz butter
6 tablespoons soured
  cream

Mix the flour with salt and pepper and use to coat the chicken joints. Melt the butter in a frying pan and brown the joints on all sides. Transfer them to a casserole and pour around the soured cream. Cover the casserole and cook in a preheated moderate oven (180 C/350 F, Gas Mark 4) for 1 hour or until the chicken joints are tender.
Note: Natural yogurt may be substituted for the soured cream.

109

Nigerian Chicken

Serves 4–5

1 boiling fowl
1 medium onion, sliced
2 to 3 streaky bacon
rashers, rinded and
diced
225 g/8 oz peanut butter
1 tablespoon wholemeal
flour
salt
pepper

Rice
boiled rice
lemon juice
grated nutmeg
chopped parsley

Garnish
hard-boiled egg slices
bacon rolls

Simmer the chicken in water to cover until it is tender. Drain, reserving the stock, and remove the skin and bones.

Skim the fat from the surface of the stock and put the fat into another saucepan. Add the onion and bacon to the fat and fry until golden brown. Add 450 ml/¾ pint of the reserved stock. Mix the peanut butter and flour with a little more stock to make a paste and add to the pan with salt and pepper. Bring to the boil.

Put the chicken meat into a casserole and pour over the peanut butter mixture. Cook in a preheated moderate oven (160 C/325 F, Gas Mark 3) for 45 minutes.

Mix hot boiled rice with lemon juice, nutmeg and parsley to taste and arrange around the edge of a warmed serving dish. Pour the chicken mixture into the centre and garnish with hard-boiled eggs and bacon rolls. Serve with chutney, sliced tomatoes, currants, chopped almonds, diced beetroot and desiccated coconut.

Chicken Liver Mould

Serves 6

75 g/3 oz butter
3 tablespoons flour
1.2 litres/2 pints milk
salt
pepper
225 g/8 oz fat bacon,
rinded and minced
225 g/8 oz chicken livers,
minced
6 eggs, beaten
1 garlic clove, crushed
1 tablespoon chopped
parsley
few sliced olives or
cooked mushrooms

Melt the butter in a saucepan. Add the flour and cook, stirring, for 2 minutes. Gradually stir in the milk, then bring to the boil, stirring well. Simmer until thickened. Add salt and pepper.

Mix together the bacon, chicken livers, eggs, garlic, parsley and salt and pepper, then add half the sauce. Turn into a greased soufflé dish and place in a roasting tin of hot water. Bake in a moderate oven (160 C/325 F, Gas Mark 3) for about 1 hour. (This can be kept hot for another hour in a low oven, covered with foil or buttered greaseproof paper.)

When ready to serve, reheat the remaining sauce and stir in the olives or mushrooms. Serve with the mould.

Almond Chicken
Serves 4

25 g/1 oz butter
2 small onions, chopped
100 g/4 oz mushrooms,
  sliced
1 tablespoon cornflour
300 ml/½ pint milk
350 g/12 oz cooked
  chicken meat, chopped
salt
pepper
¼ teaspoon ground ginger
¼ teaspoon grated nutmeg
150 g/5 oz natural yogurt
2 egg yolks
25 g/1 oz blanched
  almonds, split and
  toasted

Melt the butter in a saucepan and fry the onions and mushrooms until the onions are softened. Stir in the cornflour and cook for 1 to 2 minutes, then gradually stir in the milk. Bring to the boil, stirring. Add the chicken, salt, pepper, ginger and nutmeg and heat through gently.

Mix the yogurt with the egg yolks and add to the pan. Cook very gently until thickened, without boiling. Turn into a warmed serving dish and sprinkle with the almonds.

Southern Fried Chicken with Lemon Barbecue Sauce
Serves 5-6

flour
salt
pepper
1 × 1.5 kg/3 lb chicken,
  cut into joints
75 g/3 oz pork or bacon
  fat

Sauce
5 tablespoons olive oil
2 tablespoons lemon juice
2 tablespoons grated
  onion
1 garlic clove, crushed
  with ½ teaspoon salt
½ teaspoon black pepper
¼ teaspoon dried thyme

First make the sauce. Mix together all the ingredients, cover and leave for at least 8 hours.

Mix the flour with salt and pepper and use to coat the chicken joints. Melt the fat in a frying pan, put in the chicken joints, cover and cook gently until the joints are tender and well browned. Turn them once during cooking. Serve with the sauce.

Tarragon Chicken
Serves 4

1 × 1.5 kg/3 lb chicken
2 tablespoons chopped
*   fresh tarragon*
25 g/1 oz butter
300 ml/½ pint stock
1 tablespoon cream

Put the chicken into a casserole and rub it with half the tarragon. Add the butter and stock to the casserole, cover and cook in a preheated moderately hot oven (190 C/375 F, Gas Mark 5) for 1½ hours or until tender.

Transfer the chicken to a warmed serving dish and keep hot.

Pour the cooking liquid into a saucepan and add the remaining tarragon. Cook gently for a few minutes. Stir in the cream and pour this sauce over the chicken.

Hawaiian Chicken
Serves 4

flour for coating
salt
paprika
4 chicken pieces
1 tablespoon grated
*   orange rind*
150 ml/¼ pint orange
*   juice*
250 g/9 oz canned
*   crushed pineapple,*
*   drained*
orange segments to
garnish

Mix flour with salt and paprika and use to coat the chicken pieces. Place them in a greased casserole and sprinkle with the orange rind. Pour in the orange juice, then spread the chicken with the pineapple.

Cover the casserole and cook in a preheated moderate oven (180°C/350 F, Gas Mark 4) for 1 hour.

Serve garnished with orange segments.

Kentucky Chicken
Serves 4–5

100 g/4 oz fresh
*   breadcrumbs*
2 teaspoons salt
2 tablespoons chopped
*   parsley*
50 g/2 oz Parmesan
*   cheese, grated*
6 chicken joints or pieces,
*   skinned*
100 g/4 oz butter, melted

Mix together the breadcrumbs, salt, parsley and cheese. Dip the chicken joints in the melted butter, then coat with the breadcrumb mixture. Arrange the joints in a baking dish and pour over and around any remaining melted butter. Bake in a preheated moderate oven (180°C/350 F, Gas Mark 4) for 45 to 50 minutes or until the joints are tender and golden brown. Serve hot or cold.

Portuguese Chicken   *Serves 4–5*

*1 small boiling fowl, cut
    into joints*
25 g/1 oz butter
225 g/8 oz small onions
2 garlic cloves, crushed
1 bay leaf
*1 long strip of pared
    lemon rind*
150 g/5 oz rice
salt
pepper
175 ml/6 fl oz white wine

Smear the chicken joints with the butter and pack into a deep casserole. Surround with the onions and add the garlic, bay leaf, lemon rind, rice, salt and pepper. Pour in the wine. Cover the casserole tightly and bake in a preheated cool oven (150°C/300°F, Gas Mark 2) for 2 to $2\frac{1}{2}$ hours or until the chicken is tender.

Onorina's mid-Lent Chicken   *Serves 5–6*

1 boiling fowl
1 garlic clove
*2 onions, 1 halved and
    1 chopped*
1 thyme sprig
1 marjoram sprig
1 oregano sprig
salt
pepper
2 tablespoons olive oil
450 g/1 lb rice
*2 to 3 tablespoons grated
    Parmesan cheese*
grated rind of $\frac{1}{2}$ lemon
squeeze of lemon juice
1 or 2 eggs, beaten
*grated Parmesan cheese
    to serve*

Put the fowl in a saucepan with the garlic, halved onion, herbs, salt and pepper. Cover with water and bring to the boil. Simmer until the bird is tender – the cooking time will depend on the age of the bird. Strain off the liquid and reserve. Joint the bird and keep hot.

Heat the oil in another saucepan and fry the chopped onion with the rice until the onion is softened. Stir constantly so the rice absorbs the oil. Add salt, pepper and all of the reserved chicken cooking liquid. Simmer until the rice absorbs the liquid, then add the same amount of liquid again. Continue adding liquid in this way – in all about 1.75 litres/3 pints – until the rice is tender. Stir in the cheese and lemon rind and juice, then remove from the heat and stir in the eggs.

Spread the rice mixture on a warmed serving platter and top with the chicken joints. Serve with crusty bread and Parmesan cheese.

Note: This dish is less rich if the eggs are omitted.

113

Stewed Duck with Port Wine
Serves 5-6

*2 kg/4½ lb duck
  (approx.)
2 onions, finely chopped
herb forcemeat
3 sage leaves, chopped
120 ml/4 fl oz port wine
juice of 1 lemon
fried bread triangles to
  garnish*

Put the duck giblets in a saucepan, cover with water and bring to the boil. Add the onions and simmer to make about 300 ml/½ pint stock.

Mix the forcemeat with the sage leaves and stuff the duck. Truss and place in a flameproof casserole or heavy saucepan. Pour around the giblet stock, cover and simmer for about 2 hours, adding the port wine just before the duck is ready. Transfer the duck to a warmed serving dish and sprinkle with the lemon juice. Strain the cooking liquid around it and garnish with fried bread triangles.

Orange Duck
Serves 5-6

*2 kg/4½ lb young
  duck (approx.)
25 g/1 oz butter
300 ml/½ pint brown
  sauce
grated rind of 2 oranges
juice of 4 to 5 oranges
50 g/2 oz canned tomato
  purée
orange quarters to
  garnish*

Truss the duck. Melt the butter in a pan and brown the duck on all sides. Drain off the fat.

Mix together the brown sauce, orange rind and juice and tomato purée and pour into the pan. Cover and cook gently for 45 minutes or until the duck is tender.

Carve the duck and serve with the sauce, garnished with orange quarters.

Duck with Cherries
Serves 5-6

*2 kg/4½ lb young
  duck (approx.)
50 g/2 oz butter
150 ml/¼ pint chicken
  stock
100 ml/3 fl oz Madeira
  or sherry
salt
pepper
225 g/8 oz cherries,
  stoned
1 tablespoon cherry
  brandy*

Put the butter inside the duck, truss it and place in a roasting tin. Roast in a preheated hot oven (230°C/450°F, Gas Mark 8) for 10 minutes, then reduce the temperature to moderate (180°C/350°F, Gas Mark 4) and roast for a further 15 minutes to each 450 g/1 lb.

Transfer the duck to a warmed serving platter and keep hot. Pour the fat from the tin, then stir in the stock, Madeira or sherry, salt, pepper and cherries. Bring to the boil on top of the stove and simmer until the cherries are tender. Stir in the brandy and serve.

Roast Duck

Serves 5–6

2 kg/4½ lb young duck
(approx.)
salt
pepper
Stuffing
2 thick slices of white
bread, crumbled
milk
1 heaped teaspoon
chopped fresh sage
½ small onion, chopped
salt
pepper
¼ teaspoon grated orange
rind (optional)
1 egg, beaten

To make the stuffing, sprinkle the breadcrumbs with a little milk to moisten them, then squeeze out the excess milk. Mix in the remaining stuffing ingredients.

Stuff the inside of the duck and truss. Rub the duck all over with salt and pepper, place in a roasting tin and prick all over with a fork. Roast in a preheated hot oven (230 C/450 F, Gas Mark 8) for 10 minutes, then reduce the temperature to moderate (180 °C/350 F, Gas Mark 4) and roast for a further 15 minutes to each 450 g/1 lb. Serve with apple sauce.

Teal and Anchovies

Serves 4

2 teal
50 g/2 oz cheese, grated
4 anchovy fillets
stock
1 teaspoon dry mustard
1 teaspoon
Worcestershire sauce
1 teaspoon anchovy
essence
1 tablespoon brown sugar
little mushroom ketchup
2 tablespoons port wine
little lemon juice
watercress to garnish

Roast the teal in a preheated hot oven (220 C/425° F, Gas Mark 7) for 35 minutes or until they are almost done. Fillet them and put the fillets in a casserole. Sprinkle over the cheese and lay an anchovy on each fillet. Moisten with a little stock and bake in a preheated moderate oven (180 C/350 F, Gas Mark 4) for 45 minutes.

Mix together the mustard, Worcestershire sauce, anchovy essence, sugar, mushroom ketchup, port and 2 tablespoons stock. Stir in the liquid from the casserole. Just before serving, pour this sauce over the teal and sprinkle with a little lemon juice. Garnish with watercress.

115

Roast Goose
Serves 8

4.5 kg/10 lb goose
herb, sage or apple
* stuffing, or 2 lemons*
flour
fried apple or pineapple
* rings to garnish*

Stuff the goose, or halve one of the lemons and rub the goose all over with the juice. Peel the second lemon and place it inside the goose (to absorb some of the fat). Truss the goose and place it in a roasting tin. Sprinkle with flour and roast in a preheated moderately hot oven (200°C/400°F, Gas Mark 6) for 20 minutes. Reduce the temperature to moderate (180°C/350°F, Gas Mark 4) and continue roasting for 15 minutes to each 450 g/1 lb. A 4.5 kg/10 lb goose should take about 2½ hours, but if it is on the old and tough side, it may need 20 minutes to each 450 g/1 lb.

Serve garnished with fried apple or pineapple rings.

Note: A sour apple cooked in the tin with the goose will improve the gravy.

Roast Goose with Mashed Potato Stuffing
Serves 8–10

1 kg/2 lb potatoes,
* peeled, cooked and*
* mashed*
40 g/1½ oz butter or 3
* tablespoons double*
* cream*
salt
pepper
½ teaspoon dried sage
1 onion, parboiled and
* finely chopped*
4.5 kg/10 lb goose
* (approx.)*
flour

Mix the potatoes with the butter or cream, salt, pepper, sage and onion. Use to stuff the goose and truss. Place in a roasting tin, sprinkle with flour and roast as in the previous recipe.

Fried Crumbs

40 g/1½ oz butter
100 g/4 oz fresh
breadcrumbs

Melt the butter in a frying pan and add the breadcrumbs. Fry, stirring frequently, until the crumbs are golden brown.

Turkey Beanpot

Serves 8-10

75 g/3 oz butter
350 g/12 oz onions, sliced
2 to 3 garlic cloves,
crushed
50 g/2 oz flour
2 to 3 teaspoons chilli
powder
1 kg/2 lb 5oz canned
tomatoes
3 tablespoons tomato
paste
600 ml/1 pint stock
salt
pepper
2 teaspoons
Worcestershire sauce
900 g/2 lb cooked turkey
meat, diced
425 g/15 oz canned red
kidney beans, drained

Melt the butter in a saucepan and fry the onions and garlic until softened. Stir in the flour and chilli powder and cook for 1 minute. Add the tomatoes, tomato paste, stock, salt, pepper and Worcestershire sauce and bring to the boil, stirring. Mix in the turkey and simmer for 5 minutes. Add the beans and continue simmering gently for 20 to 30 minutes, adding a little more stock if necessary.

Alternatively, the beanpot can be transferred to a casserole and cooked in a preheated moderate oven (180 C/350 F, Gas Mark 4) for 45 minutes.

Serve with rice or buttered noodles.

Turkey Mousse

Serves 4-6

350 g/12 oz cooked
turkey meat, minced
5 tablespoons white sauce
15 g/½ oz aspic jelly
crystals
salt
pepper
150 ml/¼ pint double
cream, whipped
watercress to garnish

Pound the minced turkey until it is very smooth, then mix in the white sauce. Make up the aspic jelly to 150 ml/¼ pint, using half the water specified on the packet. Add to the turkey mixture with plenty of salt and pepper. Fold in the cream and turn into a wetted ring mould. Chill until set.

Turn out of the mould to serve, with the centre filled with watercress.

Variation: Fill the centre with a salad of tomatoes and green peppers cut into strips.

117

Roast Turkey with Spanish Stuffing

Serves 15–20

1 × 6.25 to 7.25 kg/14 to 16 lb oven ready turkey
50 g/2 oz butter, softened
salt
pepper

Stuffing

1 tablespoon oil
1 onion, finely chopped
1 garlic clove, crushed
4 streaky bacon rashers, rinded and chopped
1 small green or red pepper, cored, seeded and chopped
2 tomatoes, skinned and chopped
50 g/2 oz raisins
40 g/1½ oz long-grain rice, cooked
salt
pepper
1 tablespoon chopped parsley
1 egg, beaten

First make the stuffing. Heat the oil in a frying pan and fry the onion and garlic until softened. Add the bacon and fry until it is golden brown. Pour off the fat and stir in the pepper, tomatoes, raisins, rice, salt, pepper and parsley. Bind together with the egg and cool.

Stuff the neck end of the turkey, putting any extra stuffing into the body cavity. Truss and weigh the bird, then place it on a large piece of buttered foil. Rub the bird all over with the butter and sprinkle with salt and pepper. Wrap the foil around the bird loosely and place in a roasting tin. Roast in a preheated hot oven (230°C/450°F, Gas Mark 8) for 3¼ hours or until the turkey is cooked through. Fold back the foil for the last 20 minutes cooking to brown the breast.

If you prefer, cook by the slow roasting method in a preheated moderate oven (160°C/325°F, Gas Mark 3) for 4¼ to 4½ hours. There is no need to wrap the bird in foil.

Serve with roast potatoes, chipolata sausages, bacon rolls, gravy made from giblet stock, bread sauce and cranberry sauce or jelly.

Turkey Roll

Serves 6–7

350 g/12 oz cooked turkey meat
225 g/8 oz cooked ham
1 small onion
pinch of ground mace
½ teaspoon dried thyme
salt
pepper
50 g/2 oz fresh breadcrumbs
1 egg, beaten
browned breadcrumbs

Mince together the turkey, ham and onion, then mix in the mace, thyme, salt, pepper and fresh breadcrumbs. Bind with the egg. Pack into a greased loaf tin lined with greased greaseproof paper and cover. Steam for 1 hour. Turn out and coat with browned breadcrumbs while still warm.

Turkey en Croûte

Serves 6

*approx. 1 kg/2 lb
    turkey roast (white
    meat)*
salt
pepper
25 g/1 oz butter
1 onion, finely chopped
*75 g/3 oz fresh
    breadcrumbs*
*100 g/4 oz button
    mushrooms, chopped*
*2 tablespoons chopped
    parsley*
good pinch of dried sage
*good pinch of dried
    thyme*
1 egg, beaten
*225 g/8 oz shortcrust
    pastry*
beaten egg to glaze
*parsley or watercress to
    garnish*

Rub the turkey roast with salt and pepper. Melt the butter in a frying pan and brown the turkey roast on all sides. Remove it from the pan with 2 spoons, leaving the fat behind, and place on a sheet of foil. Wrap up loosely and place in a roasting tin. Cook in a preheated moderate oven (170 C/325°F, Gas Mark 3) for about 45 minutes or until tender. Cool slightly.

Fry the onion in the fat in the frying pan until it is softened. Remove from the heat and mix in the breadcrumbs, mushrooms, parsley, sage, thyme, plenty of salt and pepper and the egg.

Roll out the pastry to an oblong large enough to enclose the turkey. Spread the mushroom stuffing in the centre. Remove any outer skin from the turkey and place on the stuffing. Dampen the edges of the dough and wrap around the turkey, pressing the edges to seal. Place on a baking sheet, seam underneath, and decorate with the dough trimmings. Brush with beaten egg and bake in a preheated moderately hot oven (190°C/375°F, Gas Mark 5) for about 30 minutes or until the pastry is golden brown. Serve hot or cold, garnished with parsley or watercress.

Variation: Several pieces of lamb or pork fillet tied together can be used instead of turkey, as can fillet steak.

Turkey Cakes

*cooked turkey meat,
    minced*
salt
pepper
mashed potato
*dry breadcrumbs or
    seasoned flour*
fat for shallow frying

Mix the turkey with salt, pepper and enough mashed potato to form a firm mixture. Shape into cakes and coat with breadcrumbs or flour. Shallow fry until golden brown on both sides.

Turkey Fingers with Avocado Sauce

Serves 4–6

*3 to 4 turkey breast
fillets or steaks, cut
into 5 × 1 cm/½ inch
strips
salt
pepper
curry powder
flour
1 egg, beaten
golden breadcrumbs
oil for deep frying*

Avocado Sauce

*1 ripe avocado, halved
and stoned
1 garlic clove, crushed
1 tablespoon lemon juice
2 tablespoons chopped
chives
2 tomatoes, skinned,
seeded and chopped
1 to 2 tablespoons cream
(optional)
salt and pepper*

First make the sauce. Scoop the avocado flesh out of the skin and mash it with the garlic and lemon juice. Beat in the remaining sauce ingredients. Cover.

Rub the turkey strips with salt, pepper and curry powder, then coat with flour. Dip in the egg and coat with breadcrumbs. Heat the oil to 180°C/350°F, and deep fry the turkey strips, in batches, until they are golden brown. Drain on paper towels and cool. Serve cold with the sauce.

Savoury Aigrettes

Serves 4

*40 g/1½ oz butter
150 ml/¼ pint water
2 tablespoons finely
chopped onion
65 g/2½ oz flour
2 large eggs
salt and pepper
pinch of cayenne pepper
75 g/3 oz cooked bacon
or ham, finely chopped
175 g/6 oz cooked turkey
meat, finely chopped
50 g/2 oz mature
Cheddar cheese, grated
oil for deep frying*

Melt the butter in the water in a saucepan. Add the onion and bring to the boil. Remove from the heat and tip in the flour. Beat until the mixture leaves the sides of the pan. Beat in the eggs, one at a time. Add salt, pepper and cayenne, then mix in the bacon or ham, turkey and cheese.

Drop teaspoonsful of the turkey mixture into hot oil and deep fry until golden brown and crisp. Drain on paper towels and serve hot with a piquant tomato or wine sauce.

Turkey and Gammon Roast

Serves about 20

*1.75 kg/4 lb joint of
gammon or prime
collar of bacon, soaked
for several hours
4.5 to 5.5 kg/10 to 12 lb
oven ready turkey
350 g/12 oz sausagemeat
50 g/2 oz fresh
breadcrumbs
salt
pepper
2 tablespoons chopped
parsley
grated rind of 1 orange
pinch of grated nutmeg
1 small egg, beaten
softened butter*

Drain the gammon and put it in a saucepan with fresh cold water. Bring to the boil, then simmer gently, allowing 20 minutes per 450 g/ 1 lb plus 20 minutes over. Drain, then remove the skin and excess fat. Cool.

Place the turkey on a chopping board, breast side down, and pull the legs and wings free from the bird. Cut the skin from the tail to neck along the backbone, then carefully ease and cut the flesh all round from the carcass of the bird. Leave the wing and leg bones intact after breaking them from the carcass at the ball and socket joints and easing out the breast bone - taking care not to cut through the skin. Ease out the bones and lay the turkey flat, skin side down.

Mix together the sausagemeat, breadcrumbs, salt, pepper, parsley, orange rind and nutmeg and bind with the egg. Spread this stuffing down the centre of the turkey breast. Place the gammon on top, pressing it gently into the stuffing. Wrap the turkey around the gammon to enclose it and sew or skewer the flaps of turkey together. Turn the turkey breast upwards and reshape the bird with the legs and wings in the correct position. Truss, then weigh.

Place the bird in a roasting tin and smear the breast with softened butter. Sprinkle with salt and pepper. Roast in a preheated moderate oven (180°C/350°F, Gas Mark 4) for 4-4½ hours, basting several times with the fat in the tin. Cover with foil when sufficiently browned.

Serve hot or cold, cut into slices across the breast so that each slice contains gammon, stuffing and turkey.

Turkey Pasties
Makes 4

2 to 4 turkey winglets,
  skinned, boned and
  chopped
1 onion, finely chopped
75 g/3 oz sausagemeat
pinch of dried mixed
  herbs
salt
pepper
1 egg, beaten
350 g/12 oz puff pastry

Mix together the turkey meat, onion, sausage-meat, herbs, salt and pepper and bind with half the egg.

Roll out the pastry thinly and cut into four 18 cm/7 inch rounds. Divide the turkey mixture between the rounds, pressing it into flat cakes. Dampen the pastry edges and fold over. Press together to seal.

Place the pasties on a baking sheet and brush with the remaining beaten egg. Bake in a preheated hot oven (220°C/425°F, Gas Mark 7) for 10 minutes, then reduce the temperature to moderately hot (190°C/375°F, Gas Mark 5) and bake for a further 10 to 20 minutes or until well browned and puffy. Serve hot or cold.

Roast Turkey with Rice Stuffing
Serves 15–20

1 × 6.25 to 7.25 kg/14 to
  16 lb oven ready
  turkey
50 g/2 oz butter, softened
salt
pepper
Stuffing
40 g/1½ oz butter
turkey liver, chopped
1 onion, finely chopped
75 g/3 oz long-grain rice,
  cooked
75 g/3 oz raisins or
  sultanas
50 g/2 oz blanched
  almonds, chopped
2 tablespoons chopped
  parsley
salt
pepper
1 egg, beaten

First make the stuffing. Melt the butter in a frying pan and fry the liver and onion until the onion is softened. Remove from the heat and mix in the remaining stuffing ingredients. Cool.

Stuff the neck end of the turkey. Truss and weigh the bird, then place it on a large piece of buttered foil. Rub the bird all over with the butter and sprinkle with salt and pepper. Wrap the foil around the bird loosely and place in a roasting tin. Roast in a preheated hot oven (230°C/450°F, Gas Mark 8) for 3¼ hours or until the turkey is cooked through. Fold back the foil for the last 20 minutes' cooking to brown the breast.

If you prefer, cook by the slow roasting method in a preheated moderate oven (160°C/325°F, Gas Mark 3) for 4¼ to 4½ hours. There is no need to wrap the bird in foil.

Curried Turkey and Pineapple Salad

Serves 4

150 ml/¼ pint mayonnaise
1 to 2 teaspoons curry
powder
salt
pepper
6 to 8 spring onions,
sliced
226 g/8 oz canned
pineapple rings
½ teaspoon grated lemon
rind
1 green pepper, cored,
seeded, chopped and
blanched
½ red pepper, cored,
seeded, chopped and
blanched
350 g/12 oz cooked
turkey meat, diced
75 g/3 oz long-grain rice,
cooked
lettuce
watercress and tomato
wedges to garnish

Mix the mayonnaise with the curry powder, salt, pepper and spring onions. Drain the pineapple and add 2 to 3 tablespoons of the can syrup to the mayonnaise mixture. Reserve 2 pineapple rings for the garnish and chop the remainder. Add the chopped pineapple to the mayonnaise mixture with the lemon rind and green and red peppers. Mix well, then fold in the turkey and rice.

Make a bed of lettuce on a serving plate and pile the salad on top. Garnish with watercress and tomato wedges.

Turkey Schnitzel

Serves 4

4 turkey breasts
flour
1 egg, beaten
golden breadcrumbs
4 to 6 tablespoons oil
Garnish
lemon slices
anchovy fillets
capers

Put each turkey breast between two sheets of greaseproof paper and beat until thin and doubled in size. Dust each breast with flour, then dip in the egg and coat with breadcrumbs, pressing them on firmly. Chill until required.

Heat the oil in a frying pan and fry the schnitzels, two at a time, for about 3 to 4 minutes on each side or until golden brown and cooked through. Serve hot, garnished with lemon slices, anchovy fillets and capers.

Variations: Use veal escalopes, or thin quick-fry steaks, or beaten pork fillet in place of the turkey breasts.

123

Pickled Turkey and Ham Puff

Serves 4–6

40 g/1½ oz butter
1 onion, chopped
25 g/1 oz flour
300 ml/½ pint chicken stock or milk
salt
pepper
225 g/8 oz cooked turkey meat, chopped
100 g/4 oz cooked ham, chopped
4 to 6 pickled walnuts, roughly chopped, or 2 tablespoons capers
350 g/12 oz puff pastry
beaten egg or milk to glaze

Melt the butter in a saucepan and fry the onion until softened. Add the flour and cook, stirring, for 2 minutes. Gradually stir in the stock or milk and bring to the boil, stirring. Add salt, pepper, the turkey, ham and walnuts or capers and mix well. Cool.

Roll out the pastry to a 30 cm/12 inch square and cut in half. Place one half on a dampened baking sheet. Spread over the turkey mixture, leaving a 2.5 cm/1 inch border all around.

Roll out the other piece of dough until it is 30 × 18 cm/12 × 7 inches, then fold in half lengthways.

Leaving a 5 cm/2 inch margin at each end and 2.5 cm/1 inch at the cut side, make horizontal cuts into the fold at 2 cm/¾ inch intervals. Dampen the pastry margin, then place it carefully over the turkey filling, unfolding it to enclose the filling. Press the edges together, knock together and crimp. Brush with egg or milk and bake in a preheated hot oven (220°C/425°F, Gas Mark 7) for 20 minutes. Reduce the temperature to moderately hot (190°C/375°F, Gas Mark 5) and bake for a further 10 to 15 minutes or until the pastry is golden brown. Serve hot or cold.

Pheasant Marie Antoinette

Serves 2–3

1 young pheasant
sufficient fresh or canned oysters to stuff the pheasant
fat bacon rashers
300 to 450 ml/½ to ¾ pint milk
white or cream sauce to serve
pastry croûtes to garnish

Stuff the pheasant with the oysters. Line a saucepan with bacon rashers. Put in the pheasant and cover the breast with more bacon rashers. Pour in the milk and cook very gently for 50 minutes or until the pheasant is tender.

Drain the pheasant, discard the bacon and place the pheasant on a warmed serving dish. Pour over white or cream sauce and garnish with pastry croûtes.

Game Pie

Serves 8-10

*225 g/8 oz cooked ham
or bacon
175 g/6 oz pie veal
1 small onion
salt
pepper
good pinch of grated
nutmeg or ground
cinnamon
225 g/8 oz cooked game
meat, chopped
300 ml/½ pint game or
chicken stock
15 g/½ oz gelatine*

Pastry
*350 g/12 oz flour
½ teaspoon salt
100 g/4 oz lard or white
vegetable fat
150 ml/¼ pint water
beaten egg to glaze*

Mince the ham or bacon, veal and onion together, then mix in salt, pepper and the nutmeg or cinnamon.

To make the pastry, sift the flour and salt into a bowl. Melt the lard or fat in the water and bring to the boil. Add to the flour and mix to a soft dough. Knead lightly, then roll out three-quarters of the dough to a 28 cm/11 inch round. Use to line a lightly greased loose-bottomed 15 to 18 cm/6 to 7 inch diameter round cake tin or game pie mould. Spread half the minced meat mixture over the bottom and cover with the chopped game. Spread over the rest of the minced mixture and press down lightly. Roll out the remaining dough and use to cover the pie. Press the edges together to seal, and decorate the top with the dough trimmings.

Make a hole in the centre for the steam to escape. Brush with beaten egg, then bake in a preheated moderately hot oven (200°C/400°F, Gas Mark 6) for 30 minutes. Brush again with egg and reduce the temperature to moderate (180°C/350°F, Gas Mark 4). Bake for a further 1½ hours. Cover the top with foil when the pastry is sufficiently browned.

Heat the stock and dissolve the gelatine in it. Add salt and pepper and cool.

Remove the pie from the oven. As it cools, pour the stock mixture through the hole in the lid, adding more from time to time. Cool completely, then chill before removing the pie from the tin. Serve cut into slices.

Roast Marinated Venison

Serves 5–6

1 haunch of venison
1 tablespoon flour
150 ml/¼ pint soured
  cream or natural
  yogurt

Marinade
150 ml/¼ pint red wine
300 ml/½ pint water
1 garlic clove, crushed
1 tablespoon chopped
  onion
1 tablespoon chopped
  carrot
little chopped celery
few mushrooms, sliced
6 peppercorns
1 bay leaf

Mix together the ingredients for the marinade and add the venison. Cover and leave in a cool place, not the refrigerator, for 36 hours to 2 days. Turn from time to time.

When ready to cook, drain the venison. Spit roast if possible, with the marinade in a tray beneath to catch the meat drippings. Baste frequently with the marinade. Alternatively, roast in a preheated moderately hot oven (190°C/375°F, Gas Mark 5) allowing 35 minutes per pound. Baste occasionally with the marinade.

Strain the marinade into a saucepan. Mix the flour with the soured cream or yogurt and stir into the marinade. Bring to the boil, stirring well, and simmer until thickened. Serve this with the venison.

Roast Game Birds

Serves 4

2 young game birds
salt
pepper
4 fatty bacon rashers
2 knobs of butter
melted dripping or oil
flour (optional)

Garnish
watercress
lemon or orange slices

Rub the birds with salt and pepper, then cover the breasts with the bacon. Put a knob of butter inside each bird and arrange side by side in a roasting tin greased with a little dripping or oil. Brush the birds all over with dripping or oil, then roast in a preheated moderately hot oven (200°C/400°F, Gas Mark 6) for the following times, basting frequently with the fat in the tin:

Pheasant – about 1 hour
Partridge – 35 to 45 minutes
Grouse – 40 to 60 minutes
Wild duck – 20 to 60 minutes, depending on size and variety
Pigeon – 20 to 30 minutes

If liked, about 5 minutes before the end of the cooking time, remove the bacon and dredge the birds with flour. Baste with the fat in the tin and complete the cooking.

Serve with gravy and fried crumbs or game chips, and garnished with watercress and lemon or orange slices.

Casseroled Grouse

Serves 4

2 grouse
50 g/2 oz flour
50 g/2 oz butter
2 shallots, sliced
1 carrot, sliced
1 celery stalk, sliced
1 bouquet garni
salt
pepper
300 ml/½ pint stock
225 g/8 oz cooked lean
   gammon, diced
120 ml/4 fl oz red wine
watercress to garnish

Coat the grouse with 15 g/½ oz of the flour. Melt the butter in a pan and brown the grouse on both sides. Transfer them to a casserole.

Add the shallots, carrot and celery to the pan and fry until softened. Transfer to the casserole with a slotted spoon and add the bouquet garni, salt and pepper.

Add the remaining flour to the pan, adding more butter if necessary to absorb it, and cook, stirring, for 2 minutes. Gradually stir in the stock and bring to the boil. Pour into the casserole over the grouse and add the gammon. Cover and simmer gently for 2½ to 3 hours, according to the age of the birds. Add the wine towards the end of the cooking time.

Split the grouse and arrange on a warmed serving dish. Add the vegetables. Strain the cooking liquid and serve separately. Garnish with watercress.

Roast Guinea Fowl with Olive Stuffing and Soured Cream Sauce

Serves 4–5

2 young guinea fowl
salt
pepper
4 fatty bacon rashers
melted dripping or oil
flour (optional)
150 ml/¼ pint soured
   cream or natural
   yogurt

Stuffing
12 olives, stoned and
   chopped
pepper
75 g/3 oz fresh
   breadcrumbs
1 egg, beaten

Mix together the ingredients for the stuffing and use to stuff the birds. Rub them with salt and pepper, then cover the breasts with the bacon. Arrange side by side in a roasting tin greased with a little dripping or oil, then roast in a preheated moderately hot oven (200°C/400°F, Gas Mark 6) for 45 minutes or until tender. Baste frequently with the fat in the tin.

Transfer the birds to a warmed serving platter and keep hot. Pour off the fat from the tin, then stir in the soured cream or yogurt. Scrape the pan well and simmer for 1 to 2 minutes. Serve with the guinea fowl.

Casserole of Partridge and Cabbage
Serves 4

50 g/2 oz butter
2 onions, thinly sliced
2 carrots, sliced
2 mature partridges
1 medium Savoy
. cabbage, quartered
100 g/4 oz streaky bacon
in one piece
salt
pepper
pinch of dried thyme
300 ml/½ pint stock
225 g/8 oz pork sausages
chopped parsley to
garnish

Melt the butter in a frying pan and brown the onions, carrots and partridges. Meanwhile, cook the cabbage and bacon in boiling water for 6 minutes. Drain well. Remove the rind from the bacon, then cut the bacon and cabbage into smaller pieces.

Put half the cabbage in a casserole, add a little salt and pepper and put the partridges, bacon and vegetables on top. Season again, adding the thyme too. Pour in the stock and cover with the rest of the cabbage. Cover tightly and cook in a cool oven (150°C/300°F, Gas Mark 2) for 2 hours.

About 45 minutes before the casserole is ready, grill the sausages until they are browned on all sides. Add them to the casserole for the last 30 minutes of cooking.

To serve, pile the cabbage in the centre of a warmed serving dish. Put the partridges on top and surround with the bacon, vegetables and sausages. Garnish with parsley.

Partridge and Mushrooms
Serves 4

350 g/12 oz mushrooms,
sliced
50 g/2 oz butter
salt
pepper
2 young partridges
watercress to garnish

Sauce
40 g/1½ oz butter
40 g/1½ oz flour
450 ml/¾ pint stock
100 ml/3 fl oz sherry
salt
pepper

Melt the butter in a frying pan and fry 225 g/8 oz of the mushrooms until they are tender. Season with salt and pepper, then use the mushrooms to stuff the partridges. Place the partridges in a casserole and roast in a pre-heated moderately hot oven (200°C/400°F, Gas Mark 6) until the birds are browned.

Meanwhile, make the sauce. Melt the butter in a saucepan and add the flour. Cook, stirring, for 2 minutes, then gradually stir in the stock. Bring to the boil and simmer, stirring, until thickened. Stir in the sherry, salt and pepper.

Pour the sauce over the partridges and cook for a further 45 minutes or until the birds are tender. Add the remaining mushrooms for the last 15 minutes' cooking. Serve garnished with watercress.

Braised Pigeons with Oranges and Wine
Serves 4

2 young pigeons
2 tangerines or small
  oranges, peeled
4 strips of fat bacon or
  pork
25 g/1 oz lard
3 shallots, chopped
1 small onion, chopped
100 g/4 oz mushrooms,
  sliced
1 tablespoon flour
150 ml/¼ pint Marsala or
  red wine
salt
pepper
1 bouquet garni
1 teaspoon dried mixed
  herbs

Garnish
small grilled sausages
grilled bacon rolls

Put a tangerine or orange inside each bird. Cut the skin on the breast on either side by the wings and insert the strips of bacon or pork. Truss the birds.

Melt the lard in a frying pan and brown the birds on all sides. Transfer them to a casserole.

Add the shallots, onion and mushrooms to the pan and fry until softened. Sprinkle over the flour and stir well, then add the Marsala or wine, salt and pepper.

Bring to the boil, stirring well, then pour this mixture over the pigeons in the casserole. Add the bouquet garni and other herbs. Cover tightly and cook in a preheated moderately hot oven (200 C/400 F, Gas Mark 6) for 1 to 1½ hours or until the pigeons are tender. Serve garnished with sausages and bacon rolls.

Note: If the sauce is too thick, add a little stock.

Faisan Normande
Serves 2–3

1 young pheasant
salt
pepper
100 g/4 oz butter
750 g/1½ lb apples,
  peeled, cored and
  thinly sliced
4 to 5 tablespoons cream
  or top of milk

Rub the pheasant with salt and pepper. Melt the butter in a frying pan and brown the pheasant on all sides.

Put half the apples in a casserole and pour over a little of the butter from the pan. Put the pheasant in the casserole and cover with the rest of the apples. Pour over the rest of the butter from the pan and the cream or top of the milk. Cover tightly and cook in a preheated moderate oven (180°C/350°F, Gas Mark 4) for 30 minutes or until the pheasant is tender.

Casserole of Pigeons with Apples and Cider   *Serves 2–3*

25 g/1 oz butter
2 young pigeons
1 small apple, cored and sliced
1 small onion, sliced
15 g/½ oz flour
450 ml/¾ pint stock
150 ml/¼ pint cider
salt
pepper
1 bouquet garni
Garnish
fried apple rings
fried bacon rashers

Melt the butter in a flameproof casserole or heavy saucepan and brown the pigeons on all sides. Remove them from the pan and cut in half.

Add the apple and onion to the pan and fry until lightly browned. Sprinkle over the flour and cook, stirring well, for 2 minutes. Gradually stir in the stock and cider and bring to the boil. Add salt, pepper and the bouquet garni and return the pigeon halves to the casserole. Cover and cook for 2 to 2½ hours or until the pigeons are tender.

Transfer the pigeons to a warmed serving dish and keep hot. Strain the cooking liquid and return it to the pan. Boil briskly until well reduced, then pour it over the pigeons. Garnish with fried apple rings and bacon rashers.

Venison Stewed in Beer   *Serves 5–6 (depending on weight of joint)*

225 g/8 oz demerara sugar
2 tablespoons black treacle
600 ml/1 pint beer
1 joint of venison

Dissolve the sugar and treacle in the beer. Put the venison in a saucepan and pour over the liquid. Cover and bring to the boil, then simmer gently until tender, allowing about 30 minutes to each 450 g/1 lb plus 30 minutes over.

Hare Jugged in Beer   *Serves 5–6*

1 hare (with blood), cut into joints
flour
salt
pepper
50 g/2 oz beef dripping
1 onion stuck with 5 cloves
600 ml/1 pint beer
100 ml/3 fl oz port wine or sherry

Mix flour with salt and pepper and use to coat the hare joints. Melt the dripping in a frying pan and brown the joints on all sides. Transfer them to a casserole, with any fat, and add the blood, onion and beer. Cover and cook in a preheated cool oven (150 C/300 F, Gas Mark 2) for 4 to 5 hours or until the meat comes easily from the bones.

Just before serving, remove the onion and stir in the port or sherry. Serve with redcurrant jelly.

Saddle of Hare à la Crème
Serves 4

1 saddle of hare
English mustard
25 g/1 oz butter
150 ml/¼ pint stock
150 ml/¼ pint cream
Marinade
3 tablespoons olive oil
2 small onions, sliced
2 small carrots. sliced
1 tablespoon vinegar
450 ml/¾ pint red wine
1 thyme sprig
1 rosemary sprig
2 bay leaves
6 peppercorns
salt

For the marinade, heat the oil in a saucepan and fry the onions and carrots until softened. Stir in the remaining marinade ingredients and bring to the boil. Simmer for 7 minutes, then cool.

Put the hare in a bowl and pour over the marinade. Leave for 36 hours, turning occasionally.

Remove the hare, reserving the marinade, and spread it with mustard. Melt the butter in a saucepan and brown the saddle on all sides. Add the strained marinade and bring to the boil. Simmer until reduced by about one-third. Add the stock and return to the boil.

Transfer to a casserole, cover tightly and cook in a preheated moderate oven (180 C/350 F, Gas Mark 4) for 1½ to 1¾ hours or until tender.

Transfer the hare to a warmed serving dish and keep warm. Add the cream to the cooking liquid and heat through. Strain the sauce and serve with the hare.

Roast Hare
Serves 4

1 young hare, or saddle
* joint of an older hare*
stuffing (optional)
fatty bacon rashers
oil
dripping

Stuff the hare, if liked, then truss and place in a roasting tin. Cover with fatty bacon and brush with oil. Put plenty of dripping into the tin and roast in a preheated moderate oven (180°C/350°F, Gas Mark 4) for 1½ to 2 hours, depending on size, until tender. Baste frequently with the fat in the tin, and lay a piece of oiled foil loosely over the hare after 30 minutes' cooking.

Serve with a thick gravy, with a flavouring of port or sherry, if liked, and redcurrant or japonica jelly.

131

Rabbit Casserole
Serves 4

4 rabbit pieces
226 g/8 oz canned
tomatoes
600 ml/1 pint canned
condensed tomato soup
150 ml/¼ pint beef stock
½ teaspoon Bovril
1 teaspoon
Worcestershire sauce
salt
pepper
225 g/8 oz onions, sliced
225 g/8 oz carrots, sliced
100 g/4 oz mushrooms,
sliced
1 small swede, cubed
1 to 2 red or green
peppers, cored, seeded
and sliced (optional)
4 belly of pork slices

Put the rabbit pieces in a deep baking dish. Mix together the tomatoes, tomato soup, stock, Bovril, Worcestershire sauce, salt and pepper and add the vegetables. Pour into the dish. Place the pork slices on top.

Cover the dish and bake in a preheated cool oven (150°C/300°F, Gas Mark 2) for 3½ to 4 hours or until the rabbit is tender. Serve with boiled rice or baked jacket potatoes.

Herb Roll
Serves 4

225 g/8 oz flour
salt
100 g/4 oz shredded suet
2 tablespoons milk
1 egg, beaten
50 g/2 oz chopped mixed
fresh herbs
little chopped onion
(optional)
pepper
100 g/4 oz cooked rabbit
or chicken meat or
bacon, minced
2 tablespoons stock
beaten egg to glaze
knob of dripping

Sift the flour with a pinch of salt into a bowl. Add the suet and bind with the milk. Roll out this dough to 2.5 cm/1 inch thick.

Mix together the egg, herbs, onion, if used, salt and pepper and spread over the dough. Mix the meat with the stock and spread over the herb mixture. Roll up like a Swiss roll and pinch the ends with a sprinkle of flour. Place in a greased baking tin and brush with beaten egg. Add the dripping to the tin.

Bake in a preheated moderate oven (180°C/350°F, Gas Mark 4) for 45 minutes to 1 hour, basting frequently with the melted fat in the tin.

Hunter's Rabbit

Serves 4

*1 small hard cabbage,
  cored and cut
  lengthways into 6
  pieces*
25 g/1 oz fat
*450 g/1 lb chipolata
  sausages*
1 small onion, chopped
1 rabbit, jointed
*3 to 4 bacon rashers,
  rinded*
*150 ml/¼ pint game or
  chicken stock*
300 ml/½ pint dry cider
salt
pepper
1 bouquet garni

Cook the cabbage in boiling water for 5 minutes, then drain well and place in a casserole.

Melt the fat in a frying pan and fry the sausages and onion until the sausages are golden brown on all sides. Remove from the heat and drain.

Place the rabbit pieces on top of the cabbage in the casserole, then add the sausages and onion. Cover with the bacon rashers. Pour in the stock and cider and add the salt, pepper and bouquet garni.

Cover the casserole very tightly, sealing with a flour and water paste, if necessary. Cook in a preheated cool oven (150°C/300°F, Gas Mark 2) for 2½ hours.

Rabbit and Sausage Hot Pot

Serves 4–5

350 g/12 oz sausage meat
*1 rabbit or chicken,
  jointed*
1 large onion, chopped
salt
pepper
stock
*75 g/3 oz fresh
  breadcrumbs*
25 g/1 oz butter

Spread half the sausage meat on the bottom of a pie dish. Place the rabbit or chicken joints on top and sprinkle them with the onion, salt and pepper. Cover with the rest of the sausage meat. Half fill the dish with stock.

Sprinkle the breadcrumbs over the top and press them down firmly. Dot with the butter. Cover the dish with foil and bake in a preheated cool oven (150°C/300°F, Gas Mark 2) for 1½ hours. Fifteen minutes before the cooking time is up, remove the foil so that the top can brown.

133

Stuffings

Crayfish Stuffing

Enough to stuff a 3 to 4 kg/7 to 9 lb bird

liver of bird to be stuffed
100 g/4 oz calf's liver
3 crayfish tails, pounded
2 to 3 bacon rashers,
   rinded and diced
chopped parsley
sweet herbs
salt
pepper
ground allspice

Mince the two livers together finely, then mix in the remaining ingredients, adding herbs and seasoning to taste.

Apple Stuffing

Enough to stuff a 3 to 4 kg/7 to 9 lb bird

6 cooking apples, peeled,
   cored and diced
50 g/2 oz butter
salt
pepper
$\frac{1}{4}$ teaspoon grated lemon
   rind
2 heaped tablespoons
   sugar
100 g/4 oz fresh
   breadcrumbs

Melt the butter in a pan and add the apples. Cook gently, stirring frequently, until they are soft. Remove from the heat and mix in the remaining ingredients. Moisten with a little water if necessary.

Chestnut Stuffing   *Enough to stuff a 3 to 4 kg/7 to 9 lb bird*

450 g/1 lb chestnuts,
  cooked and peeled
2 bacon rashers, rinded,
  cooked and chopped
1 small onion, minced
salt
pepper
top of milk or cream

Mix together the chestnuts, bacon, onion, salt and pepper and put through a sieve or vegetable mill to make a purée. Moisten with a little top of the milk or cream if necessary.

Celery Stuffing   *Enough to stuff a 3 to 4 kg/7 to 9 lb bird*

25 g/1 oz butter
4 celery stalks, finely
  chopped
100 g/4 oz fresh
  breadcrumbs
salt
pepper
½ small onion, minced

Melt the butter in a pan and fry the celery until softened. Remove from the heat and mix in the remaining ingredients. Moisten with a little more melted butter, or bacon fat, if necessary.

New England Stuffing   *Enough to stuff a 3 to 4 kg/7 to 9 lb bird*

12 thick slices of bread,
  crusts removed, toasted
stock or water
salt
pepper
1 egg, beaten
1 tablespoon chopped
  fresh sage
1 thick slice of fat salt
  pork, finely chopped

Chop up the toast and moisten with a little stock or water. Mix in the remaining ingredients.

135

Salads

Cheese and Cabbage Salad

Serves 4–5

*450 g/1 lb white cabbage,
  cored and shredded
225 g/8 oz cheese, diced
1 medium onion, grated
5 to 6 tablespoons
  mayonnaise
chopped parsley to
  garnish*

Mix together the cabbage, cheese, onion and
mayonnaise and pile in a serving dish. Garnish
with parsley and chill before serving.
Variation: Add a little grated carrot and a few
sultanas.

Tomato and Watercress Salad

Serves 4

*1 bunch of watercress,
  chopped
225 g/8 oz tomatoes,
  skinned and sliced
150 ml/¼ pint natural
  yogurt
squeeze of lemon juice
1 teaspoon sugar
1 teaspoon French
  mustard
1 tablespoon chopped
  chives
salt
pepper*

Layer the watercress and tomatoes in a salad
bowl. Mix together the remaining ingredients
to make the dressing and pour over the
vegetables.

Mushroom Salad

Serves 4

*450 g/1 lb button
  mushrooms
200 ml/⅓ pint wine
  vinegar
2 tablespoons sugar
little grated lemon rind
juice of ½ lemon
salt
pepper
pinch of garlic powder
1 bouquet garni or 2 bay
  leaves
chopped parsley to
  garnish*

Halve any large mushrooms. Put the vinegar, sugar, lemon rind and juice, salt, pepper, garlic powder and bouquet garni or bay leaves in a saucepan and bring to the boil, stirring to dissolve the sugar. Add the mushrooms and return to the boil. Pour into a bowl, cover and cool.

Serve cold, garnished with parsley.

Tuna Bean Salad

Serves 4

*450 g/1 lb French beans
approx. 6 tablespoons
  French dressing
4 tomatoes, skinned and
  sliced
¼ cucumber, diced
1 tablespoon finely
  chopped onion
  (optional)
198 g/7 oz canned tuna
  fish, drained and flaked
salt
pepper
2 hard-boiled eggs, sliced*

Cook the beans in boiling salted water until they are just tender. Drain well and cool slightly, then toss with the dressing. Cool completely.

Add the tomatoes, cucumber, onion, if used, tuna, salt and pepper to the beans and fold together. Serve garnished with the egg slices.
Variation: Bean salad niçoise. Add 2 potatoes, peeled, cooked and diced, 6 sliced spring onions and 1 crushed garlic clove to the final mixture. Add 25 g/1 oz of drained anchovy fillets, halved lengthways, and some black or stuffed olives to the garnish.

Coleslaw
Serves 5-6

½ small white cabbage,
  cored and finely
  shredded
150 ml/¼ pint natural
  yogurt
1 tablespoon lemon juice
1 teaspoon sugar
salt
pepper

Combine the ingredients together thoroughly.

Honeyed Fresh Fruit Salad
Serves 4

1 apple, peeled, cored
  and sliced
1 banana, sliced
juice of ½ lemon
small bunch of grapes,
  skinned, halved and
  pipped
1 orange, peeled and
  segmented
cider, sherry or water
1 tablespoon clear honey

Sprinkle the banana and apple slices with the lemon juice to prevent them going brown. Mix together all the fruit in a bowl and cover with cider, sherry or water, into which the honey has been stirred. Chill for about 1 hour before serving.

Ruby Slaw
Serves 4

225 g/8 oz carrots,
  grated
225 g/8 oz cooked
  beetroot, peeled and
  grated
1 tablespoon chopped
  chives or spring onions
4 to 6 tablespoons French
  dressing or mayonnaise
salt
pepper
mustard and cress to
  garnish

Fold together the carrots, beetroot, chives or spring onions, dressing or mayonnaise, salt and pepper. Arrange on a platter and garnish with mustard and cress.

Red Bean and Apple Salad

Serves 6

*2 to 3 green-skinned
  eating apples, cored
  and diced*
*4 tablespoons French
  dressing*
salt
pepper
*little crushed garlic
  (optional)*
*40 g/1½ oz walnuts,
  roughly chopped*
*425 g/15 oz canned red
  kidney beans, drained*

Mix together the apples, dressing, salt, pepper and garlic, if using. Add the walnuts and beans and fold together. Chill lightly before serving.

Curried Celery Salad

Serves 6

*150 ml/¼ pint thick
  mayonnaise*
1 tablespoon lemon juice
1 teaspoon curry powder
salt
pepper
1 head of celery, sliced
6 spring onions, sliced
50 g/2 oz sultanas

Combine the mayonnaise, lemon juice, curry powder, salt and pepper, then fold in the celery, onions and sultanas.

Apple and Carrot Salad

Serves 4 5

4 carrots
*2 tablespoons chopped
  parsley*
salt
pepper
*4 tablespoons French
  dressing*
*3 eating apples, cored
  and chopped*
lemon juice
*3 bananas, sliced
  (optional)*

Use a potato peeler to shave the carrots into thin strips. Put these in a salad bowl and add the parsley, salt, pepper and dressing. Dip the apples in lemon juice to prevent discolouration and add to the carrot mixture. Fold together gently. Add the bananas, if using, first dipping them in lemon juice

Pineapple Slaw   *Serves 4*

*150 g/5 oz canned
  pineapple
350 g/12 oz white
  cabbage, cored and
  shredded
8 to 10 spring onions,
  chopped
50 g/2 oz walnuts,
  chopped
4 to 6 tablespoons
  mayonnaise*

Drain the pineapple syrup from the can and reserve. If using pineapple rings, chop them. Mix the pineapple with the cabbage, spring onions and walnuts. Combine the mayonnaise with 2 tablespoons of the reserved pineapple syrup, then fold into the cabbage mixture.

Tomato Salad   *Serves 4–5*

*450 g/1 lb tomatoes,
  skinned and sliced
1 tablespoon oil
1 teaspoon wine vinegar
chopped chives, garlic
  (crushed), onion
  (diced) or fresh basil*

Arrange the tomato slices in a serving dish. Mix together the remaining ingredients to make a dressing and pour over the tomatoes.

Artichoke and Potato Salad   *Serves 5–6*

*450 g/1 lb new potatoes,
  scraped
150 ml/¼ pint French
  dressing
1 tablespoon finely
  chopped onion
250 g/9 oz canned
  artichoke hearts,
  drained and chopped
12 black olives, stoned
salt
pepper
watercress to garnish*

Cook the potatoes in boiling water until they are just tender. Drain well and cool slightly, then mix with the French dressing. Leave to cool completely.

Add the onion, artichoke hearts, olives, salt and pepper to the potatoes and fold together. Turn into a bowl and garnish with a border of watercress.

Cottage Cheese, Chicken and Ginger Salad   *Serves 5-6*

450 g/1 lb cottage cheese
2 tablespoons double
   cream
100 g/4 oz cooked
   chicken meat, diced
25 g/1 oz stem ginger,
   finely chopped
salt
pepper
watercress

Beat the cottage cheese with the cream. Add the chicken, ginger, salt and pepper and mix well. Pile in the centre of a serving dish and surround with watercress.

Bean Slaw   *Serves 4*

450 g/1 lb runner beans,
   sliced
75 g/3 oz walnuts,
   chopped
4 celery stalks, chopped
2 eating apples, cored
   and chopped
2 large carrots, cut into
   thin sticks
4 to 6 tablespoons French
   dressing
2 tablespoons finely
   chopped onion to
   garnish

Cook the beans in boiling salted water until just tender. Drain, rinse in cold water and drain again. Cool.

Add the walnuts, celery, apples, carrots and dressing to the beans and fold together thoroughly. Turn into a salad bowl and garnish with the onion.

Cheese and Apple Salad   *Serves 4*

4 red-skinned eating
   apples, cored and diced
275 g/10 oz cheese, cubed
100 g/4 oz celery or
   cucumber, diced
4 tablespoons mayonnaise
   or French dressing
1 tablespoon chopped
   walnuts
watercress to garnish

Mix together the apples, cheese, celery or cucumber and mayonnaise or dressing. Pile in a salad bowl and garnish with the walnuts and watercress.

Pacific Island Salad

2 grapefruit, peeled and
segmented
4 oranges, peeled and
segmented
1 small pineapple, peeled,
cored and cubed
4 apples, cored and diced
1 banana, sliced
4 tomatoes, diced
100 g/4 oz blue cheese,
diced
100 g/4 oz Gruyère
cheese, diced
175 g/6 oz cooked ham,
diced
100 g/4 oz walnut halves
1 lettuce, shredded

Mix together all the ingedients in a large salad bowl. No dressing is needed as the fruit juices moisten the ingredients. Chill, covered, for 1 hour.

Fish Rice Salad

75 g/3 oz cooked rice
175 g/6 oz cooked fish
fillets, flaked
50 g/2 oz raisins
salt
pepper

Dressing
2 tablespoons oil
1 tablespoon wine vinegar
½ garlic clove, crushed
dried tarragon

Garnish
tomato
cucumber
parsley

Mix together the ingredients for the dressing. Add the rice, fish, raisins, salt and pepper and mix well. Pile in the centre of a serving platter and garnish with tomato, cucumber and parsley.

Crab Salad

Serves 4

350 g/12 oz frozen crab
meat, thawed
2 eating apples, peeled,
cored and diced
little lemon juice
4 celery stalks, sliced
1 × 12.5 cm/5 inch piece
cucumber, diced
lemony mayonnaise
salt
pepper
shredded lettuce to serve

Flake the crab meat, mixing together the white and brown meat. Sprinkle the apples with lemon juice to prevent them turning brown and add to the crab meat with the celery and cucumber. Fold in enough mayonnaise to make a creamy consistency and add salt and pepper. Serve on a bed of shredded lettuce in a bowl or individual glasses.

French Dressing

3 tablespoons oil
1 tablespoon wine vinegar
1 teaspoon sugar
1 teaspoon made mustard
1 teaspoon lemon juice
pinch of salt
dried tarragon (optional)

Put all the ingredients into a screwtop jar and shake until well mixed.

Sweet and Sour Salad

Serves 4

2 medium carrots, grated
2 sour apples, cored and
diced
1 celery stalk, chopped
4 dates, stoned and
chopped
15 g/½ oz raisins
50 g/2 oz walnuts,
chopped
4 tablespoons natural
yogurt
2 teaspoons lemon juice
1 teaspoon chopped fresh
mint

Mix together the carrots, apples, celery, dates, raisins and walnuts. Combine the yogurt, lemon juice and mint and fold into the salad.

143

German Potato Salad

Serves 6

*350 g/12 oz new
   potatoes, scraped and
   sliced
salt
1 tablespoon French
   dressing
bay leaves to garnish*

Dressing

*1 tablespoon sugar
1 tablespoon flour
150 ml/¼ pint water
1 tablespoon made
   mustard
150 ml/¼ pint tarragon
   vinegar
1 egg, beaten
15 g/½ oz butter
top of milk
pinch of grated nutmeg
1 tablespoon chopped
   chives*

First make the dressing. Mix together the sugar, flour, 1 tablespoon of the water and the mustard in a saucepan. Stir in the rest of the water and the vinegar and bring to the boil. Simmer, stirring, for 5 minutes. Remove from the heat and beat in the egg and butter. Leave until cold, then dilute as necessary with top of milk. Mix in the nutmeg and chives.

Cook the potatoes in boiling salted water until they are tender. Drain well and toss with the French dressing while still warm. Cool, then coat with the dressing. Serve garnished with bay leaves.

Rice Salad

Serves 5–6

*100 g/4 oz boiled Patna
   rice
1 green or red pepper,
   cored, seeded and
   finely chopped
50 g/2 oz walnuts,
   chopped
1 red dessert apple, cored
   and finely chopped
1 small celery stalk,
   finely chopped
200 g/7 oz canned
   sweetcorn, drained
50 g/2 oz sultanas
salt
3 to 4 tablespoons French
   dressing or mayonnaise*

Mix together all the ingredients.

Chicken, Grape and Rice Salad

Serves 4–5

350 g/12 oz cooked
  chicken meat, cut into
  neat pieces
100 g/4 oz green grapes,
  halved and pipped
100 g/4 oz black grapes,
  halved and pipped
175 g/6 oz boiled long-
  grain rice
diced cucumber
sliced tomatoes
grated carrot
cooked peas

Lemon Cream Dressing
1 tablespoon oil
1 tablespoon lemon juice
$\frac{1}{4}$ teaspoon grated lemon
  rind
$\frac{1}{4}$ teaspoon sugar
3 tablespoons single
  cream
salt

Paprika Dressing
4 to 5 tablespoons oil
2 tablespoons wine
  vinegar
1 teaspoon paprika
pinch of sugar
salt
pepper

Garnish
black grapes
tomatoes

Mix together the ingredients for the lemon cream dressing. Add the chicken and grapes and leave to marinate for 30 minutes.

Combine the rice, cucumber, tomatoes, carrot and peas. Mix together the ingredients for the paprika dressing and fold through the rice mixture.

Make a border of the rice mixture around a flat serving platter. Pile the chicken mixture in the centre. Garnish with grapes and tomatoes.

Continental Salad
Serves 5-6

2 medium green peppers,
cored, seeded and cut
into thin rings
450 g/1 lb tomatoes,
thinly sliced
½ cucumber, thinly sliced
Dressing
2 tablespoons oil
1 tablespoon vinegar
1 teaspoon concentrated
mint sauce
salt
pepper

Arrange the green peppers, tomatoes and cucumber in a serving dish. Mix together the dressing ingredients and pour over the vegetables.

Apple Raisin Slaw
Serves 5-6

175 g/6 oz seedless
raisins
rosé wine
3 dessert apples, cored
and diced
1 tablespoon lemon juice
½ medium cabbage, cored
and shredded
100 ml/3 fl oz
mayonnaise
salt
pepper

Put the raisins in a bowl and cover with wine. Leave for several hours or overnight.

Toss the apples with the lemon juice, then add the cabbage, raisins and wine. Add the mayonnaise, salt and pepper and toss together well. Serve immediately.

Cucumber and Tomato Salad
Serves 4-6

1 medium cucumber,
peeled and diced
225 g/8 oz tomatoes,
chopped
4 tablespoons natural
yogurt
juice of 1 lemon
1 garlic clove, crushed

Mix together the cucumber and tomatoes in a salad bowl. Combine the yogurt, lemon juice and garlic and fold into the salad.

Dutch Salad   *Serves 4–5*

2 pickled herrings, flaked
175 g/6 oz cooked
*   potato, diced*
175 g/6 oz cooked
*   beetroot, diced*
175 g/6 oz cooking
*   apples, peeled, cored*
*   and diced*
chopped onion
finely chopped fresh dill
chopped pickle
4 to 6 tablespoons French
*   dressing*
lettuce leaves

Garnish
1 dill cucumber
hard-boiled egg slices

Mix together the herrings, potato, beetroot, apples, onion, dill, pickle and dressing very lightly. Line a salad bowl with lettuce leaves and pile in the salad.

To garnish, make dill fans by cutting thin slices lengthwise down the dill cucumber leaving 5 mm/$\frac{1}{4}$ inch at one end uncut. Cut 4 or 5 strips depending on the size of the dill. Carefully flatten and spread the slices out like a fan and use as a garnish with the egg slices.

Hard-boiled Egg and Waldorf Salad   *Serves 5–6*

450 g/1 lb crisp dessert
*   apples, cored and*
*   chopped*
juice of $\frac{1}{2}$ lemon
1 celery stalk, chopped
$\frac{1}{4}$ teaspoon sugar
salt
pepper
salad cream
50 g/2 oz walnuts,
*   chopped*
1 hard-boiled egg, sliced
green and black grapes,
*   halved and pipped, to*
*   garnish*

Toss the apples with the lemon juice. Add the celery, sugar, salt, pepper, salad cream and walnuts. The ingredients should be well coated with salad cream.

Pile the salad in a dish and arrange the egg slices in a line over the centre. Garnish with grape halves.

147

Winter Salad

1 small hard cabbage,
cored and finely
shredded
¼ small red cabbage,
cored and shredded
1 green or red pepper,
cored, seeded and
sliced
1 or 2 carrots, grated
3 Jerusalem artichokes,
grated
2 dessert apples, peeled,
cored and sliced
25 g/1 oz walnuts,
chopped
¼ cucumber, chopped
4 to 6 tablespoons French
dressing
celery salt
salt
pepper
1 tablespoon chopped
chives
50 g/2 oz cheese, cut into
cubes (optional)
2 tablespoons soaked
raisins (soaked in
water, wine, cider,
etc.)

Mix together the cabbages, green or red pepper, carrots, artichokes, apples, walnuts and cucumber. Add the dressing, celery salt, salt, pepper and chives and toss well. Fold in the cheese, if using, and sprinkle with the raisins.

Pasta & Rice

Mushroom Lasagne

12 sheets of lasagne
225 g/8 oz streaky bacon
rashers, rinded and
chopped
350 g/12 oz mushrooms,
sliced
50 g/2 oz butter
50 g/2 oz flour
600 ml/1 pint milk
2 tablespoons wine
vinegar
½ teaspoon French
mustard
salt
pepper
40 g/1½ oz fresh
breadcrumbs
50 g/2 oz mature
Cheddar cheese, grated

Cook the sheets of lasagne in boiling salted water until tender. (A little oil added to the water will prevent the sheets sticking together.)

Meanwhile, fry the bacon until it has rendered most of its fat and begins to colour. Add the mushrooms and fry for a further 4 minutes. Remove from the heat and drain off the fat.

Melt the butter in a saucepan and stir in the flour. Cook, stirring, for 2 minutes, then gradually stir in the milk. Bring to the boil and simmer, stirring, until thickened. Add the vinegar, mustard, salt and pepper.

Drain the lasagne and spread the sheets on paper towels.

Make a layer of lasagne in a buttered baking dish and cover with half the mushroom mixture followed by a little of the sauce. Repeat these layers once, then cover with the remaining lasagne and sauce. Mix together the breadcrumbs and cheese and sprinkle over the top. Bake in a preheated moderately hot oven (200°C/400°F, Gas Mark 6) for 30 to 40 minutes or until golden brown.

Note: This dish can be prepared in advance and kept in the refrigerator, in which case increase the baking time to 1 to 1¼ hours. It can also be frozen for up to 2 months, and should be thawed before baking.

Spaghetti Bake
Serves 4

225 g/8 oz spaghetti or
  short-cut macaroni
1 teaspoon made mustard
salt
pepper
pinch of cayenne pepper
600 ml/1 pint cheese
  sauce
40 g/1½ oz butter
2 large onions, thinly
  sliced
100 g/4 oz mushrooms,
  sliced (optional)
175 to 225 g/6 to 8 oz
  cooked turkey meat,
  cut into thin strips
100 g/4 oz bacon rashers,
  rinded, cooked and
  chopped
1 teaspoon dried basil or
  thyme
25 g/1 oz cheese, grated

Cook the spaghetti or macaroni in boiling salted water until tender.

Meanwhile, stir the mustard, salt, pepper and cayenne into the sauce. Melt the butter in a frying pan and fry the onions until golden brown. Add the mushrooms, if using, and fry for a further 3 minutes. Drain.

Drain the spaghetti or macaroni, then arrange half of it on the bottom of a buttered 1.75 litre/3 pint baking dish. Cover with half the sauce, then add the onion mixture followed by the turkey, bacon and herbs. Cover with the rest of the pasta and pour over the remaining sauce. Sprinkle with the cheese.

Bake in a preheated moderately hot oven (200°C/400°F, Gas Mark 6) for 45 minutes or until the top is well browned and all the ingredients are heated through.

Note: This dish can be prepared in advance and kept in the refrigerator, in which case increase the baking time to 1 hour.

Tuna and Macaroni Cheese
Serves 4

225 to 275 g/8 to 10 oz
  macaroni
50 g/2 oz butter
1 onion, chopped
50 g/2 oz flour
150 ml/¼ pint milk
100 to 175 g/4 to 6 oz
  Cheddar cheese, grated
2 hard-boiled eggs,
  chopped
198 g/7 oz canned tuna
  fish, drained and flaked

Cook the macaroni in boiling salted water until tender.

Meanwhile, melt the butter in a saucepan and fry the onion until softened. Sprinkle over the flour and cook, stirring, for 2 minutes. Gradually stir in the milk and bring to the boil. Simmer, stirring, until thickened. Add most of the cheese and stir until it has melted, then fold in the eggs, tuna, salt and pepper.

Drain the macaroni and fold into the tuna mixture. Turn into a buttered flameproof serving dish and sprinkle over the remaining cheese. Brown under a preheated hot grill.

Variation: Add 1 to 2 teaspoons dried mixed herbs, oregano, basil or thyme to the sauce.

Savoury Rice and Eggs
Serves 3–4

75 g/3 oz fat bacon,
  rinded and chopped
1 medium onion, sliced
100 g/4 oz rice
250 ml/8 fl oz stock or
  water
salt
pepper
6 tomatoes, skinned and
  sliced
25 g/1 oz butter
25 g/1 oz flour
300 ml/½ pint milk
4 hard-boiled or poached
  eggs
chopped parsley to
  garnish

Fry the bacon and onion together in a saucepan until the onion is softened. Stir in the rice and cook for 2 minutes, then stir in the stock or water, salt, pepper and tomatoes. Bring to the boil, then cover and simmer for 20 minutes or until the rice is tender and the liquid has been absorbed.

Meanwhile, melt the butter in a saucepan and stir in the flour. Cook, stirring, for 2 minutes, then gradually stir in the milk. Bring to the boil and simmer, stirring, until thickened. Add salt and pepper.

Spread the rice mixture in a warmed serving dish and arrange the eggs on top. Pour over the sauce and garnish with parsley.

Egg and Prawn Risotto
Serves 4

100 g/4 oz butter
1 onion, chopped
4 bacon rashers, rinded
  and chopped
1 green pepper, cored,
  seeded and chopped
225 g/8 oz long-grain rice
600 ml/1 pint chicken
  stock
150 ml/¼ pint dry white
  wine
175 g/6 oz shelled prawns
salt
pepper
4 hard-boiled eggs,
  chopped
50 g/2 oz Parmesan
  cheese, grated

Melt the butter in a saucepan and fry the onion, bacon and green pepper until the onion is golden brown. Stir in the rice and cook for 2 minutes, then stir in the stock and wine. Bring to the boil, then cover and simmer until the rice is tender and the liquid has been absorbed.

Stir the prawns into the rice mixture with salt and pepper and heat through gently. Fold in the eggs followed by the cheese. If the risotto is too dry, add a little more butter – it must be moist.

Spaghetti with Aubergine Sauce

Serves 4

1 tablespoon oil
1 large onion, sliced
1 garlic clove, crushed
1 aubergine, approx.
225 g/8 oz, chopped
1 green pepper, cored,
seeded and chopped
425 g/15 oz canned
tomatoes
120 ml/4 fl oz red wine
½ teaspoon dried basil
225 g/8 oz spaghetti
100 g/4 oz mushrooms,
chopped
1 tablespoon tomato
paste
salt
pepper
grated Parmesan cheese
to serve

Heat the oil in a saucepan and fry the onion and garlic until golden brown. Add the aubergine, green pepper, tomatoes, wine and basil and stir well. Bring to the boil, then cover and simmer for 30 minutes.

Meanwhile, cook the spaghetti in boiling salted water until it is tender.

Add the mushrooms, tomato paste, salt and pepper to the aubergine sauce and simmer for a further 5 minutes.

Drain the spaghetti and turn into a warmed serving dish. Pour over the aubergine sauce and serve with Parmesan cheese.

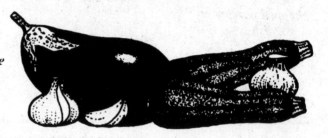

Carbonara

Serves 5–6

225 g/8 oz streaky bacon
rashers, rinded and
diced
225 g/8 oz pasta
(tagliatelle, spaghetti,
macaroni, etc.)
3 eggs, beaten
100 g/4 oz cheese, grated
salt
pepper
40 g/1½ oz butter

Fry the bacon in a frying pan until it is lightly browned.

Meanwhile, cook the pasta in boiling water until it is tender. Drain well.

Mix together the eggs, cheese, salt and pepper.

Melt the butter in the saucepan in which the pasta was cooked. Add the pasta, the bacon and the egg mixture. Heat gently, stirring together thoroughly, for about 1 minute. Do not allow the eggs to scramble: they should make a moist, soft and creamy coating for the pasta.

Beef in Beer with Noodles   *Serves 4*

2 tablespoons oil
750 g/1½ lb stewing
  steak, cubed
40 g/1½ oz flour
300 ml/½ pint brown
  stock
300 ml/½ pint brown ale
1 carrot, diced
1 small turnip, diced
  (optional)
1 onion, chopped
salt
pepper
225 g/8 oz mushrooms,
  sliced
225 g/8 oz egg noodles

Heat the oil in a saucepan and brown the steak cubes, in batches. Return all the meat to the pan and sprinkle over the flour. Cook, stirring well, for 3 minutes, then gradually stir in the stock and ale. Bring to the boil and add the carrot, turnip, if used, onion, salt and pepper. Simmer gently for 1 hour.

Add the mushrooms and simmer for a further 30 minutes or until the meat is tender.

Just before the meat is ready, cook the noodles in boiling salted water until tender. Drain and pile in a warmed serving dish. Spoon over the meat mixture and serve.

Spaghetti Romana   *Serves 4*

25 g/1 oz margarine
1 medium onion, sliced
  into rings
60 g/2¼ oz canned
  tomato purée
150 ml/¼ pint chicken
  stock
225 g/8 oz mushrooms,
  sliced
100 g/4 oz cooked ham,
  diced
½ teaspoon dried mixed
  herbs
1 bay leaf
salt
pepper
225 g/8 oz spaghetti
grated Parmesan cheese
  to serve

Melt the margarine in a saucepan and fry the onion until softened. Stir in the tomato purée, stock, mushrooms, ham, herbs, salt and pepper and bring to the boil. Simmer for 15 minutes.

Meanwhile, cook the spaghetti in boiling salted water until tender. Drain well and turn into a warmed serving dish. Remove the bay leaf from the sauce and pour over the spaghetti. Serve with Parmesan cheese.

Tuna Pasta Bake
Serves 4

100 g/4 oz short-cut
  spaghetti
25 g/1 oz margarine
25 g/1 oz flour
300 ml/½ pint milk
198 g/7 oz canned tuna
  fish, drained and flaked
100 g/4 oz Cheddar
  cheese, grated
salt
pepper
25 g/1 oz potato crisps,
  crushed
2 tomatoes, sliced

Cook the spaghetti in boiling salted water until tender.

Meanwhile, melt the margarine in a saucepan and stir in the flour. Cook, stirring, for 2 minutes, then gradually stir in the milk. Bring to the boil and simmer, stirring, until thickened.

Drain the spaghetti and fold into the sauce with the tuna, cheese, salt and pepper. Turn into a 1.2 litre/2 pint baking dish and sprinkle the crisps on top.

Bake in a preheated moderate oven (180°C/350°F, Gas Mark 4) for 20 to 30 minutes or until the top is golden brown. Serve garnished with the tomato slices.

Chicken Lasagne
Serves 6

12 sheets of lasagne
1 tablespoon oil
1 onion, sliced
100 g/4 oz mushrooms,
  sliced
2 teaspoons ground
  ginger
1 teaspoon grated nutmeg
3 bay leaves
salt
pepper
3 chicken portions,
  cooked, skinned and
  boned
1 tablespoon cornflour
450 ml/¾ pint milk
150 ml/¼ pint natural
  yogurt
100 g/4 oz Cheddar
  cheese, grated

Cook the lasagne in boiling salted water until tender. (A little oil added to the water will prevent the sheets of pasta from sticking together.)

Meanwhile, heat the oil in a saucepan and fry the onion until softened. Add the mushrooms and fry for a further 3 minutes. Stir in the spices, bay leaves, salt and pepper, then mix in the chicken (shredded or chopped). Dissolve the cornflour in the milk and add to the pan. Cook, stirring, until thickened.

Drain the lasagne and spread out on paper towels.

Make alternate layers of lasagne and the chicken mixture in a baking dish. Combine the yogurt and cheese and spread over the top. Bake in a preheated moderately hot oven (200°C/400°F, Gas Mark 6) for 30 minutes or until the top is golden brown.

Buttered Pasta
Serves 4–5

450 g/1 lb white or green noodles, spaghetti or macaroni
225 g/8 oz butter
175 to 225 g/6 to 8 oz Parmesan cheese, grated

Cook the pasta in boiling salted water until it is tender.

Put half the butter, cut into small pieces, into a warmed deep dish. Drain the pasta and tip half into the dish. Add half the cheese, then the remaining noodles, butter and cheese. Toss quickly together until the butter has melted and serve.

Cheese and Mushroom Risotto
Serves 3–4

75 g/3 oz butter
1 medium onion, sliced
175 g/6 oz rice
600 ml/1 pint hot chicken stock
2 tomatoes, skinned and chopped
salt
pepper
100 g/4 oz mushrooms, sliced
225 g/8 oz Cheddar cheese, cubed

Melt 50 g/2 oz of the butter in a saucepan and fry the onion until softened. Stir in the rice and cook for 2 minutes, then stir in the stock, tomatoes, salt and pepper. Bring to the boil, stirring, then cover and simmer until the rice is tender and the liquid has been absorbed.

Meanwhile, melt the remaining butter in a frying pan and fry the mushrooms for 3 minutes.

Stir the mushrooms and cheese into the rice mixture and serve.

Italian Pie
Serves 4

40 g/1½ oz macaroni
225 g/8 oz sausagemeat, cut into small pieces
2 medium tomatoes, skinned and sliced
salt
pepper
4 teaspoons chopped parsley
stock
450 g/1 lb mashed potato
3 tablespoons milk

Cook the macaroni in boiling salted water until tender. Drain well, then turn into a pie dish. Spread the sausage pieces on top and cover with the tomatoes. Add salt, pepper and the parsley. Pour enough stock into the dish to half fill it. Spread the mashed potato over the top and brush with the milk.

Bake in a preheated moderate oven (180°C/350°F, Gas Mark 4) for about 40 minutes or until the sausage meat is well cooked and the top is browned.

Chicken Louisiana
Serves 4

175 g/6 oz long-grain rice
450 ml/¾ pint chicken stock
1 tablespoon oil
3 streaky bacon rashers, rinded and chopped
1 large onion, thinly sliced
1 green pepper, cored, seeded and thinly sliced
400 g/14 oz canned tomatoes
350 g/12 oz cooked chicken meat, chopped
2 cooked spicy sausages or frankfurters, sliced
salt
pepper

Put the rice and stock in a saucepan and bring to the boil. Cover and simmer gently until the rice is tender and the liquid has been absorbed.

Meanwhile, heat the oil in another saucepan and fry the bacon, onion and green pepper until the onion is softened. Stir in the tomatoes, chicken, sausage or frankfurter slices, salt and pepper. Add the rice, mix well and cook for a further 10 minutes.

Liver Risotto
Serves 4–5

50 g/2 oz dripping
1 medium onion, chopped
175 g/6 oz Italian or Patna rice
600 ml/1 pint stock
1 chicken stock cube
25 g/1 oz butter or bacon dripping
50 to 75 g/2 to 3 oz bacon, chopped
225 g/8 oz liver, chopped
1 green or red pepper, cored, seeded and sliced
salt
pepper

Melt the dripping in a saucepan. Add the onion and fry until golden brown. Add the rice and cook for 3 minutes, stirring well. Stir in 150 ml/¼ pint of the stock and the stock cube and bring to the boil. Simmer gently, adding the rest of the stock gradually as it is absorbed. Continue simmering until the rice is tender and all the stock has been absorbed.

Meanwhile, melt the butter or bacon dripping in a frying pan. Add the bacon and fry until brown. Add to the rice.

Add the liver to the frying pan and fry until lightly browned. Add to the rice.

Finally, add the green or red pepper to the frying pan and fry until softened. Add to the rice with salt and pepper. Cook for a further 2 to 3 minutes for the flavours to combine, then serve

Lasagne al Forno

Serves 6

450 g/1 lb lasagne, green
or white
750 ml/1¼ pints béchamel
sauce
50 g/2 oz Parmesan
cheese, grated

Bolognese Sauce
15 g/½ oz butter
100 g/4 oz streaky bacon,
rinded and chopped
1 onion, chopped
1 large carrot, chopped
1 celery stalk, chopped
225 g/8 oz minced beef
100 g/4 oz chicken livers,
chopped
3 tablespoons tomato
purée
150 ml/¼ pint white wine
300 ml/½ pint stock
salt
pepper
pinch of grated nutmeg

First make the bolognese sauce. Melt the butter in a saucepan and fry the bacon until browned. Add the onion, carrot and celery and fry until softened. Stir in the beef and fry until browned. Add the remaining sauce ingredients, bring to the boil, cover and simmer for 30 to 40 minutes.

Meanwhile, cook the lasagne, in batches, in boiling salted water. (A little oil added to the water will prevent the sheets of pasta sticking together.) Drain on paper towels.

Make alternate layers of meat sauce, béchamel sauce and pasta in a greased baking dish, continuing until the dish is full. Finish with béchamel sauce and sprinkle over the cheese.

Bake in a preheated moderate oven (180°C/350°F, Gas Mark 4) for 30 minutes.

Rice with Bacon

Serves 4

225 g/8 oz frozen mixed
vegetables
15 g/½ oz butter
225 g/8 oz smoked
bacon, rinded and
chopped
450 g/1 lb long-grain
rice, boiled and cooled
salt
pepper
200 g/7 oz canned
pineapple rings,
drained

Cook the vegetables according to the instructions on the packet. Drain and cool.

Melt the butter in a frying pan and fry the bacon until browned. Drain and mix into the rice with salt and pepper. Allow to cool.

Pile the rice mixture on a serving plate and garnish with the vegetables and pineapple rings.

Spaghetti with Wine Sauce

Serves 4

8 large prunes
300 ml/½ pint red wine
500 g/1¼ lb pork fillet,
cut into 1 cm/½ inch
slices
2 tablespoons flour
salt
pepper
90 g/3½ oz margarine
225 g/8 oz spaghetti
1 tablespoon chopped
fresh chives
150 ml/¼ pint double
cream
1 tablespoon redcurrant
jelly
lemon juice

Soak the prunes in the wine overnight. The next day, tip the mixture into a saucepan and cook gently until the prunes are tender.

Meanwhile, mix the flour with salt and pepper and use to coat the pork slices. Melt 40 g/1½ oz of the margarine in a frying pan and brown the pork slices on all sides. Pour off the excess fat, then add 150 ml/¼ pint of the wine from the prunes. Cover and cook until the meat is tender.

Meanwhile, cook the spaghetti in boiling water until it is tender. Drain well and return to the saucepan. Add the remaining margarine, the chives, salt and pepper and toss well. Keep hot.

Mix 2 tablespoons of the wine from the pork into the cream, then stir this mixture into the pan with the redcurrant jelly. Cook gently until the sauce is smooth and glossy. Sharpen to taste with lemon juice and adjust the seasoning. Stir in the drained prunes.

Pile the spaghetti in a warmed serving dish and pour over the pork and wine sauce. Serve hot.

Macaroni Bolognese   *Serves 4*

2 tablespoons oil
1 medium onion, chopped
225 g/8 oz minced beef
50 g/2 oz mushrooms,
* chopped*
150 ml/¼ pint red wine or
* dry cider*
100 g/4 oz canned
* tomatoes, chopped*
salt
pepper
175 g/6 oz macaroni
100 g/4 oz cheese, grated

Heat the oil in a frying pan and fry the onion until softened. Add the beef and fry until it is browned, then stir in the mushrooms and wine or cider. Bring to the boil and simmer gently for 20 minutes. Add the tomatoes, salt and pepper and continue simmering.

Meanwhile, cook the macaroni in boiling water until it is tender. Drain well. Turn about three-quarters of the macaroni into a heated serving dish and pour over the sauce. Arrange the remaining macaroni around the edge and serve with the cheese.

Paella   *Serves 4*

1 tablespoon oil
4 chicken joints, skinned,
* boned and cut into*
* bite-sized pieces*
4 back bacon rashers,
* rinded and diced*
2 tomatoes, skinned and
* chopped*
1 onion, chopped
1 garlic clove, crushed
1 green pepper, cored,
* seeded and chopped*
225 g/8 oz rice
600 ml/1 pint chicken
* stock*
few strands of saffron
16 mussels, cooked
* (optional)*
12 prawns, cooked
225 g/8 oz peas, cooked
salt
pepper

Heat the oil in a heavy-based saucepan and fry the chicken pieces, bacon, tomatoes and onion until the onion is softened. Add the garlic and green pepper and fry for a further 2 to 3 minutes. Stir in the rice and cook until it absorbs the liquid, then add the stock and saffron. Bring to the boil, cover and simmer gently for about 20 minutes or until the rice is almost tender.

Add the mussels, if used, the prawns, peas, salt and pepper and heat through gently. Serve hot with a tossed green salad.

Vegetarian Pilaf
Serves 4

*50 g/2 oz butter or nut
 fat*
1 tablespoon oil
225 g/8 oz brown rice
1 medium onion, chopped
3 celery stalks, chopped
600 ml/1 pint water
50 g/2 oz sultanas
*6 pieces dry fungi or
 mushrooms, soaked
 overnight and drained*
1 teaspoon yeast extract
*100 g/4 oz salted cashews
 or peanuts*
½ teaspoon sugar
1 teaspoon grated nutmeg
1 teaspoon ground ginger
salt

To Garnish
chopped parsley
lemon slice

Melt the butter or fat with the oil in a saucepan. Add the rice and fry until pale brown. Add the onion and celery and continue frying until softened. Stir in the water, sultanas and fungi or mushrooms and bring to the boil. Cover and simmer until the rice is tender and the liquid absorbed.

Stir in the yeast extract, half the nuts, the sugar, spices and salt. Turn onto a warmed serving dish and serve garnished with the remaining nuts, parsley and a lemon slice.

Oriental Kedgeree
Serves 4

225 g/8 oz butter or lard
*450 g/1 lb unpolished
 Patna rice*
100 g/4 oz lentils, cooked
salt
*2 medium onions, thinly
 sliced*
*4 hard-boiled eggs,
 quartered*

Melt the butter or lard in a saucepan. When very hot, add the rice and fry until golden brown. Drain off the fat and reserve.

Add the lentils to the rice, with salt, and cover the mixture with boiling water. Cook gently, stirring frequently, until the rice and lentils are quite soft. Drain off any remaining water, then place the pan on the corner of the stove and shake from time to time to dry and separate the grains of rice.

Meanwhile, heat the reserved fat in a frying pan. Add the onions and fry until golden brown. Drain.

Pile the rice and lentil mixture on a warmed serving dish and garnish with the onions and egg quarters.

Macaroni and Tomato Pie

Serves 4

100 g/4 oz macaroni
25 g/1 oz margarine
1 onion, chopped
100 g/4 oz tomatoes,
  skinned and chopped
25 g/1 oz flour
300 ml/½ pint milk
salt
pepper
2 hard-boiled eggs, sliced
100 g/4 oz shortcrust
  pastry

Cook the macaroni in boiling water until it is tender.

Meanwhile, melt the margarine in a saucepan. Add the onion and tomatoes and cook until the onion is softened. Stir in the flour and cook for 2 minutes, then gradually stir in the milk. Bring to the boil and simmer, stirring, until thickened. Add salt and pepper.

Drain the macaroni well and fold into the tomato sauce. Turn into a baking dish. Arrange the egg slices on top.

Roll out the dough and use to cover the dish. Decorate with the dough trimmings. Bake in a preheated moderately hot oven (200°C/400°F, Gas Mark 6) for 35 minutes or until the pastry is golden brown.

Rice with Chopped Pork

Serves 4–6

450 g/1 lb rice, boiled
  and cooled
310 g/11 oz canned
  chopped pork, diced
2 tomatoes, chopped
50 g/2 oz carrots,
  chopped
75 g/3 oz sultanas
1 piece of cucumber,
  diced
½ teaspoon sugar
1 to 2 tablespoons
  chopped chives
½ red pepper, cored,
  seeded and chopped
½ green pepper, cored,
  seeded and chopped

Garnish
radishes
cucumber slices
tomatoes

Mix together all the ingredients and chill for at least 12 hours. Serve on a flat dish garnished with radishes, cucumber slices and tomatoes.

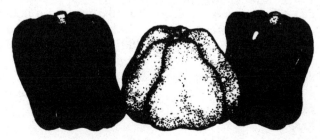

Cottage Cheese with Noodles

Serves 4–6

100 g/4 oz noodles
50 g/2 oz butter
225 g/8 oz cottage cheese
  with chives
150 g/5 oz soured cream
2 tablespoons grated
  Parmesan cheese
salt
pepper
2 eggs, beaten
parsley sprigs or
  watercress to garnish

Cook the noodles in boiling water until they are tender. Drain well.

Melt the butter in another saucepan and mix in the cottage cheese and soured cream. Remove from the heat and fold in the noodles, followed by the Parmesan cheese, salt, pepper and eggs. Turn into a greased baking dish and bake in a preheated moderately hot oven (190°C/375°F, Gas Mark 5) for 45 minutes. Garnish with parsley or watercress to serve.

Pasta Fritters

Serves 4

2 tablespoons chopped
  cooked noodles
2 eggs, beaten
2 tablespoons diced
  cooked ham
1 tablespoon chopped
  parsley
1 tablespoon grated
  Parmesan cheese
oil for deep frying

Mix together the noodles, eggs, ham, parsley and cheese. Drop a spoonful of the mixture into hot oil, allow it to spread out and set, then deep fry until golden brown. Drain the fritters on paper towels and serve hot.

Savoury Rice

Serves 4–5

50 g/2 oz margarine
100 g/4 oz boiled rice
1 large onion, chopped
225 g/8 oz sausage,
  cooked and sliced
200 g/7 oz canned
  shrimps, drained
1 hard-boiled egg,
  chopped
salt
pepper

Melt the margarine in a saucepan. Add the rice and onion and cook, stirring, until golden brown. Stir in the remaining ingredients and tip the mixture into a baking dish.

Bake in a preheated moderately hot oven (200°C/400°F, Gas Mark 6) for 30 to 40 minutes.

Variation: A 300 g/11 oz can of mushroom or chicken soup may be added.

Meat and Macaroni Mould

Serves 4

75 g/3 oz short-cut
   macaroni
175 g/6 oz cooked meat,
   chopped
1 teaspoon chopped
   parsley
1 tablespoon minced
   onion
salt
pepper
1 egg, beaten
little gravy
40 g/1½ oz dry
   breadcrumbs

Cook the macaroni in boiling water until it is tender. Drain well, then add the meat, parsley, onion, salt and pepper. Mix together and bind with the egg and enough gravy to make a soft consistency.

Grease a pudding basin and coat with the breadcrumbs. Tip in the macaroni mixture. Steam for 2 hours.

Macaroni with Green Pepper and Mushrooms

Serves 4

50 g/2 oz butter
1 large onion, chopped
225 g/8 oz mushrooms,
   sliced
1 green pepper, cored,
   seeded and chopped
salt
pepper
225 g/8 oz macaroni
225 g/8 oz cheese, grated
2 tomatoes, sliced, to
   garnish

Melt the butter in a frying pan and fry the onion until softened. Add the mushrooms, green pepper, salt and pepper and continue frying until cooked.

Meanwhile, cook the macaroni in boiling water until it is tender. Drain well.

Mix together the macaroni and vegetables in a flameproof serving dish. Sprinkle over the cheese and bake in a preheated moderate oven (180°C/350°F, Gas Mark 4) for 15 minutes or until the cheese has melted and is golden brown. Alternatively, the dish may be grilled. Garnish with tomato slices before serving.

Eggs & Cheese

Egg and Onion Pie
Serves 4

50 g/2 oz butter
450 g/1 lb spring onions
  or leeks, finely chopped
2 to 3 eggs, beaten
salt
pepper
100 g/4 oz shortcrust
  pastry

Melt the butter in a frying pan and fry the onions or leeks until just softened. Tip them into a shallow pie dish or plate and spread out. Mix the eggs with salt and pepper and pour into the dish. Roll out the dough and use to cover the dish.

Bake in a preheated moderate oven (180°C/350°F, Gas Mark 4) for 30 to 40 minutes or until the pastry is golden brown. Serve hot or cold.

Note: A little chopped bacon can be fried with the onions.

Eggs en Cocotte
Serves 4

1 × 275 g/10 oz packet
  frozen creamed spinach
4 eggs
4 tablespoons single
  cream
salt
pepper
100 g/4 oz Cheddar
  cheese, grated

Cook the spinach according to the directions on the packet. Cool slightly, then divide it between four cocotte or ramekin dishes. Break an egg into each dish and coat with the cream. Add salt and pepper and sprinkle over the cheese.

Place the ramekins in a shallow baking dish of warm water and bake in a preheated moderate oven (180°C/350°F, Gas Mark 4) for 25 to 40 minutes or until the eggs are just set and the cheese is melted and golden brown.

164

Egg Croquettes   *Serves 6*

50 g/2 oz butter
50 g/2 oz flour
300 ml/½ pint milk
50 g/2 oz strong Cheddar
  cheese, grated
4 hard-boiled eggs, finely
  chopped
salt
pepper
2 eggs, beaten
1 tablespoon water
dry breadcrumbs for
  coating
oil for deep frying

Melt the butter in a saucepan and add the flour. Cook, stirring, for 2 minutes, then gradually stir in the milk. Bring to the boil and simmer, stirring, until thick. Stir in the cheese until melted. Remove from the heat and fold in the hard-boiled eggs, salt and pepper. Spread the mixture on a buttered plate and leave to cool.

Divide the egg mixture into 12 to 14 portions and shape each into a ball with floured hands. Mix the beaten eggs with the water. Dip the balls into the egg mixture, then coat in breadcrumbs. Deep fry for 3 to 4 minutes or until golden brown. Drain on paper towels and serve hot or cold.

Basic Cheese Soufflé   *Serves 4–5*

25 g/1 oz butter
15 g/½ oz plain flour
150 ml/¼ pint milk
3 eggs, separated
salt
pepper
100 g/4 oz Cheddar
  cheese, grated

Melt the butter in a saucepan and stir in the flour. Cook, stirring, for 1 minute, then gradually stir in the milk. Cook, stirring, until thickened. Remove from the heat and cool a little, then stir in the egg yolks, salt, pepper and cheese.

Whisk the egg whites until stiff and fold into the cheese mixture. Spoon into a buttered 15 cm/6 inch casserole or soufflé dish. Bake in the centre of a preheated moderately hot oven (190°C/375°F, Gas Mark 5) for 25 to 30 minutes or until risen and golden brown. Serve immediately.

Variations: To the cheese mixture, before folding in the egg whites, add 50 g/2 oz shelled prawns, or 50 to 100 g/2 to 4 oz cooked flaked haddock, or 100 g/4 oz chopped cooked ham, or 75 g/3 oz sliced cooked mushrooms.

165

Cheese and Potato Bake
Serves 4

750 g to 1 kg/1½ to 2 lb potatoes, peeled and thinly sliced
2 large onions, thinly sliced
1 medium aubergine, thinly sliced
225 g/8 oz Cheddar cheese, thinly sliced
225 g/8 oz collar bacon, rinded and diced
salt
pepper
½ teaspoon dried oregano
226 g/8 oz canned tomatoes

Arrange two-thirds of the potatoes, the onions, aubergines, half the cheese and the bacon in thin layers in a buttered casserole. Add salt and pepper to the layers. Sprinkle the oregano on top and cover with the undrained tomatoes. Arrange the remaining potatoes and cheese in overlapping slices on top. Cover the casserole and cook in a preheated moderate oven (180°C/350°F, Gas Mark 4) for about 1½ hours or until the potatoes are almost tender.

Uncover the casserole and bake for a further 20 to 30 minutes to brown the top.

Asparagus Savouries
Serves 4

450 g/1 lb fresh or canned asparagus spears
4 slices of buttered toast
4 slices of processed cheese
cayenne pepper and chopped parsley to garnish

If using fresh asparagus, cook in boiling salted water until tender and drain well. Divide the asparagus spears between the toast and cover with the cheese slices.

Cook under a preheated hot grill until the cheese starts to melt. Garnish with a sprinkling of cayenne and parsley.

Cheese and Potato Pie
Serves 4

1 kg/2 lb potatoes, peeled and sliced
225 g/8 oz cheese, grated
2 eggs
salt
pepper
300 ml/½ pint milk
50 g/2 oz butter, melted

Make alternate layers of potato slices and cheese in a buttered baking dish, ending with cheese. Beat together the eggs, salt, pepper, milk and butter and pour into the dish. Bake in a preheated moderate oven (180°C/350°F, Gas Mark 4) for 1 hour. Serve hot.
Variations: Add 1 medium grated or finely chopped onion, or 1 or 2 sliced tomatoes, or 75 g/3 oz lightly fried chopped bacon.

Cheese Pudding
Serves 4

*225 g/8 oz white bread,
crusts removed and
diced
175 g/6 oz Cheddar
cheese, grated
3 eggs
600 ml/1 pint tepid milk
salt
pepper*

Mix together the bread and cheese. Beat the eggs with the milk, salt and pepper and mix into the bread and cheese. Pour into a buttered 1.2 litre/2 pint pie dish. Bake in a preheated moderately hot oven (190°C/375°F, Gas Mark 5) for 50 minutes.

Cheese and Tomato Flan
Serves 4–5

*25 g/1 oz butter
1 medium onion, chopped
3 tomatoes (about 225 g/
8 oz), skinned and
chopped
100 g/4 oz Cheddar
cheese, grated
salt
pepper
2 eggs, beaten
1 × 18 cm/7 inch baked
flan case, made from
shortcrust pastry*

Melt the butter in a frying pan and fry the onion until softened. Mix together the tomatoes, cheese, salt, pepper and eggs and stir in the onion. Pour into the flan case.

Bake in a preheated moderate oven (180°C/350°F, Gas Mark 4) for 45 to 50 minutes or until the filling is set and golden. Serve hot or cold.

Variations: Omit the tomatoes and use 100 g/4 oz fried chopped mushrooms, and add 150 ml/$\frac{1}{4}$ pint milk to the mixture. Or omit the tomatoes and use 100 g/4 oz chopped cooked ham, and add 150 ml/$\frac{1}{4}$ pint milk to the mixture.

Cheesy Onions
Serves 4

4 large Spanish onions
Stuffing
*50 g/2 oz fresh
breadcrumbs
100 g/4 oz Cheddar
cheese, grated
1 tablespoon chutney or
sweet pickle
1 egg, beaten
salt
pepper*

Cook the onions in boiling water for 15 minutes. Drain and cool, then remove the centres carefully with a spoon. Chop the centres.

Mix together all the stuffing ingredients and add the chopped onion centres. Use to stuff the onions and place them in a buttered baking dish. Bake in a preheated moderate oven (180°C/350°F, Gas Mark 4) for 45 to 50 minutes or until the onions are very tender and the stuffing is golden brown.

167

Cheese and Spinach Eggs
Serves 4

*450 g/1 lb spinach,
  cooked, well drained
  and chopped
4 hard-boiled eggs,
  halved
25 g/1 oz butter
25 g/1 oz flour
300 ml/½ pint milk
100 g/4 oz cheese, grated
cayenne pepper*

Spread the spinach out in a buttered baking dish. Arrange the egg halves on the spinach, cut sides down.

Melt the butter in a saucepan and add the flour. Cook, stirring, for 2 minutes, then gradually stir in the milk. Bring to the boil and simmer, stirring, until thickened. Stir in the cheese until melted.

Pour the cheese sauce over the eggs and sprinkle the top with a little cayenne. Bake in a preheated moderate oven (180 °C/350°F, Gas Mark 4) for 30 minutes or until the cheese sauce is bubbling.

Apple and Cheese Flan
Serves 4–5

*2 medium cooking apples,
  peeled, cored and
  sliced
2 cloves
50 g/2 oz sugar
1 tablespoon cornflour
2 tablespoons cold water
1 × 18 cm/7 inch baked
  flan case, made from
  shortcrust pastry
75 g/3 oz Cheddar
  cheese, grated*

Put the apples, cloves and sugar in a saucepan and stew gently until the apples are tender. Sieve or blend to a purée. Dissolve the cornflour in the water in the cleaned saucepan, then stir in the apple purée. Bring to the boil, stirring, and cook for 1 minute.

Pour the apple mixture into the flan case and sprinkle the cheese on top. Cook under a preheated grill until the top is golden brown.

Cheesy Eggs
Serves 4

*175 g/6 oz Cheddar
  cheese, grated
40 g/1½ oz flour
1 teaspoon salt
1 egg, beaten
1½ tablespoons milk
4 hard-boiled eggs
dry breadcrumbs for
  coating
fat for deep frying*

Mix together the cheese, flour, salt, beaten egg and milk. Using wet hands, coat the hard-boiled eggs completely with the cheese mixture, then roll them in the breadcrumbs.

Deep fry for 2 to 3 minutes or until golden brown. Drain on paper towels and serve hot or cold.

Cheese and Ham Aigrettes

Makes about 24

50 g/2 oz choux pastry
75 g/3 oz Cheddar
cheese, grated
25 g/1 oz cooked ham,
chopped
1 teaspoon finely chopped
onion
salt
cayenne pepper
oil for deep frying
grated cheese to serve

Mix the dough with the cheese, ham, onion, salt and cayenne until smooth. Heat the oil to 180°C/350°F. Drop small spoonsful of the mixture into the oil and deep fry for about 4 to 5 minutes or until golden brown. Drain on paper towels and serve hot, sprinkled with grated cheese.

Cheese Curry

Serves 3–4

25 g/1 oz butter
1 medium onion, chopped
2 teaspoons curry powder
25 g/1 oz flour
300 ml/½ pint stock
25 g/1 oz sultanas, or
1 tablespoon mixed
pickle
225 g/8 oz Cheddar
cheese, cubed

Melt the butter in a saucepan and fry the onion until golden. Add the curry powder and flour and cook, stirring, for 2 minutes. Gradually stir in the stock and bring to the boil. Simmer, stirring, until thickened. Stir in the sultanas or pickle, then fold in the cheese. Serve hot with plain boiled rice.

Eggs and Rice Supreme

Serves 4

350 g/12 oz hot boiled
long-grain rice
4 hard-boiled eggs,
halved lengthways
knob of butter
dash of Worcestershire
sauce
salt
pepper
300 ml/½ pint white sauce
½ teaspoon made mustard
100 g/4 oz cheese, grated

Divide the rice between four flameproof serving dishes. Keep hot.

Remove the yolks from the eggs and mash with the butter, Worcestershire sauce, salt and pepper. Stuff the egg white halves with this mixture, then place two halves in each dish on the rice. Mix the white sauce with the mustard and pour over the top. Sprinkle with the cheese.

Brown under a hot grill for about 3 minutes.

169

Cheese and Sweetcorn Flan

Serves 5–6

175 g/6 oz shortcrust
  pastry
150 g/5 oz cheese, grated
15 g/½ oz butter
1 small onion, chopped
75 g/3 oz streaky bacon
  rashers, rinded and
  chopped
200 g/7 oz canned
  sweetcorn, drained
2 eggs, beaten
150 ml/¼ pint milk
3 tablespoons cream
salt
pepper

Mix the dough with 50 g/2 oz of the cheese until well combined. Roll out the dough and use to line an 18 cm/7 inch flan ring.

Melt the butter in a frying pan and fry the onion and bacon until the onion is softened. Remove from the heat and stir in the sweetcorn. Add the egg, milk, cream, salt and pepper and mix well. Stir in the remaining cheese.

Pour the sweetcorn mixture into the pastry case. Bake in a preheated moderately hot oven (200°C/400°F, Gas Mark 6) for 30 to 35 minutes or until the filling is set and the pastry is golden brown.

Tomato Soufflés au Gratin

Serves 4

396 g/14 oz canned
  tomatoes
½ teaspoon dried oregano
50 g/2 oz butter or
  margarine
2 small onions, finely
  chopped
4½ tablespoons flour
approx. 150 ml/¼ pint
  milk
4 eggs, separated
100 g/4 oz Cheddar
  cheese, grated
salt
pepper

Drain the tomatoes, reserving the can juice. Chop the tomatoes and mix in the oregano. Divide the tomatoes between four buttered 350 ml/12 fl oz soufflé dishes or ovenproof serving dishes.

Melt the fat in a saucepan and fry the onions until softened. Sprinkle over the flour and cook, stirring, for 2 minutes. Make the reserved tomato juice up to 300 ml/½ pint with the milk and gradually stir into the onion mixture. Bring to the boil, stirring, and simmer until thickened. Remove from the heat and cool slightly, then beat in the egg yolks, cheese, salt and pepper until the mixture is smooth.

Whisk the egg whites until stiff and fold into the cheese and tomato sauce. Spoon into the soufflé dishes on top of the tomatoes. Bake in a preheated moderate oven (180°C/350°F, Gas Mark 4) for 35 to 40 minutes or until well risen and lightly browned. Serve immediately.

Cheese and Bacon Slice
Serves 4

175 g/6 oz puff pastry
made English mustard
50 g/2 oz cheese, grated
50 g/2 oz bacon, rinded
  and diced
beaten egg to glaze

Roll out the dough into an 18 cm/7 inch square and cut into two oblongs. Place one oblong on a baking sheet. Spread it lightly with mustard, to within 1 cm/½ inch of the edges, then sprinkle over the cheese and bacon.

Fold the second oblong in half lengthways and cut across the fold every 1 cm/½ inch to within 1 cm/½ inch of the edge to form slats. Dampen the edges of the oblong on the baking sheet and place the other oblong on top. Flake and decorate the edges, then brush all over with beaten egg. Bake in a preheated hot oven (220˚C/425°F, Gas Mark 7) for 15 to 20 minutes or until the pastry is risen and golden brown.

Scotch Eggs
Serves 3

3 hard-boiled eggs
flour for coating
225 g/8 oz sausagemeat
1 egg, beaten
4 tablespoons dry
  breadcrumbs
oil for deep frying
watercress or parsley
  sprigs to serve

Coat the eggs in flour, then cover with the sausagemeat. Flour again, then dip in the beaten egg and coat with the breadcrumbs. Deep fry until golden brown and drain on paper towels. Cut each egg in half and serve on a bed of watercress or parsley.

Peppered Eggs
Serves 4

1 medium onion, thinly
  sliced
1 red pepper, cored,
  seeded and sliced
225 g/8 oz green beans,
  sliced
8 eggs
2 tablespoons milk
salt
pepper

Put the onion, red pepper and beans in a saucepan and cover with water. Bring to the boil and simmer until the vegetables are just tender. Drain well and spread out in a buttered baking dish.

Beat the eggs with the milk, salt and pepper and pour over the vegetables. Bake in a preheated moderately hot oven (190°C/375°F, Gas Mark 5) for 25 minutes or until the egg mixture is set. Serve hot, cut into wedges.

Golden Eggs

Serves 6

6 hard-boiled eggs,
  chopped
750 g/1½ lb potatoes,
  peeled, cooked and
  mashed
75 g/3 oz cheese, grated
2 tablespoons chopped
  spring onions or chives
salt
pepper
2 eggs, beaten
dry breadcrumbs for
  coating
oil for deep frying

Mix together the hard-boiled eggs, potatoes, cheese, spring onions or chives, salt and pepper. Form into egg shapes, then dip in the beaten eggs and coat with breadcrumbs. Deep fry until golden brown and drain on paper towels. Serve hot or cold.

Cheese Hot Pot

Serves 4–5

350 g/12 oz lamb's liver,
  cut into 2.5 cm/1 inch
  pieces
300 ml/½ pint milk
25 g/1 oz flour
salt
pepper
50 g/2 oz butter or
  margarine
450 g/1 lb onions, thinly
  sliced
150 ml/¼ pint stock
2 tablespoons tomato
  purée
450 g/1 lb potatoes,
  peeled, cooked and
  sliced
100 g/4 oz cheese, grated
chopped parsley to
  garnish

Soak the liver in the milk for 1 hour. Drain off the milk and reserve. Mix the flour with salt and pepper and use to coat the liver pieces.

Melt the fat in a frying pan and fry the onions gently until they are softened. Add the liver pieces and brown on all sides. Gradually stir in the stock, tomato purée and reserved milk and bring to the boil, still stirring.

Pour into a 1.2 litre/2 pint casserole. Arrange the potato slices on top to cover and sprinkle with the cheese. Bake in a preheated moderately hot oven (190°C/375°F, Gas Mark 5) for 20 to 30 minutes or until the top is golden brown. Serve garnished with parsley.

Basic Cheese Sauces

Thin Pouring Sauce
25 g/1 oz butter
25 g/1 oz flour
900 ml/1½ pints milk
225 g/8 oz cheese, grated

Pouring Sauce
25 g/1 oz butter
25 g/1 oz flour
600 ml/1 pint milk
175 g/6 oz cheese, grated

Coating Sauce
25 g/1 oz butter
25 g/1 oz flour
300 ml/½ pint milk
75 g/3 oz cheese, grated

Very Thick Sauce
25 g/1 oz butter
25 g/1 oz flour
150 ml/¼ pint milk
50 g/2 oz cheese, grated

Melt the butter in a saucepan and add the flour. Cook, stirring, for 2 minutes, then gradually stir in the milk. Bring to the boil and simmer, still stirring, until thickened. Add the cheese and stir until it melts and the sauce is smooth.

Use a thin pouring sauce as a basis for soups; a pouring sauce with pasta or vegetables; a coating sauce to cover fish, eggs, meat, vegetables, etc.; a very thick sauce as a basis for soufflés.

Bacon and Egg Pie
Serves 5–6

100 g/4 oz streaky bacon rashers, rinded and diced
3 eggs
Pastry
100 g/4 oz flour
40 g/1½ oz lard
½ teaspoon bicarbonate of soda
milk to mix

For the pastry, sift the flour into a bowl and rub in the lard. Dissolve the soda in a little milk and add to the flour mixture. Mix to a smooth dough, adding more milk as necessary. Divide the dough in half. Roll out one half and use to line an 18 cm/7 inch pie plate. Spread the bacon dice over the bottom of the pastry case and break the eggs on top. Roll out the rest of the dough and use to cover the pie.

Bake in a preheated moderately hot oven (190°C/375°F, Gas Mark 5) for 40 minutes or until the pastry is golden brown.

173

Scalloped Eggs

Serves 4

4 hard-boiled eggs,
halved
15 g/½ oz butter
salt
pepper
50 g/2 oz shelled shrimps

Mayonnaise

2 egg yolks
½ teaspoon English
mustard powder
¼ to ½ teaspoon salt
shake black pepper
150 ml/¼ pint oil
(cooking or olive)
1 to 2 tablespoons
vinegar

Tartare Sauce

150 ml/¼ pint mayonnaise
1 tablespoon chopped
parsley
2 teaspoons chopped
capers
2 teaspoons chopped
gherkins

Scoop out the egg yolks, keeping the whites intact, and mash the yolks with the butter, salt and pepper. Chop 2 or 3 of the shrimps and mix into the yolk mixture. Fill the egg whites with the yolk mixture, arrange them on a dish and top with the remaining whole shrimps.

To make the mayonnaise, beat the egg yolks and seasoning with a whisk. Add the oil a drop at a time until it has all been incorporated. Beat in the vinegar to taste.

To make the tartare sauce, blend all the ingredients, including the mayonnaise, together. Pour the sauce over the eggs and garnish with parsley, chives and cucumber.

Egg Cobbler

Serves 3–4

4 hard-boiled eggs,
chopped
100 g/4 oz cooked bacon
or ham, chopped
300 ml/½ pint coating
cheese sauce (made
with mature Cheddar)
100 g/4 oz butter, melted
50 to 75 g/2 to 3 oz fresh
breadcrumbs
1 tomato, sliced
salt
pepper

Mix together the eggs, bacon or ham and sauce. Combine the butter and breadcrumbs. Make alternate layers of the two mixtures in a buttered baking dish, ending with breadcrumbs. Arrange the tomato slices on top and sprinkle with salt and pepper.

Bake in a preheated moderately hot oven (190°C/375°F, Gas Mark 5) for 15 minutes. Serve hot.

Anchovy Eggs

Serves 4

*4 hard-boiled eggs,
halved
25 g/1 oz butter
salt
cayenne pepper
anchovy essence
2 large slices of buttered
brown bread
8 thin tomato slices
chopped parsley to
garnish*

Scoop the yolks out of the eggs, keeping the whites intact, and mash the yolks with the butter, salt, cayenne and anchovy essence to taste. Put the yolk mixture into a forcing bag and press into the egg whites.

Cut four rounds from each slice of bread. Place a tomato slice on each round and an egg half on top. Garnish with parsley.

Cheese Dip

*175 g/6 oz processed
cream cheese spread
5 tablespoons mayonnaise
2 tablespoons creamed
horseradish
3 tablespoons finely
chopped onion*

Mix the ingredients together thoroughly and serve with potato crisps or thin cheese biscuits. Any flavoured processed cheese may be used.

Cheese Patties

Serves 4

*225 g/8 oz flaky pastry
beaten egg to glaze
parsley sprigs and tomato
wedges to garnish*
Filling
*150 ml/$\frac{1}{4}$ pint coating
cheese sauce (made
with 100 g/4 oz
cheese)
1 egg, scrambled
salt
pepper
1 teaspoon chopped
chives*

Roll out the dough to 5 cm/2 inches thick and cut out 7.5 cm/3 inch rounds. Place the rounds on a baking sheet and mark out lids from the centre of each with a smaller pastry cutter, cutting about halfway through the dough. Arrange on a baking sheet. Brush with beaten egg and bake in a preheated hot oven (230°C/450°F, Gas Mark 8) for 15 to 20 minutes or until crisp and golden brown. Take off the lids and scoop out any soft inside.

Mix together the sauce, egg, salt, pepper and chives. Use to fill the pastry cases and garnish with parsley and tomatoes. Warm through before serving or serve cold.

Eggs in Aspic
Serves 4

*1 × 25 g/1 oz packet
aspic jelly crystals
4 hard-boiled eggs, sliced
lengthways
4 cooked carrots, cut into
strips or slices
chopped parsley to
garnish*

Make up the aspic jelly according to the instructions on the packet. Pour a little of the aspic into the bottom of a serving dish and chill until set.

Arrange the egg slices and carrots on the aspic, then carefully pour over the remaining aspic. Chill again until set. Turn out to serve, garnished with parsley.

Welsh Cheese Savouries
Makes 6

*1 hard-boiled egg,
chopped
50 g/2 oz cheese, grated
2 tablespoons French
dressing
6 baked vol-au-vent cases
cocktail onions to garnish*

Mix together the egg and cheese and bind with the dressing. Divide between the pastry cases and garnish with onions.

Cheese Triangles
Serves 4

Cheese Pastry
*40 g/1½ oz flour
25 g/1 oz butter
50 g/2 oz cheese, grated
pinch of cayenne pepper
beaten egg to glaze*
Filling
*50 g/2 oz plain or
smoked cooked
haddock fillet, skinned
and chopped
15 g/½ oz butter
25 g/1 oz cheese, grated
½ egg, beaten
salt
pepper*

For the pastry, sift the flour into a bowl and rub in the butter and half the cheese. Stir in the cayenne and bind to a dough with a little water. Allow to rest for 10 minutes. Meanwhile, mix together the filling ingredients.

Roll out the dough to about 3 mm/⅛ inch thick and cut out 5 cm/2 inch rounds. Divide the filling between the rounds. Brush the edges of the rounds with beaten egg and fold into three to make triangles.

Place the triangles on a baking sheet and brush all over with beaten egg. Sprinkle with the rest of the cheese. Bake in a preheated moderately hot oven (190°C/375°F, Gas Mark 5) for 10 to 15 minutes or until the triangles are golden brown.

Quiche Lorraine

Serves 5–6

175 g/6 oz shortcrust
   pastry
6 streaky bacon rashers,
   rinded and halved
1 small onion, chopped
100 g/4 oz cheese, thinly
   sliced
2 eggs
salt
pepper
cayenne pepper
150 ml/¼ pint single
   cream or top of milk
25 g/1 oz butter, melted
1 tomato, sliced
   (optional)

Roll out the dough and use to line an 18 cm/7 inch flan tin. Fry the bacon with the onion until the onion is softened, then spoon into the pastry case. Cover with the cheese slices. Beat the eggs with salt, pepper, cayenne, the cream and butter and pour over the cheese. Arrange the tomato slices on top (optional).

Bake in a preheated moderately hot oven (200 C/400 F, Gas Mark 6) for 40 minutes or until the filling is set and golden brown. Serve hot or cold.

Aberdeen Toasties

Serves 4

175 g/6 oz haddock
   fillets, cooked, skinned
   and flaked
150 ml/¼ pint coating
   cheese sauce
2 egg yolks
salt
pepper
4 slices of buttered toast

Put the haddock, sauce, egg yolks, salt and pepper into a saucepan and heat gently, stirring. Pour on to the toast and, if liked, brown under the grill.

Egg and Mint Pie

Serves 6

225 g/8 oz shortcrust
   pastry
4 to 5 eggs
salt
pepper
1 tablespoon chopped
   fresh mint

Divide the dough in half. Roll out one piece and use to line an 18 cm/7 inch flan tin. Break the eggs into the pastry case and sprinkle them with salt, pepper and the mint. Roll out the remaining dough and cover the pie.

Bake in a preheated moderate oven (180 C/350 F, Gas Mark 4) for 40 to 45 minutes or until the pastry is golden brown. Serve hot or cold.

Cheese Croustades

Serves 4

*100 g/4 oz shortcrust
   pastry*
*50 g/2 oz Parmesan
   cheese, grated*
25 g/1 oz butter, melted
1 egg
1 egg yolk
salt
cayenne pepper

Roll out the dough and use to line small patty tins. Mix together the cheese, butter, egg, egg yolk, salt and cayenne and divide between the patty tins. Bake in a preheated moderate oven (180°C/350°F, Gas Mark 4) for 25 minutes or until the egg mixture is set and the pastry is golden brown.

Spanish Omelette

Serves 1

2 tablespoons oil
*2 small potatoes, peeled
   and diced*
*1 small onion, finely
   chopped*
3 eggs, beaten
salt
pepper

Heat the oil in a frying pan and fry the potatoes and onion gently until they are cooked and tender, but not brown. Beat the eggs with salt and pepper and pour into the pan. Cook until the bottom of the omelette is set, then turn over and cook the other side. (This can be done by reversing the omelette onto a plate and sliding it back into the pan.) Alternatively, cook the top under the grill.

Note: Other vegetables, such as cooked peas, green beans, peppers, leeks or tomatoes may be used as available, and pieces of cooked ham or bacon added.

Cheese Butterflies

Makes 20

*100 g/4 oz shortcrust
   pastry*
*25 g/1 oz Cheddar or
   Parmesan cheese,
   grated*
50 g/2 oz cream cheese
cayenne pepper
chopped chives
cheese and celery spread

Roll out the dough and cut out rounds about 3.5 cm/1½ inches in diameter. Place them on a baking sheet and bake in a preheated moderately hot oven (200°C/400°F, Gas Mark 6) for 15 minutes or until golden brown. Cool.

Mix together the cheese and cream cheese and beat in cayenne, chives and cheese and celery spread to taste. Spread the cheese mixture over half the pastry rounds. Cut or break the remaining pastry rounds in half and place them on top to represent butterfly wings.

Eggs Florentine
Serves 2

1 × 100 g/4 oz packet
  frozen chopped spinach
1 teaspoon cornflour
1 tablespoon milk
salt
pepper
2 eggs, poached
300 ml/½ pint coating
  cheese sauce
25 g/1 oz cheese, grated
toast triangles to garnish

Cook the spinach according to the directions on the packet. Dissolve the cornflour in the milk and add to the spinach with salt and pepper. Stir well and pour into a flameproof dish. Spread out the spinach, then place the eggs on top. Pour over the sauce and sprinkle with the cheese. Cook under a preheated grill until the top is golden brown. Serve hot, garnished with toast triangles.

Cheddar Cheese Puffs
Serves 4

300 ml/½ pint water
25 g/1 oz butter
100 g/4 oz flour
salt
cayenne pepper
100 g/4 oz cheese, grated
2 eggs, beaten
oil for deep frying

Put the water and butter in a saucepan and bring to the boil, stirring to melt the butter. Add the flour, salt and cayenne and stir until the mixture leaves the sides of the pan. Remove from the heat and beat in the cheese and eggs.

Drop spoonsful of the paste into hot oil and deep fry until golden brown. Drain on paper towels and serve hot.

Chicken and Egg Mousse
Serves 4

1½ teaspoons gelatine
150 ml/¼ pint hot water
175 g/6 oz minced
  chicken
2 hard-boiled eggs,
  chopped
1 tablespoon chopped
  parsley
salt
pepper
150 ml/¼ pint double
  cream
sliced olives, cucumber,
  tomatoes, etc. to
  garnish

Dissolve the gelatine in the hot water. Mix together the chicken, eggs, parsley, salt and pepper, then stir in the gelatine mixture. Whip the cream and fold into the chicken mixture. Pour into a dampened mould or serving dish and chill until set.

Turn out to serve, garnished with olives, cucumber, tomatoes, etc.

Egg Cutlets

Serves 4

25 g/1 oz margarine
25 g/1 oz flour
150 ml/¼ pint milk
1 egg yolk
1 tablespoon chopped
  cooked ham
3 hard-boiled eggs,
  chopped
1 teaspoon chopped
  parsley
4 mushrooms, chopped
salt
pepper
1 egg, beaten
dry breadcrumbs for
  coating
oil for shallow frying
cooked macaroni to
  garnish

Melt the margarine in a saucepan and add the flour. Cook, stirring, for 2 minutes, then gradually stir in the milk. Cook, stirring, until thickened. Remove from the heat and beat in the egg yolk, followed by the ham, hard-boiled eggs, parsley, mushrooms, salt and pepper. Spread the mixture on a dampened plate and cool.

Shape the egg mixture into cutlets. Dip in the beaten egg and coat in breadcrumbs. Fry in shallow fat and serve hot, garnished with a few pieces of macaroni.

European Omelette

Serves 3–4

8 eggs
200 g/8 oz canned
  ratatouille
40 g/1½ oz butter, or 2
  tablespoons oil

Beat the eggs lightly and mix in the ratatouille. Melt the butter, or heat the oil, in a large frying pan. Pour in the egg mixture and cook until the omelette is just set. Slide on to a warmed serving plate and serve hot.

Cheese Crumble
Serves 4–5

*350 g/12 oz haddock
fillets, skinned
300 ml/½ pint milk
2 hard-boiled eggs, sliced
75 g/3 oz butter or
margarine
150 g/5 oz flour
100 g/4 oz cheese, grated
1 tablespoon chopped
parsley
salt
pepper
parsley sprig to garnish*

Put the haddock in a saucepan and pour over the milk. Cook gently for 15 to 20 minutes or until the fish will flake easily. Drain off the milk and reserve. Flake the fish and place it in a baking dish. Arrange the egg slices on top.

Make the milk up to 300 ml/½ pint with more milk if necessary. Melt 25 g/1 oz of the fat in a saucepan and add 25 g/1 oz of the flour. Cook, stirring, for 2 minutes, then gradually stir in the milk. Bring to the boil and simmer, still stirring, until thickened. Add 50 g/2 oz of the cheese, the parsley, salt and pepper and stir until the cheese has melted. Pour this sauce over the eggs in the dish.

Rub the remaining fat into the remaining flour until the mixture resembles breadcrumbs. Stir in the rest of the cheese and sprinkle over the sauce.

Bake in a preheated moderate oven (180°C/350°F, Gas Mark 4) for 15 to 20 minutes or until the top is crisp and golden. Serve hot, garnished with a sprig of parsley.

Cheese and Asparagus Flan
Serves 5–6

*50 g/2 oz margarine
150 g/5 oz wholemeal
flour*

Filling
*290 g/10½ oz canned
asparagus spears,
drained
75 g/3 oz cheese, grated
3 eggs
150 ml/¼ pint single
cream
salt
pinch of cayenne pepper*

Rub the margarine into the flour and bind with a little water into a dough. Roll out the dough and use to line a 20 cm/8 inch flan tin. Bake blind in a preheated moderately hot oven (200°C/400°F, Gas Mark 6) for 10 minutes.

Arrange the asparagus spears on the bottom of the flan case and sprinkle over the cheese. Beat together the eggs, cream, salt and cayenne and pour into the flan case. Bake for a further 30 minutes. Serve hot or cold.

Prawn Cheesebake

Serves 4

100 g/4 oz shelled prawns
300 ml/½ pint coating
  cheese sauce (page 173)
275 g/11 oz canned
  sweetcorn, drained
2 celery stalks, finely
  chopped
3 spring onions, chopped
salt
pepper
225 g/8 oz long-grain rice

Stir most of the prawns into the sauce, then fold in the sweetcorn, celery and spring onions. Add salt and pepper. Pour into a greased baking dish, cover and bake in a preheated moderately hot oven (190°C/375 F, Gas Mark 5) for 25 minutes.

Meanwhile, cook the rice in boiling salted water until tender. Drain, if necessary, and arrange around the edge of a warmed serving dish. Pour the prawn sauce into the centre and garnish with the remaining prawns.

Cheese and Kipper Flan

Serves 4–5

100 g/4 oz shortcrust
  pastry
2 eggs
150 ml/¼ pint milk
100 g/4 oz cheese, grated
225 g/8 oz kipper fillets,
  flaked
pepper

Roll out the dough and use to line a 20 cm/8 inch flan tin.

Beat together the eggs and milk, then mix in the cheese, kippers and pepper. Pour into the flan case and bake in a preheated moderate oven (180°C/350 F, Gas Mark 4) for 45 minutes or until the filling is set and golden brown. Serve hot or cold.

Surprise Eggs

Serves 4

4 eggs, separated
4 tablespoons double
  cream
salt
pepper
100 g/4 oz Parmesan
  cheese, grated

Whisk the egg whites until stiff and divide between four buttered ramekin or individual baking dishes. Make a deep depression with the back of a spoon in each dish and slip in the egg yolk. Cover with the cream and sprinkle with salt, pepper and cheese. Bake in a preheated hot oven (230°C/450°F, Gas Mark 8) for 8 to 10 minutes.

Vegetables

Creamy Beans with Carrots
Serves 4

225 g/8 oz young carrots, sliced
salt
pepper
450 g/1 lb runner beans, stringed and sliced
2 tablespoons oil
1 tablespoon chopped fresh mint
2 to 3 tablespoons fresh or soured cream

Put the carrots into a saucepan with salt and pepper and add just enough water to cover. Bring to the boil, cover and simmer for 5 minutes.

Drain off a little of the water, then add the beans and oil. Mix well, bring back to the boil and re-cover. Simmer for a further 10 to 12 minutes or until the vegetables are tender.

Drain off the liquid and stir in the mint and cream.

Cauliflower Soufflé
Serves 4

15 g/½ oz butter
2 tomatoes, skinned and sliced
1 cauliflower, cooked and divided into florets
2 to 3 eggs, separated
1 tablespoon milk
50 g/2 oz cheese, grated
½ teaspoon dry mustard
salt
pepper

Melt the butter in a saucepan and add the tomatoes and cauliflower. Cook gently for 5 minutes.

Meanwhile, beat the egg yolks with the milk and 25 g/1 oz of the cheese. Add the mustard and salt and pepper. Whisk the egg whites until stiff and fold into the yolk mixture.

Turn the cauliflower mixture into a greased soufflé dish and sprinkle over the remaining cheese. Spoon the egg mixture on top. Bake in a preheated moderately hot oven (190°C/375° F, Gas Mark 5) for 20 to 30 minutes. Serve immediately.

Onion Cake

potatoes, peeled and
  sliced
chopped onion
butter
salt
pepper

Make a layer of potato slices on the bottom of a well-buttered cake tin. Sprinkle with onion and dot with butter. Add salt and pepper to taste, then repeat the layers until the tin is full. Finish with a layer of potatoes spread with butter. Cover with a lid or a heatproof plate and bake in a preheated moderate oven (180°C/350°F, Gas Mark 4) for 1 hour.

Variation: Grated cheese may be added.

Leeks Lucullus

Serves 4

8 leeks, trimmed and
  chopped
8 potatoes, peeled
100 g/4 oz cream or
  demi-sel cheese
100 g/4 oz butter or
  margarine
125 g/5 oz cheese, grated
salt
pepper
8 bacon rashers, rinded
  and grilled

Cook the leeks and potatoes in boiling salted water until they are tender. Drain well, then rub through a sieve. Beat the cream or demi-sel cheese into the purée, then add the butter or margarine, 100 g/4 oz of the cheese and pepper.

Turn the mixture into a shallow flameproof serving dish. Sprinkle over the remaining cheese and brown under the grill. Serve garnished with the bacon.

Young Marrows au Gratin

Serves 4

3 or 4 small marrows,
  peeled and chopped
salt
pepper
65 g/2½ oz butter
3 tablespoons cream
1 egg
50 g/2 oz cheese, grated

Put the marrows in a saucepan with salt, pepper and a very little water. Cook gently until the marrows are tender. Drain if necessary and turn into a heated ovenproof serving dish. Mix together 50 g/2 oz of the butter, the cream and egg and fold into the marrows. Add a little of the cheese and salt and pepper. Sprinkle the remaining cheese over the top and dot with the rest of the butter. Cook in a preheated hot oven (220°C/425°F, Gas Mark 7) for 5 to 10 minutes or until lightly browned.

Baked Beans
Serves 6–8

*750 g/1½ lb dried medium
haricot beans, soaked
overnight*
2 pig's trotters
salt
pepper
*6 to 8 medium potatoes,
peeled*

Drain the beans and tip into a pottery crock. Add the trotters and pour in just enough water to reach the level of the beans. Cover tightly and cook in a preheated cool oven (140°C/275°F, Gas Mark 1) for 8 hours or overnight.

Forty-five minutes before the beans have finished cooking, add salt and pepper, then put the potatoes on top to cover the beans. Finish the cooking, uncovered.

Spinach Tartlets
Serves 4

*225 g/8 oz spinach,
cooked and finely
chopped*
salt
pepper
¼ teaspoon grated nutmeg
1 large egg, beaten
*3 tablespoons cream or
top of milk*
*100 g/4 oz mature
Cheddar cheese, grated*
*175 to 225 g/6 to 8 oz
shortcrust pastry*

Mix together the spinach, salt, pepper, nutmeg, egg, cream and all but about 2 tablespoons of the cheese. Roll out the dough and use to line four individual Yorkshire pudding tins or eight patty tins, crimping the edges. Fill with the spinach mixture and sprinkle over the remaining cheese.

Bake in a preheated moderately hot oven (200°C/400°F, Gas Mark 6) for 30 minutes or until the pastry is golden and the filling is just firm to the touch. Serve hot, warm or cold.

Glazed Carrots
Serves 5–6

750 g/1½ lb carrots
25 g/1 oz butter
*½ teaspoon finely chopped
parsley*
2 sugar lumps
salt
pepper
*600 ml/1 pint stock or
water*

Slice the carrots into rounds, then cut the rounds into thin slices about twice as thick as a matchstick. Put into a saucepan with the remaining ingredients and bring quickly to the boil. Cover and simmer for 20 minutes or until tender.

185

Creamy Baked Courgettes   *Serves 4*

25 g/1 oz butter
225 g/8 oz streaky bacon
 rashers, rinded and
 chopped
2 onions, sliced
450 g/1 lb courgettes,
 sliced
salt
pepper
grated nutmeg
150 ml/¼ pint single
 cream
25 to 50 g/1 to 2 oz
 flaked almonds, toasted
chopped parsley to
 garnish

Melt the butter in a frying pan and fry the bacon and onions until beginning to colour. Add the courgettes and mix together thoroughly, then pour off the excess fat and turn into a baking dish. Season well with salt, pepper and nutmeg and bake in a preheated moderate oven (180°C/350°F, Gas Mark 4) for about 30 minutes or until the courgettes are tender.

Pour over the cream and return to the oven to heat through. Sprinkle over the almonds and garnish with parsley.

Leek Pudding   *Serves 4*

225 g/8 oz flour
¼ teaspoon salt
1 teaspoon baking
 powder
100 g/4 oz chopped suet
450 g/1 lb leeks, finely
 chopped

Sift the flour, salt and baking powder into a bowl and mix in the suet. Add the leeks, then bind to a sticky dough with cold water. Turn the dough into a greased pudding basin, filling it three-quarters full. Cover and steam for 2 hours.

Turn out and serve with a good gravy.

Guernsey Bean Jar   *Serves 5-6*

450 g/1 lb small dried
 beans, soaked
 overnight
1 pig's trotter or piece of
 shin beef
1 onion
chopped parsley
salt
600 ml/1 pint slightly
 thickened stock

Drain the beans and put into a saucepan with fresh cold water. Bring to the boil and simmer until tender. Drain again and tip into a stone jar or earthenware dish. Add the remaining ingredients and cover tightly. Bake in a preheated cool oven (140°C/275°F, Gas Mark 1) for 4 to 5 hours.

Runner Beans with Cream   *Serves 4*

*750 g to 1 kg/1½ to 2 lb
  runner beans*
salt
*4 tablespoons cream or
  top of milk*

Cook the beans in boiling salted water until they are just tender. Drain well and turn into a heated ovenproof serving dish. Stir in the cream and warm in a preheated moderate oven (180°C/350°F, Gas Mark 4) for a few minutes before serving.

Baked Spinach Puffs   *Serves 4*

Pastry
*50 g/2 oz butter or
  margarine*
150 ml/¼ pint water
65 g/2½ oz flour, sifted
salt
pepper
pinch of cayenne pepper
2 eggs, beaten

Filling
25 g/1 oz butter
1 tablespoon oil
1 onion, thinly sliced
*100 g/4 oz mushrooms,
  chopped*
*225 g/8 oz frozen
  spinach, thawed and
  drained*
salt
pepper
*grated nutmeg or ground
  mace*
225 g/8 oz cottage cheese
*4 tablespoons single
  cream*
*50 g/2 oz Lancashire or
  Gouda cheese, grated*

For the pastry, melt the fat in the water, then bring to the boil. Add the flour all at once and beat over a gentle heat until the mixture is smooth and forms a ball. Cool a little, then beat in salt, pepper and the cayenne followed by the eggs, adding them a little at a time until the mixture is smooth and glossy.

Put 3 to 4 spoonsful of the pastry dough, well spaced apart, onto two greased baking sheets. Cover the puffs with an inverted tin so that no steam can escape during baking. Bake in a preheated moderately hot oven (200°C/400°F, Gas Mark 6) for about 50 minutes or until the puffs move when the baking sheet is lightly shaken. The puffs will treble in size. Keep warm while you make the filling.

Melt the butter with the oil in a saucepan and fry the onion until softened. Add the mushrooms and cook for a further 3 minutes. Stir in the spinach and heat through for 3 minutes. Season well with salt, pepper and nutmeg or mace, then stir in the cottage cheese and cream. Heat gently.

Arrange the puffs in a lightly greased baking dish and cut off the tops. Fill with the spinach mixture and replace the tops. Sprinkle with the grated cheese and return to the oven. Bake for 5 minutes or until really hot and the cheese has melted.

187

Pecan and Celery Casserole   *Serves 4*

25 g/1 oz margarine
2 tablespoons oil
1 onion, sliced
2 leeks, sliced
6 celery stalks, sliced
25 g/1 oz flour
300 ml/½ pint vegetable
    stock
300 ml/½ pint milk
salt
pepper
pinch of cayenne pepper
½ teaspoon
    Worcestershire sauce
175 to 225 g/6 to 8 oz
    shelled pecan nuts

Melt the margarine with the oil in a flameproof casserole and fry the onion and leeks until softened. Add the celery and cook for a further 3 to 4 minutes. Stir in the flour and cook for 1 minute, then gradually add the stock and milk. Bring to the boil, stirring. Add salt, pepper, the cayenne, Worcestershire sauce and nuts and mix well.

Cover the casserole and either simmer gently on top of the stove for about 40 minutes or transfer to a preheated moderate oven (180°C/350°F, Gas Mark 4) and cook for 40 minutes. Adjust the seasoning and serve with brown rice.

Variation: Shelled walnuts can be used in place of the pecans, and half the milk can be replaced by natural yogurt to give a more piquant flavour.

Carrot and Potato Amandine   *Serves 4*

450 g/1 lb carrots, sliced
450 g to 750 g/1 to 1½ lb
    potatoes, peeled
salt
1 tablespoon oil
1 large onion, sliced
1 garlic clove, crushed
    (optional)
450 ml/¾ pint cheese
    sauce
50 g/2 oz flaked almonds
75 g/3 oz mature
    Cheddar cheese, grated
chopped parsley to
    garnish

Cook the carrots and potatoes in boiling salted water for 10 minutes. Drain and place in a casserole. Heat the oil in a frying pan and fry the onion and garlic, if used, until softened. Mix the onion with the carrots and potatoes. Pour over the cheese sauce.

Combine the almonds and cheese and sprinkle on top. Bake in a preheated moderately hot oven (200°C/400°F, Gas Mark 6) for about 45 minutes or until well browned on top. Sprinkle liberally with parsley and serve with a mixed salad.

Vegetable Pie with Nut Pastry

Serves 5-6

2 tablespoons corn oil
2 onions, chopped
350 g/12 oz carrots,
  peeled and diced
225 g/8 oz peas or beans,
  diced
100 g/4 oz celery,
  chopped
25 g/1 oz butter or
  margarine
25 g/1 oz flour
yeast extract

Pastry

250 g/9 oz flour
100 g/4 oz fat
75 g/3 oz ground Brazil
  nuts, hazelnuts,
  walnuts or cashew nuts

Heat the oil in a frying pan and fry the onions until softened. Remove from the heat. Cook the carrots, peas or beans and celery in boiling salted water until tender. Drain off the water, reserving 300 ml/$\frac{1}{2}$ pint.

Melt the butter or margarine in another saucepan and stir in the flour. Cook for 2 minutes, then gradually stir in the reserved vegetable cooking water. Bring to the boil and simmer, stirring, until thickened. Fold in the onions, carrots, peas or beans and celery and add yeast extract to taste. Turn into a baking dish and cool.

Meanwhile, make the pastry. Sift the flour into a bowl and rub in the fat until the mixture resembles breadcrumbs.

Mix in the nuts, then bind to a dough with cold water. Roll out the dough and use to cover the baking dish. Bake in a preheated hot oven (220°C/425°F, Gas Mark 7) for 20 minutes or until the pastry is browned.

Ratatouille

Serves 4

25 g/1 oz butter
2 tablespoons oil
2 aubergines, sliced
3 courgettes, sliced
1 green or red pepper,
  cored, seeded and
  sliced
$\frac{1}{4}$ to $\frac{1}{2}$ cucumber, sliced
4 tomatoes, skinned and
  sliced
2 onions, sliced
salt
pepper
1 to 3 garlic cloves,
  peeled and crushed

Melt the butter with the oil in a flameproof casserole. Add the remaining ingredients and stir well. Cover tightly and transfer to a preheated moderate oven (180°C/350°F, Gas Mark 4). Cook for 1 to 1$\frac{1}{2}$ hours or until all the vegetables are very tender. Alternatively, the ratatouille may be cooked gently on top of the stove.

Braised Red Cabbage
Serves 5-6

40 g/1½ oz lard
1 medium red cabbage,
  cored and shredded
1 apple, peeled, cored
  and chopped
300 ml/½ pint cold water
150 ml/¼ pint vinegar
salt
1 tablespoon brown sugar
1 teaspoon cornflour

Melt the lard in a saucepan and add the cabbage. Toss until coated with the fat, then stir in the apple, water, vinegar and salt. Bring to the boil and simmer for about 1 hour or until tender. If necessary, add more water or vinegar to the pan.

Stir in the sugar. Dissolve the cornflour in a little water and add to the pan. Simmer, stirring, until thickened. Serve with rabbit or pork.

Vegetable Pie
Serves 5

450 g/1 lb potatoes,
  peeled and thinly sliced
175 g/6 oz streaky bacon
  rashers, rinded and
  chopped
225 g/8 oz carrots, sliced
50 g/2 oz mushrooms,
  sliced
3 tomatoes, sliced
1 onion, chopped
100 g/4 oz Cheddar
  cheese, grated
2 eggs
300 ml/½ pint milk
salt
pepper
½ teaspoon dried oregano
½ teaspoon grated nutmeg

Make alternate layers of potato, bacon, carrot, mushroom, tomato, onion and cheese in a greased 1.2 litre/2 pint baking dish. Repeat the layers until the dish is full, ending with cheese.

Mix together the eggs, milk, salt, pepper and oregano and pour into the dish. Sprinkle with the nutmeg and bake in a preheated moderate oven (180°C/350°F, Gas Mark 4) for 50 minutes.

Italian Peppers

Serves 4

25 g/1 oz butter
1 onion, chopped
2 streaky bacon rashers,
  rinded and chopped
450 g/1 lb lean minced
  pork
25 g/1 oz fresh
  breadcrumbs
1 teaspoon dried tarragon
salt
pepper
275 g/10 oz canned
  condensed tomato soup
4 green peppers
2 tablespoons water
good dash of
  Worcestershire sauce

Melt the butter in a frying pan and fry the onion and bacon until softened. Stir in the pork and fry until it is lightly browned. Add the breadcrumbs, tarragon, salt, pepper and 2 tablespoons of the undiluted soup and mix well.

Cut the stalk ends off the peppers and remove the white pith and seeds. Fill the peppers with the pork mixture and stand them in a casserole. Mix together the remaining soup, the water, Worcestershire sauce and salt and pepper. Pour this around the peppers.

Cover the casserole and cook in a preheated moderate oven (180°C/350°F, Gas Mark 4) for 45 minutes to 1 hour or until tender.

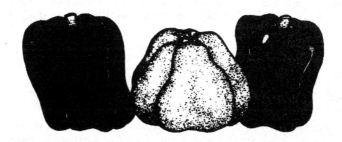

Neeps 'n Tatties

Serves 4–6

450 g/1 lb swede, peeled
  and diced
225 g/8 oz potatoes,
  peeled and diced
salt
pepper
grated nutmeg
25 g/1 oz butter
chopped parsley to
  garnish

Cook the swede and potatoes in boiling salted water until tender. Drain well, then mash very thoroughly. Season well with salt, pepper and nutmeg, then beat in the butter. Serve hot garnished with parsley.

Variation: Turnips may be used in place of swede.

191

Pipérade
Serves 4–5

50 g/2 oz butter
1 shallot, finely chopped
1 to 2 garlic cloves,
  crushed
2 large green peppers,
  cored, seeded and
  shredded
225 g/8 oz ripe tomatoes,
  skinned, seeded and
  chopped
salt
pepper
4 eggs
2 tablespoons milk
Garlic Croûtes
2 slices of bread, crusts
  removed
25 g/1 oz butter
½ garlic clove, crushed

Melt the butter in a saucepan and fry the shallot and garlic until lightly browned. Add the green peppers and cook for 5 minutes, then stir in the tomatoes with salt and pepper. Cook gently until soft and pulpy.

Beat the eggs with the milk, salt and pepper and add to the pan. Continue cooking gently, stirring occasionally, until the eggs are just set and scrambled.

Meanwhile, cut each slice of bread into 4 triangles. Mash the butter with the garlic and spread on the bread triangles. Grill until crisp.

Turn the pipérade into a warmed serving dish and surround with the croûtes.

Variation: Split open a French loaf, lengthways, and remove the soft crumbs. Spread with garlic or herb butter and bake in a preheated moderate oven (180°C/350°F, Gas Mark 4) until the butter has melted and the bread is crisp. Cool the loaf, then fill with the pipérade and serve cold.

Provençal Beans
Serves 4

25 g/1 oz butter
2 tablespoons oil
2 onions, thinly sliced
2 garlic cloves, crushed
350 g/12 oz tomatoes,
  skinned and sliced
450 g/1 lb French or
  runner beans
1 teaspoon dried
  marjoram or mixed
  herbs
salt
pepper
100 g/4 oz Cheddar
  cheese, grated

Melt the butter with the oil in a saucepan and fry the onions until softened. Add the garlic and tomatoes and cook for a further 2 to 3 minutes, then stir in the beans, herbs, salt and pepper. Cover and simmer very gently until the beans are tender.

Turn into a flameproof serving dish and sprinkle over the cheese. Brown quickly under the grill.

Potatoes and Onions au Gratin

Serves 4-6

225 g/8 oz potatoes,
  peeled and diced
salt
450 g/1 lb button onions
450 ml/¾ pint white sauce
pepper
25 g/1 oz cheese, grated

Cook the potatoes in boiling salted water until just tender. Meanwhile, cook the onions in another pan of boiling salted water until tender.

Heat the white sauce and season well with salt and pepper. Drain the potatoes and onions and fold into the sauce. Turn into a baking dish and sprinkle over the cheese. Bake in a preheated moderately hot oven (200°C/400°F, Gas Mark 6) for about 20 minutes. Serve with any roast joint, grill or casserole.

Baked Tomatoes

Serves 2-4

450 g/1 lb tomatoes,
  sliced
1 garlic clove, crushed
2 onions, chopped
1 tablespoon chopped
  fresh basil
salt
pepper
25 g/1 oz fresh
  breadcrumbs
25 g/1 oz butter

Put the tomato slices in a buttered baking dish with the garlic. Mix together the onions and basil and sprinkle over the tomatoes, with salt and pepper. Cover with the breadcrumbs and dot with the butter. Bake in a preheated moderate oven (180°C/350°F, Gas Mark 4) for 20 minutes.

Carrots – Algerian Style

Serves 6

1 kg/2 lb carrots, cut into
  1 cm/½ inch slices
5 tablespoons olive oil
½ teaspoon cumin seeds
3 garlic cloves, finely
  chopped
½ teaspoon dried thyme
1 bay leaf
salt
pepper
1 teaspoon lemon juice

Cook the carrots in boiling water for 15 minutes. Drain, reserving 150 ml/¼ pint of the cooking liquor.

Put the oil in another saucepan with the cumin, garlic, thyme, bay leaf, salt and pepper. Cook gently for 10 minutes, then stir in the reserved cooking liquor. Cover and simmer for a further 15 to 20 minutes.

Add the carrots and stir into the sauce. Heat through for 2 to 3 minutes, then sprinkle over the lemon juice. Remove the bay leaf and serve.

Mushroom and Onion Pie
Serves 6–8

Filling
25 g/1 oz butter or margarine
1 tablespoon oil
175 g/6 oz onions, thinly sliced
1 large carrot, coarsely grated
175 g/6 oz mushrooms, sliced
salt
pepper
½ teaspoon dried oregano
1 large egg, beaten
4 tablespoons milk

Pastry
100 g/4 oz wholemeal flour
50 g/2 oz self-raising flour
1 teaspoon salt
50 g/2 oz lard or white fat
25 g/1 oz margarine

Garnish
watercress
tomato slices

To make the filling, melt the fat with the oil in a frying pan and fry the onions until softened. Add the carrot and mushrooms and cook for a further 3 minutes. Season well with salt and pepper and add the oregano, then remove from the heat and cool.

Meanwhile make the pastry. Mix the sifted flours and salt together, then rub in the fats until the mixture resembles breadcrumbs. Bind to a dough with cold water. Roll out the dough and use to line a 23 cm/9 inch flan tin or ring.

Spoon the mushroom filling into the pastry case. Beat together the egg and milk and pour over the top. Bake in a preheated moderately hot oven (200°C/400°F, Gas Mark 6) for 35 to 40 minutes or until the pastry is golden and the filling is firm. Serve hot or cold, garnished with watercress and tomato slices.

Latkes (Potato Pancakes)
Serves 4–5

450 g/1 lb potatoes, peeled and grated
1 onion, grated
salt
pepper
½ teaspoon chopped parsley
1 egg, separated
1 tablespoon flour
fat for shallow frying

Drain the liquid from the grated potatoes, then mix in the onion, salt, pepper, parsley and egg yolk. Mix in the flour. Whisk the egg white until stiff and fold into the potato mixture.

Form the mixture into flat cakes and shallow fry until golden brown on both sides and cooked through.

Savoury Onion Pasty

Serves 4–5

Oatmeal Pastry
75 g/3 oz self-raising
flour
½ teaspoon salt
75 g/3 oz medium
oatmeal
50 g/2 oz mixed
margarine and lard
beaten egg or milk
to glaze
Filling
225 g/8 oz spring onions
or 1 medium leek, cut
into 5 mm/¼ inch
pieces
salt
pepper
1 bacon rasher, rinded
and diced
25 g/1 oz cheese, grated
1 egg
150 ml/¼ pint milk

To make the pastry, sift the flour and salt into a bowl. Mix in the oatmeal, then rub in the fat until the mixture resembles breadcrumbs. Bind to a dough with cold water. Divide the dough in half and roll out each half into a round. Use one round to line an 18 cm/6 inch sandwich tin or baking dish.

Sprinkle the spring onion or leek pieces over the bottom of the pastry case and season well with salt and pepper. Scatter over the bacon and cheese. Mix together the egg and milk and pour on top.

Place the second pastry round on top and pinch the dampened edges together to seal. Decorate the top with dough trimmings, then brush with beaten egg or milk. Bake in a preheated hot oven (220°C/425°F, Gas Mark 7) for 10 minutes, then reduce the heat to moderate (180°C/350°F, Gas Mark 4) and continue baking for 50 minutes or until the pastry is golden. Serve hot or cold.

Stuffed Peppers

Serves 4

4 green peppers
225 g/8 oz boiled long-
grain rice
50 g/2 oz butter, melted
2 tomatoes, skinned and
chopped
4 hard-boiled eggs,
chopped
½ teaspoon turmeric
9 lovage seeds, ground
2 tablespoons chopped
chives
salt
pepper
50 g/2 oz cheese, grated
(optional)

Cut the tops off the peppers and scoop out the white pith and seeds.

Mix together the rice, butter, tomatoes, eggs, turmeric, lovage, chives, salt and pepper. Use to stuff the peppers. Arrange the peppers in a greased baking dish so they stand upright. Sprinkle the tops with grated cheese, if using.

Bake in a preheated moderate oven (180°C/350°F, Gas Mark 4) for 20 to 30 minutes or until the peppers are tender.
Note: Other vegetables, such as aubergines, large continental tomatoes, etc., can be stuffed in this way.

Duchesse Potatoes
Serves 4

450 g/1 lb potatoes,
  peeled
1 tablespoon milk
25 g/1 oz butter
1 egg, beaten

Cook the potatoes in boiling water until they are tender. Drain well, then sieve to make a smooth purée. Add the milk, butter and half the egg and beat well. Put into a forcing bag and pipe onto a greased baking sheet. Brush with the rest of the beaten egg, then bake in a preheated hot oven (220°C/425°F, Gas Mark 7) for 15 minutes.

Vichy Cabbage
Serves 6

25 g/1 oz butter or
  margarine
1 to 2 onions, chopped
1 tablespoon chopped
  parsley
150 ml/¼ pint stock
1 cabbage, cored and
  shredded
salt
pepper

Melt the fat in a saucepan. Add the onions and parsley and fry until the onions are softened. Add the stock and bring to the boil. Stir in the cabbage, cover and simmer for 3 minutes.
  Add salt and pepper, stir well and cook for a further 3 minutes. Drain the cabbage and serve.

Vegetable Marrow Hongroise
Serves 4-5

25 g/1 oz butter
1 medium marrow,
  peeled, seeded and cut
  into slivers
1 tablespoon finely
  chopped onion
1 tablespoon vinegar
pinch of dill seed, finely
  crushed, or chopped
  fresh dill leaves
salt
pepper
1 teaspoon sugar
1 teaspoon paprika
1 heaped teaspoon flour

Melt three-quarters of the butter in a frying pan. Add the marrow and cook, turning frequently, until the marrow is soft and melting. Lift the marrow out with a slotted spoon.
  Add the onion to the pan and fry until softened. Stir in the vinegar, dill, salt, pepper, sugar and paprika, then return the marrow to the pan. Mix well and cook gently for 2 minutes.
  Mash the remaining butter with the flour to make a paste and add to the pan in small pieces, stirring well. Simmer until thickened, then serve.

Spinach Roulade

Serves 4

450 g/1 lb spinach
15 g/½ oz butter
4 eggs, separated
salt
pepper
Filling
50 g/2 oz Parmesan or
 Cheddar cheese, grated
5 tablespoons tomato
 paste

Cook the spinach in a covered pan until tender (there should be enough water left on the leaves after washing so you won't need to add any). Press out any excess water, then sieve or blend the spinach to a purée. Add the butter, egg yolks, salt and pepper and beat well until smooth.

Whisk the egg whites until stiff and fold into the spinach mixture. Spread out the mixture in a foil-lined Swiss roll tin or baking tin, making a layer about 1 cm/½ inch deep. Bake in a preheated moderately hot oven (200°C/400°F, Gas Mark 6) for 10 minutes or until firm to the touch.

Meanwhile, mix together the cheese and tomato paste.

Spread the filling over the spinach roulade and roll up like a Swiss roll. Serve immediately, cut into slices.

Variation: Instead of the filling above, use 100 g/4 oz cooked sliced mushrooms mixed with 150 ml/¼ pint white sauce.

Artichoke Soufflé

Serves 4–5

1 kg/2 lb Jerusalem
 artichokes, peeled
40 g/1½ oz butter
2 tablespoons plain flour
300 ml/½ pint milk
3 eggs, separated
3 tablespoons grated
 cheese
salt
pepper

Steam the artichokes until tender. This will take about 45 minutes.

Meanwhile, melt the butter in a saucepan. Add the flour and cook, stirring, for 2 minutes. Gradually stir in the milk and bring to the boil. Simmer, stirring, until thickened. Remove from the heat and beat in the egg yolks, cheese, salt and pepper.

Slice the artichokes and place them in a baking dish. Whisk the egg whites and fold into the cheese mixture. Spoon on top of the artichokes. Bake in a preheated moderately hot oven (200°C/400°F, Gas Mark 6) for 30 minutes.

Note: Many other vegetables are excellent prepared this way.

Savoury Stuffed Aubergines
Serves 2

2 firm aubergines, halved lengthways
salt
100 g/4 oz button mushrooms, chopped
1 tablespoon oil
1 medium onion, finely chopped
1 garlic clove, crushed
100 g/4 oz Cheddar cheese, grated
pepper

Scoop out the aubergine flesh, leaving shells about 5 mm/¼ inch thick. Sprinkle the flesh and shells with salt and leave to drain for 30 minutes.

Rinse the flesh and shells and pat dry with paper towels. Chop the flesh. Mix the mushrooms with the flesh.

Heat the oil in a frying pan and fry the onion until softened. Add the aubergine flesh and mushroom mixture and the garlic and fry gently for 5 minutes. Stir in 75 g/3 oz of the cheese, salt and pepper.

Fill the aubergine shells with the mixture and sprinkle over the remaining cheese. Put the aubergines in a baking dish and bake in a preheated moderate oven (180°C/350°F, Gas Mark 4) for 30 minutes or until tender.

Cauliflower Cake
Serves 6

100 g/4 oz fresh breadcrumbs
200 ml/⅓ pint milk or white stock
25 g/1 oz butter
1 cauliflower, cooked and divided into florets
2 eggs, separated
salt
pepper
2 tablespoons browned breadcrumbs
parsley, or tomatoes and grated cheese to garnish

Put the fresh breadcrumbs and milk or stock in a saucepan and stir over a low heat until the mixture boils and thickens. Stir in the butter and cauliflower. Remove from the heat and mix in the egg yolks, salt and pepper.

Whisk the egg whites and fold into the cauliflower mixture.

Grease an 18 cm/7 inch plain mould or cake tin and coat it with the browned breadcrumbs. Spoon in the cauliflower mixture. Place the mould or tin in a roasting tin of hot water and bake in a preheated moderate oven (180°C/350°F, Gas Mark 4) for 30 to 40 minutes or until well risen and firm to the touch.

Turn out onto a warmed serving dish and garnish with parsley, or tomatoes and grated cheese.

Fruit of the Earth Salad

Serves 4

4 large potatoes
100 g/4 oz cheese, grated
4 tomatoes, sliced
2 lettuce hearts,
  quartered
3 celery stalks, chopped
2 large carrots, grated
2 tablespoons chopped
  chives

Bake the potatoes in their jackets in a pre-heated moderately hot oven (200°C/400°F, Gas Mark 6) for 1½ hours or boil them in their jackets until tender.

Slice the potatoes in half lengthways and place, cut sides up, in the grill pan. Sprinkle with the cheese and arrange the tomato slices on top. Grill until the cheese has melted and is bubbling.

Place the potato halves on a serving dish and surround with the lettuce heart quarters. Mix together the celery and carrots and arrange in piles on the dish. Sprinkle over the chives.

Parsnips au Gratin

Serves 2–3

2 large parsnips, chopped
  but not peeled
40 g/1½ oz butter or
  margarine
175 g/6 oz cheese, grated
15 g/½ oz dry
  breadcrumbs, crumbled
  shredded wheat or
  cornflakes

Steam the parsnips until tender. Mash them with a fork to a purée and beat in 25 g/1 oz of the fat and the cheese. Spread the parsnip mixture in a flameproof serving dish and sprinkle over the breadcrumbs or cereal. Dot with the rest of the butter. Brown under a hot grill.

Bacon and Potato Savoury

Serves 4

25 g/1 oz dripping
100 g/4 oz bacon scraps,
  chopped
1 medium onion, chopped
450 g/1 lb potatoes,
  peeled and chopped
salt
pepper
250 ml/8 fl oz stock or
  vegetable water
chopped parsley to
  garnish

Melt the dripping in a saucepan and add the bacon and onion. Fry until softened but not brown. Add the potatoes and fry, stirring occasionally, until they take up all the fat. Add salt, pepper and the stock or water and mix well. Cover and cook gently until the vegetables are tender. Serve hot, garnished with parsley.

199

Vegetable Casserole

Serves 6

225 g/8 oz frozen
  chopped spinach
225 g/8 oz frozen
  chopped broccoli
2 teaspooons cider
  vinegar
275 g/10 oz canned
  condensed cream of
  asparagus or
  mushroom soup
salt
pepper
1 tablespoon dried onion
  flakes, soaked
226 g/8 oz canned
  tomatoes, drained and
  chopped
100 g/4 oz cheese, grated

Cook the spinach and broccoli in separate pans for half the cooking time specified on the packets. Add 1 teaspoon vinegar to each pan.

Mix the soup with salt and pepper. Drain the spinach and broccoli and stir into the soup. Turn into a greased baking dish and top with the onion flakes and tomatoes. Sprinkle over the cheese.

Bake in a preheated moderate oven (160°C/325°F, Gas Mark 3) for 40 minutes or until the top is golden brown.

Salsify in Tomato Sauce

Serves 4

450 g/1 lb salsify
salt
grated Parmesan cheese
  to serve

Sauce
25 g/1 oz margarine
1 onion, sliced
2 mushrooms, sliced
15 g/½ oz flour
2 tomatoes, skinned and
  chopped
pinch of mixed herbs
salt
pepper
150 ml/¼ pint stock

Cook the salsify in boiling salted water until tender.

Meanwhile, make the sauce. Melt the margarine in a saucepan and fry the onion until softened. Add the mushrooms and fry for 2 minutes, then stir in the flour. Add the tomatoes, herbs, salt, pepper and stock and bring to the boil, stirring. Simmer for 10 minutes.

Drain the salsify, then peel and slice. Add to the sauce and simmer for a further 10 minutes. Serve with Parmesan cheese.

Note: Scorzonera, courgettes, kohlrabi and fennel may be prepared in the same way.

Floddies
Serves 2

*1 large potato, peeled
and grated
1 tablespoon grated
cheese
1 egg, beaten
flour
dry mustard, salt,
chopped parsley or
chives, dried herbs,
etc., to taste
oil or fat for shallow
frying*

Mix together the potato, cheese and egg, then add enough flour to make a pancake mixture. Add whatever seasoning you like.

Fry spoonsful of the mixture until golden brown on both sides. Drain and serve hot.

Cabbage and Apple Savoury
Serves 5–6

*1 cabbage, cored and
shredded
5 or 6 apples, peeled,
cored and sliced
salt
pepper
sugar
300 ml/½ pint stock
15 g/½ oz butter*

Put a little water in a pie dish and make alternate layers of cabbage and apple in the dish. Sprinkle the cabbage with salt and pepper and the apple with sugar. Pour in the stock and dot the butter over the top. Cover tightly and bake in a preheated moderate oven (180°C/ 350 F, Gas Mark 4) for 2 to 3 hours.

Saddled Celery
Serves 4

*1 head of celery
4 bacon rashers, rinded
300 ml/½ pint cheese
sauce
25 g/1 oz cheese, grated*
Garnish
*tomato slices
parsley*

Cook the celery in boiling water until tender. Drain well and divide into four bundles. Wrap a bacon rasher around each bundle and arrange them in a baking dish. Pour over the sauce and sprinkle the cheese on top.

Bake in a preheated moderately hot oven (190 C/375 F, Gas Mark 5) for 30 to 40 minutes. Serve garnished with tomato slices and parsley.

201

Outdoor Eating

Lamb Shashlik
Serves 6

*750 g/1½ lb boneless
  lamb, from the leg or
  shoulder, trimmed of
  excess fat and cut into
  1 cm/½ inch cubes
1 onion, thinly sliced
salt
pepper
juice of 1 lemon
2 tablespoons white wine
  or cider
6 small tomatoes
6 button mushrooms
melted butter or dripping
savoury boiled rice to
  serve*

Put the lamb cubes in a dish and scatter over
the onion slices. Sprinkle with salt, pepper,
lemon juice and wine or cider, then cover and
leave overnight.

When ready to cook, thread the lamb cubes
onto skewers, alternating them with tomatoes
and mushrooms. Brush with butter or dripping
and grill for 15 minutes, turning frequently.
Serve on a bed of savoury rice.

Shrimp and Yogurt Dip
Serves 6–8

*90 g/3½ oz canned
  shrimps, drained and
  chopped
150 g/5 oz natural
  yogurt
pepper
sherry*

Mix together the shrimps and yogurt. Add
pepper and sherry to taste. Serve with carrot
sticks, crisps and small savoury biscuits.

202

Horseradish Cottage Dip

Serves 4

*3 tablespoons redcurrant
   or mint jelly
4 teaspoons creamed
   horseradish
225 g/8 oz cottage cheese
150 ml/¼ pint double
   cream, whipped
salt
pepper*

Melt the jelly gently, then cool slightly. Add to the horseradish, then mix in the cottage cheese. Fold in the whipped cream and salt and pepper to taste. Serve with cocktail biscuits, sticks of carrot or celery.

Picnic Pies

Serves 8

*225 g/8 oz boneless veal
100 g/4 oz bacon
225 g/8 oz pork sausages,
   skinned
pinch of ground mace
salt
pepper
450 g/1 lb puff pastry
2 hard-boiled eggs, sliced
beaten egg to glaze*

Mince the veal and bacon together, then mix in the sausage meat, mace, salt and pepper.

Roll out the dough and use two-thirds of it to line patty tins. Put a spoonful of the meat mixture into each tin and place an egg slice on top. Cover with the rest of the meat mixture. Use the rest of the dough to make pastry lids and brush with beaten egg.

Bake in a preheated hot oven (220°C/425°F, Gas Mark 7) for 45 minutes, then reduce the temperature to moderate (160°C/350°F, Gas Mark 4) and continue baking for 25 minutes.

Bacon Picnic Roll

Serves 5–6

*6 back bacon rashers,
   rinded
450 g/1 lb sausage meat
1 apple, peeled, cored
   and finely chopped
2 tablespoons finely
   chopped onion
½ teaspoon dried sage
3 hard-boiled eggs*

Finely chop two of the bacon rashers. Mix the chopped bacon with the sausage meat, apple, onion and sage. Spread out the mixture on a floured surface to a 23 cm/9 inch square. Place the eggs in a line on the square, then roll up. Wrap the remaining bacon rashers around the roll, then wrap in foil and place on a baking sheet.

Bake in a preheated moderate oven (180 C/350 F, Gas Mark 4) for about 1¼ hours. Fifteen minutes before the end of cooking, fold back the foil so that the roll can brown. Cool completely before slicing.

203

Pork Kebabs
Serves 4

450 g/1 lb pork fillet, cut
into 2.5 cm/1 inch
cubes
350 g/12 oz canned
pineapple cubes
1 tablespoon vinegar
2 tablespoons oil
1 teaspoon
Worcestershire sauce
salt
pepper
1 green or red pepper,
blanched, cored, seeded
and cut into squares
100 g/4 oz small button
mushrooms
bay leaves
boiled rice to serve

Put the pork cubes in a shallow dish. Drain the pineapple, reserving 2 tablespoons of the can syrup. Mix the syrup with the vinegar, oil, Worcestershire sauce, salt and pepper and pour over the pork cubes. Leave to marinate for at least 30 minutes, turning occasionally.

When ready to cook, thread the pork cubes onto skewers alternately with the pineapple cubes, pepper squares and mushrooms. Add 2 bay leaves to each skewer.

Grill gently for about 15 minutes, turning frequently and brushing with the marinade to keep the meat moist. Serve with rice and a green salad.

Sausages Western Style
Serves 6

750 g/1½ lb chipolata
sausages
chutney
15 g/½ oz butter
1 onion, chopped, or 1
tablespoon dried onion
flakes
425 g/15 oz canned
baked beans in tomato
sauce
198 g/7 oz canned
condensed tomato
soup, or 100 g/4 oz
canned tomato purée
salt
pepper
100 g/4 oz cheese, grated

Split the sausages open lengthways and spread the cut surfaces with chutney. Close the sausages together again.

Melt the butter in a frying pan and fry the fresh onion, if using, until softened. Add the sausages and fry gently, turning twice, until browned all over. Add the beans, soup or tomato purée, salt, pepper and the onion flakes if using and mix well, then cover and simmer gently for 15 minutes.

Scatter the cheese over the top and continue cooking until it has melted. Serve with mashed potatoes.

Fish Cooked in Parcels

Serves 4

4 cutlets or portions of white fish
lemon juice
little soy sauce or dried tarragon
salt
pepper

Cut out four squares of foil large enough to enclose a cutlet or portion and grease them with butter. Put the fish on the foil and sprinkle with lemon juice, soy sauce or tarragon, salt and pepper. Wrap the foil securely around the fish.

Poach the fish parcels in a shallow pan of hot water for 20 to 30 minutes, according to the thickness of the fish. Serve in the parcels, to be unwrapped at the table.

Fried Chicken Maryland

Serves 4

50 g/2 oz flour
salt
pepper
4 chicken joints
100 g/4 oz butter, or 8 tablespoons oil
3 bacon rashers, rinded and cut into strips
300 ml/½ pint single cream
4 canned pineapple rings
chopped parsley to garnish

Mix the flour with salt and pepper and use to coat the chicken joints. Melt the butter or heat the oil in a frying pan. Add the chicken joints and brown on all sides. Add the bacon, then cover the pan and continue cooking gently until the chicken is tender.

Gradually stir the cream into the juices in the pan and cook gently until thickened. Do not boil. Add the pineapple rings and heat through. Adjust the seasoning and garnish with chopped parsley. Serve with sweetcorn and fried bananas.

Curried Cream Cheese Dip

Serves 8–10

225 g/8 oz cream cheese
150 g/5 oz natural yogurt
4 tablespoons mayonnaise
3 to 4 teaspoons curry powder
2 teaspoons finely grated onion
salt
1 tablespoon sultanas

Beat the cheese with the yogurt and mayonnaise until smooth. Add the curry powder, onion and salt and mix well. Pile into a dish and sprinkle over the sultanas. Serve with cocktail biscuits, sticks of carrot or celery.

Beef Cooked in Beer

Serves 5–6

25 g/1 oz flour
salt
pepper
750 g/1½ lb stewing
steak, cut into 5 cm/2
inch cubes
2 tablespoons oil
2 onions, sliced
1 teaspoon dried garlic
300 ml/½ pint brown ale
or water
1 beef stock cube
pinch of dried mixed
herbs
pinch of grated nutmeg
4 tablespoons tomato
purée
225 g/8 oz carrots or
mixed root vegetables,
sliced or chopped

Mix the flour with salt and pepper and use to coat the steak cubes. Heat the oil in a saucepan or pressure cooker and add the steak cubes, onions and garlic. Fry until the steak cubes are browned on all sides. Stir in the ale or water, stock cube, herbs, nutmeg and tomato purée and bring to the boil. If using a pressure cooker, bring to pressure and cook for 15 minutes. In a saucepan, cover and simmer for 1 hour.

Add the vegetables and stir well. With a pressure cooker, bring to pressure again and cook for a further 5 minutes. In a saucepan, cook for a further 30 minutes. Adjust the seasoning and serve.

Liver Kebabs with Onion Rice

Serves 4

4 lean bacon rashers,
rinded
225 g/8 oz calf's liver,
cut into 2 thick slices
and then into cubes
8 button mushrooms
4 tomatoes, halved
oil
salt
pepper

Onion Rice

25 g/1 oz butter
1 onion, finely chopped
225 g/8 oz long-grain rice
600 ml/1 pint stock

Stretch the bacon rashers, then cut each in half crossways. Roll up. Thread the bacon rolls onto skewers alternately with the liver cubes, mushrooms and tomato halves. Brush with oil and sprinkle with salt and pepper. Set aside.

For the rice, melt the butter in a saucepan. Add the onion and fry until softened. Stir in the rice, then add the stock and bring to the boil. Cover and simmer gently for about 20 minutes or until the rice is tender and the stock has been absorbed.

Meanwhile, grill the liver kebabs for about 10 to 15 minutes, turning occasionally.

Spoon the rice into a warmed serving dish and place the kebabs on top.

Quick Goulash

Serves 4

1 tablespoon oil
1 onion, chopped, or 1
  tablespoon dried onion
  flakes
25 g/1 oz cornflour
450 g/1 lb canned
  stewed steak
100 g/4 oz tomato purée
2 teaspoons paprika
1 tablespoons dried red
  and green peppers
150 g/5 oz natural yogurt

Heat the oil in a saucepan and fry the fresh onion, if using, until softened. Stir in the cornflour and cook until the oil is absorbed. Stir in the stewed steak, tomato purée, paprika, peppers and onion flakes, if using. Cook gently for 10 to 20 minutes.

Stir in the yogurt just before serving, with boiled rice or creamed potatoes.

Raised Picnic Pie

Serves 8–10

225 g/8 oz raw pie veal
  or cooked ham
1 small onion
6 stuffed olives, sliced, or
  1 tablespoon capers
salt
pepper
good pinch of ground
  mace or grated nutmeg
450 g/1 lb hot water
  crust pastry, made with
  1 lb flour, 1 level
  teaspoon salt and 6 oz
  lard (see page 125)
225 g/8 oz sausage meat
350 g/12 oz cooked
  chicken or turkey
  meat, diced
beaten egg to glaze
2 teaspoons gelatine
approx. 300 ml/½ pint
  stock

Mince together the veal or ham and onion. Add the olives or capers, salt, pepper and spice and mix well.

Roll out three-quarters of the dough and use to line a greased 20 to 23 cm/8 to 9 inch loose-based cake tin or game pie mould. Lay the sausagemeat on the bottom, then cover with the chicken or turkey, pressing it down slightly. Add the minced mixture.

Roll out the rest of the dough and place on top of the pie. Press the dampened edges together to seal. Make a hole in the centre and decorate the top with the dough trimmings. Brush with beaten egg.

Bake in a preheated moderately hot oven (200°C/400°F, Gas Mark 6) for 30 minutes. Brush again with beaten egg, reduce the temperature to moderate (160°C/325°F, Gas Mark 3) and continue baking for 1 hour if using ham, or 1¼ to 1½ hours if using veal. Cover the pie with greaseproof paper or foil when it is browned.

Dissolve the gelatine in the stock. As the pie cools, fill it with the stock mixture through the hole in the lid. Cool completely, then chill.

Lamb on the Spit
Serves 8

*1.5 to 1.75 kg/3 to 4 lb
  boned and rolled leg of
  lamb
juice of 1 lemon
120 ml/4 fl oz oil
1 tablespoon chopped
  fresh rosemary*

Sauce
*25 g/1 oz butter
2 onions, chopped
250 ml/8 fl oz tomato
  ketchup
250 ml/8 fl oz apple juice
2 tablespoons brown
  sugar
3 tablespoons
  Worcestershire sauce
2 tablespoons cider
  vinegar
salt
pepper*

Put the lamb in a polythene bag. Mix together the lemon juice, oil and rosemary and add to the bag. Tie the bag closed, then leave to marinate for at least 4 hours, or overnight, turning occasionally.

To make the sauce, melt the butter in a saucepan. Add the onions and fry until softened. Stir in the remaining sauce ingredients and bring to the boil. Simmer for 30 minutes.

Drain the lamb and put it on the spit. Cook over hot coals for 2 to 3 hours, turning every 20 to 30 minutes and basting with the sauce.

Hot Lemon and Barbecue Dip
Serves 4

*100 g/4 oz butter
1 garlic clove, crushed
4 teaspoons flour
2 tablespoons sugar
½ teaspoon dried thyme
¼ teaspoon Tabasco sauce
grated rind of 1 lemon
4 to 6 tablespoons lemon
  juice
150 ml/¼ pint chicken
  stock
salt
pepper
hot cooked baby
  chipolatas to serve*

Melt the butter in a saucepan and fry the garlic for 1 minute. Stir in the flour and cook for 2 minutes. Add the sugar, thyme, Tabasco, lemon rind and juice, stock, salt and pepper and bring to the boil, stirring. Cover and simmer gently for 15 minutes.

Serve hot as a dip for baby chipolatas.

Beefburgers with Onion and Cheese *Serves 4*

450 g/1 lb minced beef
50 g/2 oz Cheddar
  cheese, grated
4 thin onion slices
salt
pepper

Divide the beef into eight portions and shape into flat patties. Top half of the patties with cheese and onion and place the remaining patties on top. Press the edges together to seal. Sprinkle with salt and pepper.

Grill for 3 to 4 minutes on each side. Serve with tomato wedges and crisps or jacket potatoes, or put each beefburger into a split soft bread roll.

Peach Surprise *Serves 2*

2 ripe peaches, skinned,
  halved and stoned
2 tablespoons sherry or
  brandy (optional)
sugar
150 g/5 oz natural yogurt
cream and/or chopped
  nuts to decorate

Put the peach halves into individual dishes and sprinkle with the sherry or brandy, if using, and a little sugar to taste. Pour over the yogurt. Top with cream and/or chopped nuts.

Corned Beef Hash *Serves 4*

1 can condensed oxtail
  soup, or 1 × 600 ml/1
  pint packet oxtail soup
  mix
1 × 100 g/4 oz packet
  dried or frozen mixed
  vegetables
4 potatoes, peeled and
  sliced
1 tablespoon onion flakes
350 g/12 oz canned
  corned beef, diced
salt
pepper

Make the soup up to 450 ml/¾ pint with water in a saucepan. Bring to the boil, stirring well, then add the vegetables and simmer for 10 minutes or until they are tender. Add the corned beef, salt and pepper and cook for a further 5 minutes.

209

Salmon Loaf

Serves 4

1 hard-boiled egg, sliced
225 g/8 oz fresh or
* canned salmon, flaked*
100 g/4 oz fresh
* breadcrumbs*
knob of margarine
1 teaspoon vinegar
120 ml/4 fl oz hot milk
2 eggs, beaten
salt
pepper
parsley to garnish

Arrange the egg slices on the bottom of a greased 500 g/1 lb loaf tin. Mix together the salmon, breadcrumbs, margarine, vinegar, milk, eggs, salt and pepper and press into the tin.

Bake in a preheated moderate oven (180°C/350°F, Gas Mark 4) for 30 minutes. Cool.

When cold, turn out of the tin and serve garnished with parsley.

Leek and Cheese Dip

Serves 4

225 g/8 oz cottage cheese
150 g/5 oz soured cream
* cream*
1 × 600 ml/1 pint packet
* leek soup mix*
2 tablespoons chopped
* parsley*
2 tablespoons lemon juice

Blend together the cottage cheese, soured cream and leek soup mix. Add the parsley and lemon juice and mix well. Chill for up to 1 hour before serving, with crisps, celery curls and small oatcakes.

Hamburgers

Serves 4

2 slices of bread, crusts
* removed*
450 g/1 lb lean braising
* steak*
2 garlic cloves
1 medium onion,
* quartered*
salt
pepper
1 teaspoon dry mustard
1 egg, beaten
4 baps, split and toasted

Moisten the bread with a little water, then squeeze out the excess water. Mince together the steak, garlic, onion and bread, then mix well together with salt, pepper and the mustard. Mix in the egg. Divide into four portions and shape into patties.

Grill the hamburgers over hot coals. Put a hamburger into each bap and serve with sliced onions, tomatoes and pickles, if you like.

Puddings & Desserts

Lemon Sponge Ring
Serves 4–6

100 g/4 oz margarine
100 g/4 oz caster sugar
2 eggs, beaten
100 g/4 oz self-raising flour, sifted
1 tablespoon lemon juice
150 ml/¼ pint double cream
150 ml/¼ pint single cream
2 tablespoons lemon curd
15 g/½ oz plain chocolate, grated

Cream together the margarine and sugar. Beat in the eggs, then fold in the flour and lemon juice. Put the mixture into a greased and floured 23 cm/9 inch savarin ring tin. Bake in a preheated moderate oven (180 C/350 F, Gas Mark 4) for 25 minutes or until firm and golden. Turn out onto a wire rack and cool.

Whip the creams together until thick. Place the cake on a serving plate and spread the lemon curd over it. Top with the whipped cream and sprinkle over the grated chocolate.

Chestnut Dessert
Serves 6

750 g/1½ lb chestnuts, shells nicked or
300 g/12 oz canned chestnut purée
40 g/1½ oz butter
75 g/3 oz caster sugar
100 g/4 oz bitter chocolate

Cook the chestnuts in boiling water until they are tender, then remove the shells and skins. Sieve the chestnuts to make a purée.

Cream together the butter and sugar, then beat in the chestnut purée. Melt the chocolate gently in a heatproof basin over a pan of hot water. Add to the chestnut mixture and blend well. Turn into a lightly oiled and bottom-lined tin. Keep in a cool place until ready to serve. Serve with fresh cream and fruit.

211

Martha Washington Pie
Serves 6–8

150 g/5 oz shortening
150 g/5 oz sugar
2 eggs, beàten
300 g/11 oz flour
2 teaspoons baking
  powder
¼ teaspoon salt
200 ml/⅓ pint milk
1 teaspoon vanilla
  essence
50 g/2 oz walnuts,
  chopped
150 ml/¼ pint double
  cream
little caster sugar to taste
glacé cherries and citron
  to decorate

Cream together the shortening and sugar. Beat in the eggs. Sift together the flour, baking powder and salt and add to the creamed mixture alternately with the milk. Beat in the vanilla essence and walnuts.

Divide the mixture between two 18 cm/7 inch greased sandwich tins. Bake in a preheated moderately hot oven (190°C/375F, Gas Mark 5) for 45 minutes. Cool.

Whip the cream with caster sugar to taste. Turn the cakes out of the tins and sandwich them together with half the cream. Spread the remaining cream over the top. Decorate with glacé cherries and thin strips of citron.

Floating Island
Serves 4–6

4 eggs, separated
pinch of salt
275 g/10 oz caster sugar
50 g/2 oz sugared
  almonds, crushed
300 ml/½ pint milk
glacé cherries or grated
  chocolate to decorate
  (optional)

Beat the egg whites with the salt until stiff. Add 100 g/4 oz of the sugar and beat again until stiff, then fold in anotȟer 100 g/4 oz sugar. Butter and sugar a fairly deep 20 cm/8 inch square baking tin and spread a little of the meringue over the bottom. Cover with a sprinkling of crushed sugared almonds. Continue making layers in this way, ending with almonds.

Place the tin in a roasting tin of hot water and bake in a preheated moderately hot oven (190°C/375°F, Gas Mark 5) for 30 to 45 minutes. Cool slightly, then turn out the meringue.

Put the egg yolks, milk and remaining sugar in a heavy-based saucepan and heat gently, stirring, until the custard is thick. Cool, then chill.

Place the meringue in a serving dish and pour around the custard. Decorate the meringue with glacé cherries or grated chocolate, if you like.

Oldbury Tarts
Makes 6

450 g/1 lb flour
75 g/3 oz margarine
200 ml/⅓ pint boiling water
75 g/3 oz lard
small gooseberries
brown sugar

Sift the flour into a bowl. Make a well in the centre and put in the fat. Pour the boiling water over the fat, then mix and knead into a pliable dough. Cool slightly.

Form two-thirds of the dough into walnut-sized balls. Form the remaining third of the dough into balls half this size. Roll out the larger balls into rounds the size of a saucer and spread out to dry a little. Roll out the smaller balls to rounds half this diameter.

When the large rounds are fairly firm to handle, pleat them round to stand up about 2.5 cm/1 inch at the sides. Cover the bottom with gooseberries and add 1 tablespoon of brown sugar to each. Put the smaller rounds on top and press firmly to seal. Decorate by pinching the join between your finger and thumb to give a scalloped effect. Place on a greased baking sheet.

Leave overnight to become firm, then bake in a preheated hot oven (220°C/425°F, Gas Mark 7) for 10 minutes.

Monmouth Pudding
Serves 4

175 g/6 oz shortcrust pastry
apricot jam
600 ml/1 pint milk
100 g/4 oz fresh breadcrumbs
2 tablespoons sugar
25 g/1 oz butter
2 eggs, beaten
1 tablespoon lemon juice
grated rind of 1 lemon

Roll out the dough and use to line an 18 cm/7 inch pie dish. Spread the bottom with apricot jam.

Bring the milk to the boil. Mix together the breadcrumbs and sugar in a bowl and pour over the milk. Leave to stand for 5 minutes, then return to the saucepan. Heat gently, stirring, for 3 minutes. Remove from the heat and stir in the butter until melted. Cool slightly, then beat in the eggs and lemon juice and rind. Pour into the pastry case.

Bake in a preheated moderately hot oven (200°C/400°F, Gas Mark 6) for 35 minutes or until brown.

213

Golden Pudding

Serves 4–5

50 g/2 oz margarine
50 g/2 oz brown sugar
2 tablespoons golden
    syrup
1 teaspoon vanilla
    essence
2 eggs, beaten
200 g/7 oz self-raising
    flour
½ teaspoon mixed spice
100 ml/3 fl oz milk
3 tablespoons granulated
    sugar
1 tablespoon grated
    orange rind

Lemon Sauce

1 tablespoon cornflour
75 g/3 oz sugar
300 ml/½ pint boiling
    water
pinch of salt
1 teaspoon grated lemon
    rind
3 tablespoons lemon juice
25 g/1 oz margarine

Cream together the margarine and brown sugar. Beat in the syrup and vanilla, then the eggs. Sift together the flour and spice and add to the creamed mixture alternately with the milk. Beat until smooth. Turn into a greased shallow 20 cm/8 inch tin. Mix together the granulated sugar and orange rind and sprinkle over the top.

Bake in a preheated moderate oven (160°C/325°F, Gas Mark 3) for 30 minutes.

Meanwhile, make the sauce. Put the cornflour and sugar in a saucepan and stir in the boiling water. Bring to the boil and simmer, stirring frequently, for 15 minutes. Stir in the remaining sauce ingredients and keep warm.

Cut the pudding into oblongs and serve with the sauce.

Variation: For orange sauce, use only 200 ml/ ⅓ pint water and 1 tablespoon lemon juice. Substitute orange for lemon rind and add 5 tablespoons orange juice.

Coconut Slices

Makes 16

225 g/8 oz self-raising
    flour
pinch of salt
100 g/4 oz margarine
75 g/3 oz sugar
1 egg, beaten
2 tablespoons red jam
100 g/4 oz desiccated
    coconut
1 tablespoon milk

Sift the flour and salt into a bowl. Rub in the margarine, then mix in 25 g/1 oz of the sugar. Bind with half the egg and a little water to a stiff paste. Roll out the paste and use to line a 23 × 30 cm/9 × 12 inch Swiss roll tin. Spread over the jam.

Mix together the coconut, milk and remaining sugar and spread on top of the jam. Press the mixture down lightly. Bake in a preheated moderate oven (180°C/350°F, Gas Mark 4) for 20 to 30 minutes. Cool, then cut into slices to serve.

Raspberry Meringue

Serves 4

4 large eggs, separated
225 g/8 oz caster sugar
225 g/8 oz plain
  chocolate, broken into
  pieces
150 ml/¼ pint double
  cream
2 tablespoons milk
2 tablespoons sugar
450 g/1 lb fresh or frozen
  and thawed raspberries

Cover three baking sheets with foil and lightly oil them. Mark a 20 cm/8 inch circle on each.

Whisk the egg whites until stiff. Add 100 g/ 4 oz of the sugar and continue whisking until stiff. Fold in a further 100 g/4 oz sugar.

Spread or pipe the meringue into rounds on the circles marked on the baking sheets. Dry out in a cool oven (140°C/275°F, Gas Mark 1) for about 4 hours. Cool, then remove carefully from the foil.

Melt the chocolate gently in a heatproof basin over a pan of hot water. Whip the cream and milk together until thick, then stir in the remaining 2 tablespoons sugar.

Place one meringue round on a flat plate and spread with half the chocolate. Cover with one-third of the cream and raspberries. Place another meringue round on top and spread with the remaining chocolate. Add another third of the cream and raspberries. Put the third meringue round on top and decorate with the remaining cream and raspberries.

Variation: Use drained canned mandarin oranges instead of raspberries.

Summer Soufflé

Serves 4

225 g/8 oz sugar
150 ml/¼ pint water
5 egg whites
300 ml/½ pint mixed
  raspberry and
  strawberry purée
  (made by sieving the
  fruit)
300 ml/½ pint double
  cream
flaked toasted almonds to
  decorate

Dissolve the sugar in the water in a saucepan, then bring to the boil. Boil until a sugar thermometer registers 115°C/240°F.

Whisk the egg whites until stiff. Very gradually beat in the sugar syrup and continue beating until the mixture is cool. Stir in the fruit purée. Whip the cream until thick and fold in.

Turn into an 18 to 20 cm/7 to 8 inch diameter soufflé dish and chill for 2 to 3 hours. Sprinkle with flaked almonds just before serving.

215

Apple Amber

Serves 4-6

*150 g/5 oz shortcrust
pastry
750 g/1½ lb cooking
apples, peeled, cored
and sliced
grated rind and juice of 1
orange
sugar, golden syrup or
honey to sweeten
25 g/1 oz margarine
2 eggs, separated
50 g/2oz caster sugar
caster sugar for
sprinkling
glacé cherries or orange
slices to decorate*

Roll out the dough and use to line a shallow 20 cm/8 inch pie dish. Bake blind in a preheated moderately hot oven (190°C/375°F, Gas Mark 5) for 20 minutes or until set and lightly browned.

Meanwhile, stew the apples with the orange juice and a little water to prevent sticking. Sweeten to taste with sugar, syrup or honey, then add the margarine and egg yolks and mix well. Turn the mixture into the pastry case and cool.

Whisk the egg whites until stiff, then fold in the caster sugar. Spread or pipe the meringue over the apple filling and dredge with caster sugar.

Bake in a moderate oven (180°C/350°F, Gas Mark 4) for 15 to 20 minutes or until the meringue is lightly browned and crisp. Decorate with glacé cherries or orange slices before serving.

Raspberry Soufflé

Serves 4

*1 × 450 g/1 lb jar, or
400 g/14 oz canned,
raspberries
15 g/½ oz gelatine
1 small can evaporated
milk, chilled
caster sugar to taste
food colouring (optional)
1 egg white
whipped cream, fruit,
crystallized flowers,
etc., to decorate*

Tie a paper collar around an 18 cm/7 inch soufflé dish so that it stands about 5 cm/2 inches above the rim.

Drain the raspberries, reserving the syrup. Make the syrup up to 300 ml/½ pint with water. Dissolve the gelatine in this liquid and allow to cool.

Sieve the fruit to a purée. Whip the milk until it is stiff. Gradually beat in the jelly mixture, then fold in the raspberry purée. Sweeten to taste and add food colouring if you like. Whisk the egg white until stiff and fold into the raspberry mixture. Turn into the soufflé dish.

Chill until set. Carefully remove the paper collar and decorate before serving.

Westmorland Currant ¡Pasty
Serves 4

Pastry
225 g/8 oz flour
¼ teaspoon salt
1 teaspoon caster sugar
50 g/2 oz butter
50 g/2 oz lard
caster sugar for
* sprinkling*

Filling
50 g/2 oz butter
175 g/6 oz currants
½ teaspoon ground
* allspice*
¼ teaspoon ground
* cinnamon*
good pinch of ground
* mace*
grated rind of ½ lemon
50 g/2 oz soft brown
* sugar*
1 tablespoon rum

To make the pastry, sift the flour, salt and sugar into a bowl. Rub in the fat (not too much as the finished pastry should be rather flaky) and bind to a dough with cold water. Divide the dough in half and roll out each portion into a square. Place one square on a greased baking sheet.

For the filling, melt the butter in a saucepan and stir in the currants, spices, lemon rind and sugar. Cook gently until the sugar has dissolved, then remove from the heat and cool slightly.

Stir the rum into the filling and spread it evenly over the square of dough on the baking sheet, leaving a 1 cm/½ inch margin around the edges. Brush the margin with water and place the other dough square on top. Press the edges together to seal and prick all over with a fork.

Bake in a preheated hot oven (220 °C/425 F, Gas Mark 7) for 15 minutes or until set, then reduce the heat to moderately hot (180 °C/375 F, Gas Mark 5) and continue baking for 20 minutes or until golden brown. Dredge thickly with caster sugar and allow to cool. Serve in good-sized squares.

Feast Plum Pudding
Serves 6–8

1 × 450 g/1 lb loaf of
* bread*
225 g/8 oz raisins
225 g/8 oz currants
50 g/2 oz candied lemon
* peel*
100 g/4 oz sugar
100 g/4 oz shredded suet
1 nutmeg, grated
2 eggs, beaten

Soak the bread in water to cover overnight. The next day, drain it, pressing out excess moisture. Mix well with the remaining ingredients. Turn into a greased deep baking dish or 1 kg/2 lb loaf tin and cover. Bake in a preheated very cool oven (120ºC/250°F, Gas Mark ½) for 4 hours, or send to a bakehouse oven and bake all night.
Note: This was usually eaten cold at village feasts.

Gâteau St. Honoré à la Crème

Serves 4–6

*175 g/6 oz shortcrust
  pastry
apricot jam
65 g/2½ oz choux pastry
whipped cream*

Filling
*225 g/8 oz canned
  raspberries or
  strawberries
1 teaspoon gelatine
1 tablespoon sugar*

Roll out the dough and use to line an 18 cm/ 7 inch flan tin. Bake blind in a preheated moderately hot oven (190°C/375°F, Gas Mark 5) for 20 minutes or until set and lightly browned. Cool, then spread the bottom with apricot jam.

Pipe the choux pastry onto a greased baking sheet in 12 to 16 small buns. Bake in a preheated moderately hot oven (200°C/400°F, Gas Mark 6) for 25 to 30 minutes or until puffed up and golden brown. Slit open and cool. When cool, fill with whipped cream. Arrange the buns around the edge of the pastry case.

For the filling, drain the fruit, reserving the syrup. Make the syrup up to 150 ml/¼ pint with water if necessary. Dissolve the gelatine in this mixture, then add the sugar. Cool until on the point of setting, then carefully fold in the fruit. Spoon into the centre of the gâteau. When set, decorate with more whipped cream.

Jamaica Rum Pie

Serves 4

Crust
*100 g/4 oz digestive
  biscuits, crushed
¼ teaspoon ground
  cinnamon
50 g/2 oz butter, melted*

Filling
*1 teaspoon gelatine
2 tablespoons water
3 egg yolks
150 g/5 oz caster sugar
3 tablespoons rum
200 ml/⅓ pint double
  cream, whipped
grated chocolate to
  decorate*

Mix together the ingredients for the crust and press evenly over the bottom and sides of an 18 cm/7 inch round shallow pie dish. Bake in a preheated cool oven (150°C/300°F, Gas Mark 2) for 10 to 15 minutes. Alternatively, do not bake the crust; just chill it until set.

For the filling, dissolve the gelatine in the water. Beat the egg yolks and sugar together, then mix in the rum and gelatine. Fold in the cream. Spoon into the crust and chill for 2 to 3 hours or until set. Decorate with grated chocolate before serving.

Pineapple Upside-down Pudding
Serves 4

*2 tablespoons golden
syrup
225 g/8 oz canned
pineapple rings
few glacé cherries
100 g/4 oz butter or
margarine
50 g/2 oz sugar
2 eggs, beaten
100 g/4 oz self-raising
flour, sifted
1 teaspoon arrowroot*

Spread the syrup over the bottom of a greased 18 cm/7 inch baking dish. Drain the pineapple, reserving the syrup, and arrange on the bottom. Put a cherry in the centre of each pineapple ring.

Cream together the fat and sugar. Beat in the eggs, then fold in the flour. Pour this mixture over the pineapple in the dish. Bake in a preheated moderate oven (180 C/350 F, Gas Mark 4) for 30 to 40 minutes.

Just before the pudding is ready, make the sauce. Dissolve the arrowroot in a little of the reserved pineapple syrup, then add to the rest of the syrup in a saucepan. Bring to the boil, stirring, and simmer until clear and thickened.

Turn out the pudding upside-down onto a dish and serve with the sauce.

Brown Bread Ice Cream
Serves 6

*100 g/4 oz brown bread,
crust removed
450 ml/¾ pint double
cream
100 g/4 oz icing sugar,
sifted
½ teaspoon vanilla essence
50 g/2 oz granulated
sugar
3 tablespoons water*

Put the bread slices on a baking sheet and dry out in a preheated very cool oven (120 C/250 F, Gas Mark ½) for about 1 hour or until crisp. Make into fine crumbs with a blender, or crush with a rolling pin.

Whip the cream until thick. Fold in the icing sugar and vanilla essence and turn into a rigid container or freezing tray. Freeze for 1 hour or until the edges have begun to set.

Meanwhile, dissolve the granulated sugar in the water in a saucepan. Bring to the boil and boil for 2 minutes without stirring. Remove from the heat. Stir in the breadcrumbs and leave to cool.

Turn the semi-frozen ice cream into a bowl and beat until smooth. Mix in the breadcrumb mixture. Return to the freezing container and freeze until solid.

Mansfield Gooseberry Pie

Serves 6

pastry made with 450 g/
1 lb flour and 225 g/8 oz
home-rendered lard
1 kg/2 lb gooseberries,
trimmed
2 tablespoons demerara
sugar
2 teaspoons butter
little redcurrant jelly,
melted

Glaze
1 tablespoon sugar
1 tablespoon water

Roll out two-thirds of the dough, not too thinly, and use to line a 18 cm/7 inch round cake tin or pork pie ring. Fill with the gooseberries and sprinkle with the demerara sugar. Dot with the butter.

Roll out the rest of the dough to make a lid. Place on top of the pie and press together the dampened edges to seal. Decorate the top with the dough trimmings.

Bake in a preheated hot oven (220°C/425°F, Gas Mark 7) for 15 minutes, then reduce the temperature to moderate (180 C/350°F, Gas Mark 4) and bake for a further 30 minutes.

About 10 minutes before the pie has finished baking, mix together the sugar and water for the glaze and brush over the pie.

Make a hole in the top of the pie and pour in a little melted redcurrant jelly. Leave to cool in the tin.

Note: This pie was probably made originally as the Warden pies mentioned by Shakespeare. In the 1920's, the baker's shops were stacked with delicious pies at the time of Mansfield Fair, which was held in the Market Place in July.

Apple Horseshoe

Serves 6

225 g/8 oz shortcrust or
flaky pastry
2 to 3 apples, peeled,
cored and thinly sliced
50 g/2 oz butter or
margarine
25 g/1 oz browned
breadcrumbs
100 g/4 oz brown sugar
50 g/2 oz currants
beaten egg to glaze
chopped almonds to
decorate

Roll out the dough to a thin oblong or square. Cover with a layer of apples. Melt the fat in a saucepan and stir in the breadcrumbs, sugar and currants. Spread this mixture over the apples.

Roll up the dough like a Swiss roll and curve into a horseshoe. Place on a greased baking sheet and brush with beaten egg. Sprinkle with almonds. Bake in a preheated moderately hot oven (200°C/400°F, Gas Mark 6) for 35 to 40 minutes or until the pastry is nicely browned. Lower the heat if it seems to be browning too quickly.

Serve hot or cold, in thick slices.

Sussex Pond Pudding
Serves 4–6

450 g/1 lb flour
1 teaspoon salt
225 g/8 oz shredded suet
100 g/4 oz mixed dried
*   fruit*
½ teaspoon mixed spice
350 g/12 oz brown sugar
*   pieces*
275 g/10 oz butter

Sift the flour and salt into a bowl. Mix in the suet, then bind to a dough with cold water. Divide the dough into two portions, one about one-third larger than the other. Take about one-third from the larger portion and reserve for the lid. With the remainder of the larger portion, line a greased 1.2 litre/2 pint pudding basin.

Roll out the smaller portion of dough to a strip as wide as the depth of the basin. Sprinkle this with the fruit, mixed spice and 100 g/4 oz of the sugar. Dot with 50 g/2 oz of the butter. Roll up the strip like a Swiss roll and stand upright in the centre of the lined basin.

Sprinkle the remaining sugar into the basin around the fruit roll, then add the remaining butter, cut into small pieces. Use the reserved piece of dough to make a lid and press the edges together to seal.

Steam or boil for 2 hours. Turn out and serve with whipped cream.

Tarte Viennoise
Serves 4

100 g/4 oz flaky pastry
150 g/6 oz cream cheese,
*   sieved, or soured cream*
1 egg, separated
50 g/2 oz caster sugar
2 tablespoons rum or
*   brandy*
1 egg white
caster sugar for
*   sprinkling*

To Decorate
fresh or canned apricot
*   halves*
jam glaze
whipped cream

Roll out the dough and use to line an 18 cm/7 inch flan tin.

Mix together the cream cheese or soured cream, egg yolk, sugar and rum or brandy. (If very stiff – if using cream cheese – add a little cream.) Beat the 2 egg whites until stiff and fold into the creamed mixture. Spoon into the flan case and smooth the top. Sprinkle with a little caster sugar.

Bake in a preheated moderately hot oven (200 C/400 F, Gas Mark 6) for 30 minutes. Cool.

When cool, place apricot halves over the filling and spread with jam glaze. Decorate with whipped cream. Serve warm or cold.

Chocolate Fudge Pudding

Serves 8–10

250 g/9 oz flour
1 teaspoon baking
powder
50 g/2 oz cornflour
25 g/1 oz cocoa powder
175 g/6 oz caster sugar
175 g/6 oz margarine
3 eggs, beaten
100 ml/3 fl oz milk
Sauce
45 g/1¾ oz cocoa powder
175 g/6 oz granulated
sugar
600 ml/1 pint water

Sift the flour, baking powder, cornflour, cocoa and sugar into a bowl. Rub in the margarine, then mix in the eggs and milk. Beat well. Turn into a deep 18 cm/7 inch baking tin.

For the sauce, mix the cocoa and sugar with a little of the water, then add to the rest of the water in a saucepan. Bring to the boil, stirring. Simmer for 5 minutes. Remove from the heat and cool slightly, then pour over the mixture in the tin.

Bake in a preheated moderately hot oven (190°C/375°F, Gas Mark 5) for about 40 minutes. Turn out upside-down onto a dish to serve.

George I Christmas Pudding

Makes 3 puddings

450 g/1 lb flour
1 teaspoon salt
1 heaped teaspoon mixed
spice
½ nutmeg, grated
675 g/1½ lb finely grated
suet
450 g/1 lb sugar
450 g/1 lb browned fresh
breadcrumbs
450 g/1 lb prunes, halved
and stoned
450 g/1 lb chopped mixed
peel
450 g/1 lb small raisins
450 g/1 lb sultanas
450 g/1 lb currants
450 g/1 lb eggs, weighed
in their shells
300 ml/½ pint milk
juice of 1 lemon
100 ml/3 fl oz brandy

Sift the flour, salt and spice into a bowl. Mix in the suet, sugar and breadcrumbs, then add the dried fruit. Beat together the eggs, milk, lemon juice and brandy and add to the bowl. Mix well. Spoon into three greased 600 ml/1 pint pudding basins.

Boil for 8 hours. When ready to serve, boil again for 2 hours. Serve with rum butter.

Conversation Tarts
Makes 20

50 g/2 oz butter
50 g/2 oz sugar
1 egg
2 egg yolks
50 g/2 oz ground
  almonds
15 g/½ oz flour
few drops of almond
  essence
225 g/8 oz puff pastry
beaten egg to glaze
50 g/2 oz thin royal icing
flaked almonds to
  decorate

Cream together the butter and sugar. Gradually beat in the egg and egg yolks, then add the ground almonds, flour and almond essence and mix well.

Roll out three-quarters of the dough thinly and use to line boat-shaped tins or small patty tins. Brush with beaten egg and fill with the almond mixture. Roll out the remaining dough thinly and use to cover the tins. Spread the tops with royal icing and sprinkle with almonds.

Bake in a preheated moderately hot oven (200°C/400°F, Gas Mark 6) for 10 minutes, then reduce the heat to moderate (180°C/350°F, Gas Mark 4) and bake for a further 10 minutes.

Bananas Poached in Cider
Serves 4

300 ml/½ pint cider
25 g/1 oz brown sugar
2 tablespoons lemon juice
4 large bananas, halved
  lengthways
double cream and
  chopped nuts to
  decorate

Put the cider, sugar and lemon juice in a wide pan and bring to the boil, stirring to dissolve the sugar. Boil for 5 minutes. Add the bananas, cover and simmer gently for 5 minutes, turning once.

Turn the bananas and cider syrup into a serving dish. Cool, then chill. Serve topped with cream and nuts.

Tipsy Strawberries
Serves 4

450 g/1 lb strawberries,
  hulled
2 tablespoons brandy
3 egg whites
175 g/6 oz caster sugar

Put the strawberries in an ovenproof serving dish. Sprinkle over the brandy. Whisk the egg whites until stiff. Whisk in half the sugar, then fold in the remainder. Pile the meringue onto the strawberries.

Bake in a preheated moderately hot oven (200°C/400°F, Gas Mark 6) for 15 minutes.

Serve hot or cold with cream.

River's Plum Pudding with Audley End Sauce   *Serves 4–5*

*1 egg and its weight in
butter, sugar and flour*
*225 g/8 oz early River's
plums, halved and
stoned*
soft brown sugar
Sauce
50 g/2 oz cornflour
600 ml/1 pint milk
50 g/2 oz butter
40 g/1½ oz sugar
1 egg, beaten
*5 tablespoons cream or
top of milk*
*1 tablespoon soft brown
sugar*

Cream together the butter and sugar. Beat in the egg, then fold in the sifted flour. Spread half the mixture on the bottom of a greased small glass pie dish. Cover with the plum halves, cut sides down, and sprinkle with brown sugar. Spread over the remainder of the creamed mixture.

Bake in a preheated moderate oven (180 C/350°F, Gas Mark 4) for 30 to 45 minutes or until golden brown and firm.

Meanwhile, make the sauce. Dissolve the cornflour in a little of the milk. Put the rest of the milk in a saucepan and bring to the boil. Add the cornflour mixture, butter and sugar and simmer, stirring, for 4 to 5 minutes. Beat the egg with the cream or top of milk, and gradually stir into the sauce. Whisk well, then pour into a buttered flameproof serving dish. Sprinkle over the brown sugar and caramelize under a hot grill. Serve hot or cold, with the pudding.

Mince Pies   *Makes 12*

Pastry
100 g/4 oz flour
*50 g/2 oz mixed butter
and lard*
25 g/1 oz caster sugar
1 egg yolk
Filling
175 g/6 oz mincemeat
100 g/4 oz butter
25 g/1 oz caster sugar
1 egg yolk
100 g/4 oz flour, sifted
*angelica and glacé
cherries to decorate
(optional)*

For the pastry, sift the flour into a bowl and rub in the fat. Stir in the sugar, then bind to a dough with the egg yolk and a little cold water. Roll out the dough and use to line 12 patty tins.

Divide the mincemeat between the tins. Cream together the butter and sugar. Beat in the egg yolk, then mix in the flour. Put the mixture into a piping bag fitted with a No. 2 star tube and pipe a ring on each pie, leaving a small hole in the centre. Decorate with a holly leaf cut from angelica and holly berries from glacé cherries, if you like.

Bake in a preheated moderately hot oven (200°C/400°F, Gas Mark 6) for 25 minutes or until golden brown.

Coffee Hedgehog
Serves 4

100 g/4 oz butter or margarine
100 g/4 oz caster sugar
100 g/4 oz fresh white breadcrumbs
4 tablespoons black coffee
approx. 300 ml/½ pint double cream
1 tablespoon chopped almonds, toasted

Cream together the fat and sugar. Mix the breadcrumbs and coffee and add to the creamed mixture. Beat well, then press into a greased 600 ml/1 pint basin. Leave overnight.

The next day, turn out onto a serving plate. Whip the cream and use to cover the cake. Decorate with the almonds.

Syllabub
Serves 2–3

150 ml/¼ pint mixed orange juice and sherry
caster sugar to taste
300 ml/½ pint double cream
1 egg white

Sweeten the orange juice and sherry to taste. Add the cream and whip until fluffy. Whisk the egg white until stiff and fold in. Serve in glasses.

Macaroon Pineapple Cream
Serves 4–6

2 eggs, separated
300 ml/½ pint milk
100 g/4 oz caster sugar
2 teaspoons gelatine
100 ml/3 fl oz water
¼ teaspoon vanilla essence
150 ml/¼ pint double cream

To Decorate
small macaroons
fresh, canned or crystallized pineapple
chopped nuts

Put the egg yolks, milk and sugar in a heavy-based saucepan and cook gently, stirring, until the custard is thick. Remove from the heat.

Dissolve the gelatine in the water. Add to the custard with the vanilla essence and allow to cool but not set.

Whip the cream until thick and fold into the custard mixture. Whisk the egg whites until stiff and fold in.

Decorate the bottom of a serving dish with macaroons, pineapple and nuts and spoon in the cream. Decorate the top.

Fruit Flummery

Serves 5–6

900 ml/1½ pints milk
pinch of salt
40 g/1½ oz semolina
2 large eggs, separated
75 g/3 oz caster sugar
125 g/5 oz apple purée
little grated lemon rind
or juice

Warm the milk with the salt in a saucepan. Sprinkle over the semolina and stir well. Cream the egg yolks and sugar together and add to the pan. Bring to the boil, stirring well, and simmer gently for 10 minutes.

Remove from the heat and mix in the apple purée and lemon rind or juice. Whisk the egg whites until stiff and fold in the semolina mixture. Turn into individual glasses and chill until set.

Apple Cream

Serves 4

50 g/2 oz granulated
sugar
150 ml/¼ pint water
1 strip of lemon rind
450 g/1 lb dessert apples,
peeled, cored and
chopped
15 g/½ oz cornflour
2 eggs, separated
2 tablespoons cream
juice of ½ lemon
7 sponge fingers, halved
crossways
100 g/4 oz caster sugar
2 red dessert apples,
cored and sliced, to
decorate

Put the granulated sugar, water and lemon rind in a saucepan and heat, stirring to dissolve the sugar. Add the apples and poach for 10 minutes. Drain the apples, reserving 150 ml/¼ pint of the syrup.

Dissolve the cornflour in a little of the syrup. Heat the rest of the syrup and stir in the cornflour. Simmer, stirring, until thickened. Stir in the egg yolks, cream and lemon juice.

Line a 600 ml/1 pint soufflé dish with the sponge fingers, cut sides against the bottom. Fill the centre with alternate layers of apples and the cream mixture.

Whisk the egg whites until stiff and fold in the caster sugar. Pipe onto the dish, making sure the filling is covered. Bake in a preheated very cool oven (120°C/250°F, Gas Mark ½) for 50 minutes or until the meringue is firm.

Fit the red apple slices between the sponge fingers and cool.

Manchester Tart

Serves 4–6

175 g/6 oz flaky pastry
raspberry or strawberry
*   jam*
pared rind of 1 lemon
300 ml/½ pint milk
50 g/2 oz fresh
*   breadcrumbs*
50 g/2 oz butter
2 eggs, separated
75 g/3 oz caster sugar
1 tablespoon brandy
caster sugar for dredging

Roll out the dough and use to line a 20 cm/ 8 inch pie dish. Spread the bottom with jam.

Put the lemon rind and milk in a saucepan and bring to the boil. Remove from the heat and strain over the breadcrumbs. Leave to stand for 5 minutes, then beat in the butter, egg yolks, 25 g/1 oz of the sugar and the brandy. Pour into the pastry case. Bake in a preheated moderately hot oven (190°C/375°F, Gas Mark 5) for 45 minutes.

Whisk the egg whites until stiff and fold in the remaining sugar. Spread the meringue over the top of the filling and dredge with sugar. Bake for a further 15 minutes or until the meringue is browned. Serve cold with cream.

Rum Butter

Serves 4–6

450 g/1 lb butter, melted
750 g/1½ lb brown sugar
2 teaspoons grated
*   nutmeg*
100 ml/3 fl oz rum

Mix together the butter, sugar and nutmeg, then add the rum. Beat until the mixture starts to thicken. Pour into a bowl and leave to set.

Gooseberry Mould

Serves 4–5

450 g/1 lb gooseberries
100 g/4 oz caster sugar
2 eggs, separated
300 ml/½ pint milk
15 g/½ oz gelatine
green food colouring
whipped cream to
*   decorate*

Stew the gooseberries with the sugar and a very little water to prevent sticking. Sieve the gooseberry mixture to make a purée.

Put the egg yolks, milk and gelatine in a heavy-based saucepan and cook gently, stirring, until thick. Remove from the heat and cool, then mix in the gooseberry purée and a little food colouring. Whisk the egg whites until stiff and fold in the gooseberry mixture.

Spoon into a dampened mould and chill until set. Turn out to serve, decorated with whipped cream. Accompany with shortbread fingers.

Pumpkin Pie
Serves 4–6

*175 g/6 oz shortcrust
pastry
450 g/1 lb prepared
pumpkin, cooked
2 eggs, separated
5 tablespoons caster
sugar
150 ml/¼ pint milk
pinch of salt
¼ teaspoon ground ginger
¼ teaspoon grated nutmeg*

Roll out the dough and use to line an 18 cm/ 7 inch flan tin.

Sieve the cooked pumpkin to make 300 ml/ ½ pint purée. Mix the purée with the egg yolks and 3 tablespoons of the sugar, then beat in the milk, salt and spices. Turn into the pastry case.

Bake in a preheated moderately hot oven (200°C/400°F, Gas Mark 6) for 40 minutes or until the filling is set and golden brown.

Whisk the egg whites until stiff. Fold in the remaining 2 tablespoons sugar and spread the meringue over the top of the filling. Return to the oven, turn off the oven and leave to brown the meringue lightly.

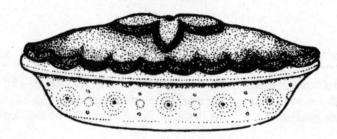

Border Tart
Serves 4–6

*150 g/6 oz shortcrust
pastry
50 g/2 oz margarine
50 g/2 oz sugar
1 egg, beaten
175 g/6 oz sultanas
25 g/1 oz walnuts,
chopped
milk or beaten egg to
glaze
glacé icing to decorate*

Roll out the dough and use to line an 18 cm/7 inch sandwich tin.

Cream together the margarine and sugar, then beat in the egg. Add the sultanas and walnuts and mix well. Spoon into the pastry case and spread out. Roll out the dough trimmings and cut into strips. Use these to decorate the top of the tart, then fold over the edge of the dough lining the tin, all round on top of the fruit. Brush the dough with milk or beaten egg.

Bake in a preheated moderate oven (180°C/350°F, Gas Mark 4) for 20 minutes. Cool, then decorate between the strips of pastry with water icing.

Orange and Lemon Ice Cream
Serves 6–8

6 egg yolks
225 g/8 oz caster sugar
finely grated rind and
    juice of 2 small
    oranges
finely grated rind and
    juice of 1 lemon
300 ml/½ pint double
    cream
crystallized or fresh fruit
    and whipped cream to
    decorate

Put the egg yolks and sugar in a heatproof basin over a pan of hot water and whisk until the mixture is light, creamy and thick. Gradually whisk in the fruit rinds and juices. Remove from the heat. Cool.

Whip the cream until thick and fold into the whisked mixture. Turn into a 1.2 litre/2 pint basin, cover and freeze until hard.

To serve, turn out onto a serving plate and decorate with crystallized or fresh pieces of orange and lemon and whipped cream. Leave to thaw at room temperature for 5 minutes before serving.

Note: If you prefer, spoon or scoop the ice cream from the basin instead of turning it out.

Chocolate Mousse
Serves 4

100 g/4 oz plain
    chocolate, broken into
    pieces
4 eggs, separated
whipped cream, flaked
    chocolate or toasted
    almonds to decorate

Melt the chocolate gently in a heatproof basin over a pan of hot water. Remove from the heat and stir in the egg yolks. Cool. Whisk the egg whites until stiff and fold in the chocolate mixture.

Turn into a serving dish or individual dishes and chill until set. Decorate before serving.

Kentish Fruit Salad
Serves 8

225 g/8 oz sugar
600 ml/1 pint water
150 g/5 oz dessert apples,
    peeled and sliced
150 g/5 oz William
    pears, peeled and sliced
100 g/4 oz Malling
    Promise raspberries
100 g/4 oz strawberries
100 g/4 oz Kentish red
    cherries, stoned
1 tablespoon lemon juice

Dissolve the sugar in the water in a saucepan. Add the apples and pears and cook gently until tender. Transfer the fruit to a glass bowl with a slotted spoon.

Add the raspberries and strawberries to the pan and poach gently. Transfer to the bowl.

Add the cherries to the pan and poach gently, then tip into the bowl. Stir in the lemon juice and cool. Serve cold with cream.

Quick Orange Mousse
Serves 4

300 g/11 oz canned mandarin oranges
15 g/½ oz gelatine
2 eggs, separated
50 g/2 oz caster sugar

Drain the oranges, reserving the syrup. Make the syrup up to 300 ml/½ pint with water. Dissolve the gelatine in this liquid and cool.

Divide the orange segments between four individual serving dishes, reserving a few segments for decoration.

Mix together the egg yolks and sugar and stir in the gelatine mixture. Whisk the egg whites until stiff and fold in the gelatine mixture. Pour into the dishes and chill until set. Decorate with the reserved orange segments before serving.

Strawberry Ring
Serves 6

100 g/4 oz butter
50 g/2 oz demerara sugar
100 g/4 oz flour, sifted
50 g/2 oz walnuts, chopped
15 g/½ oz gelatine
4 tablespoons water
450 g/1 lb strawberries, hulled and thickly sliced
1 teaspoon lemon juice
175 g/6 oz caster sugar
300 ml/½ pint double cream, whipped

To Decorate
150 ml/¼ pint double cream, whipped
1 large strawberry, sliced

Rub together the butter, demerara sugar, flour and walnuts as if making pastry. Scatter the mixture over the bottom of a shallow baking tin. Bake in a preheated moderately hot oven (200°C/400°F, Gas Mark 6) for 10 to 15 minutes or until golden brown. Cool, then crumble into a bowl.

Dissolve the gelatine in the water. Put one-quarter of the strawberries into a saucepan with the lemon juice and sugar and mash well. Bring to the boil, then remove from the heat and stir in the gelatine. Strain a little of this mixture into a 1.5 litre/2½ pint ring mould, to coat the bottom. Chill until set. Let the remainder of the strawberry jelly cool but not set.

Fold the remaining strawberry slices into the whipped cream. When the jelly is on the point of setting, fold in the strawberries and cream. Immediately make alternate layers of the strawberry mixture and the crumbs in the ring mould, starting with strawberry and ending with crumbs. Chill until set.

Turn the ring out of the mould onto a serving platter. Pipe the whipped cream for the decoration around the base of the ring and add the strawberry slices.

Butterscotch Pie

Serves 6

175 g/6 oz shortcrust pastry
225 g/8 oz demerara sugar
50 g/2 oz butter
600 ml/1 pint milk
2 eggs, separated
1 tablespoon cornflour
100 g/4 oz caster sugar

Roll out the dough and use to line an 18 cm/ 7 inch flan tin. Bake blind in a preheated moderately hot oven (190°C/375°F, Gas Mark 5) for 20 minutes or until the pastry is golden brown and set. Cool.

Put the demerara sugar and butter in a saucepan and heat gently, stirring, until the sugar and butter have melted. Remove from the heat.

Warm the milk in another saucepan. Mix together the egg yolks and cornflour and add to the milk. Cook gently, stirring, until thick. Remove from the heat and mix in the sugar and butter mixture. Pour into the pastry case.

Whisk the egg whites until stiff and fold in the caster sugar. Spread over the filling.

Bake in a preheated moderately hot oven (180°C/375°F, Gas Mark 5) for 35 minutes or until lightly browned on top.

Pwdin Watcyn Wynne

Serves 4–6

275 g/10 oz fresh breadcrumbs
225 g/8 oz chopped suet
75 g/3 oz sugar
3 eggs, beaten
pinch of salt
grated rind and juice of 2 lemons

Sauce
75 g/3 oz butter
75 g/3 oz brown sugar
grated rind of ½ lemon
pinch of grated nutmeg
100 ml/3 fl oz sherry or Madeira

Mix all the ingredients for the pudding together and put into a basin. Cover and boil for 3 hours.

Just before the pudding is ready, make the sauce. Melt the butter in a saucepan. Add the sugar, lemon rind, nutmeg and sherry or Madeira and heat through gently. Do not boil.

Turn out the pudding and serve with the sauce.

Note: Watcyn Wynne was a noted preacher and poet from Carmarthenshire.

Banana Whip
Serves 5–6

4 bananas
1 tablespoon caster sugar
grated rind and juice of 1
   lemon
75 g/3 oz porridge oats
300 ml/½ pint single
   cream
grated chocolate to
   decorate

Mash the bananas, then add the sugar, lemon rind and juice, oats and cream and mix well. Spoon into a serving dish and decorate.

Grapefruit Sorbet
Serves 6

100 g/4 oz caster sugar
250 ml/8 fl oz water
175 ml/6 fl oz canned
   frozen concentrated
   grapefruit juice,
   thawed
finely grated rind and
   juice of 1 large
   grapefruit
2 egg whites
mint sprigs to decorate

Dissolve the sugar in the water in a saucepan, then bring to the boil. Boil for 1 minute, then cool. Stir in the concentrated grapefruit juice and fresh grapefruit rind and juice. Pour into a rigid container or freezer tray and freeze until mushy.

Turn the grapefruit mixture into a bowl and beat until smooth. Whisk the egg whites until stiff and fold into the grapefruit mixture. Return to the container or freezer tray and cover. Freeze until solid.

Serve the sorbet in glasses or cleaned out halved grapefruit shells, decorated with mint.

Old-fashioned Treacle Tart
Serves 4–6

5 to 6 tablespoons golden
   syrup
50 g/2 oz fresh white
   breadcrumbs
finely grated rind of ½ to
   1 lemon
1 teaspoon lemon juice
150 g/5 oz rich shortcrust
   pastry

Put the syrup into a saucepan with the breadcrumbs, lemon rind and juice and heat gently until just melted. Cool.

Roll out the dough and use to line a 20 cm/ 8 inch pie plate. Pour in the syrup mixture. Roll out the dough trimmings and cut into long narrow strips. Lay these in a lattice pattern over the filling.

Bake in a preheated moderately hot oven (200°C/400°F, Gas Mark 6) for 25 to 30 minutes or until the pastry is lightly browned. Serve hot or cold.

Burchett's Green Pudding   *Serves 6*

100 g/4 oz butter
100 g/4 oz caster sugar
2 egg yolks
3 tablespoons strong
  black coffee
6 to 8 trifle sponge cakes,
  sliced thinly
2 tablespoons brandy or
  sherry (optional)
300 ml/½ pint thin custard
whipped cream and
  blanched almonds to
  decorate

Cream together the butter and sugar, then beat in the egg yolks. Gradually beat in the coffee. Spread the slices of sponge cake with the coffee mixture and layer in a small basin. Cover and chill for at least 24 hours.

Turn out the cake into a serving bowl and sprinkle with the brandy or sherry, if using. Cover with the custard, then decorate with whipped cream and almonds.

Baked Bananas   *Serves 4*

4 large or 6 medium
  bananas, halved
  lengthways
25 g/1 oz butter
50 g/2 oz brown sugar
grated rind and juice of 1
  orange
grated rind and juice of 1
  lemon
2 to 3 tablespoons rum
  (optional)

Arrange the bananas in a buttered baking dish. Dot with the butter and sprinkle with the sugar and orange and lemon rinds. Mix together the fruit juices and rum, if using, and pour over the top. Bake in a preheated moderate oven (160°C/325°F, Gas Mark 3) for 30 minutes. Serve hot or cold.

Caramel Soufflé
Serves 3–4

2 tablespoons golden
  syrup
20 g/¾ oz gelatine
300 ml/½ pint water
3 egg whites
Sauce
1 egg yolk
1 tablespoon golden syrup
150 ml/¼ pint cream

Heat the syrup gently until golden brown. Dissolve the gelatine in the water and add to the syrup gradually, stirring to prevent lumps forming. Cool until beginning to set.

Whisk the egg whites until stiff and fold in the syrup mixture. Spoon into a lightly oiled dish or mould. Chill until set.

To make the sauce, mix together the egg yolk and syrup, then stir in the cream.

Turn out the soufflé onto a serving dish and pour over the sauce.

Gooseberry Swansdown
Serves 6

450 g/1 lb gooseberries,
  cooked
1 tablespoon lemon juice
1 tablespoon gelatine
150 ml/¼ pint hot water
2 eggs, separated
100 g/4 oz sugar
food colouring (optional)
whipped cream, etc., to
  decorate

Sieve the gooseberries to a purée and stir in the lemon juice. Dissolve the gelatine in the water and add to the gooseberry purée. Beat the egg yolks with half the sugar and add to the gooseberry mixture. Whisk the egg whites with the remaining sugar until stiff and fold in the gooseberry mixture. If you like, add a little food colouring.

Turn into a serving dish and chill until set. Decorate before serving.

Chocolate Custard Pots
Serves 4–6

75 g/3 oz plain chocolate,
  broken into pieces
25 g/1 oz butter
2 eggs, separated
1 egg yolk
2 tablespoons sweet
  sherry or white wine
whipped cream and
  chopped pistachio nuts
  to decorate

Melt the chocolate gently with the butter in a heatproof basin placed over a pan of hot water. Remove from the heat and beat in the egg yolks. Stir in the sherry or wine. Cool.

Whisk the egg whites until stiff and fold in the chocolate mixture. Turn into a serving dish or individual dishes and chill until set. Decorate before serving.

Biscuits, Cakes & Breads

Golden Syrup Biscuits

Makes 30

25 g/1 oz butter or margarine
2 tablespoons golden syrup
½ teaspoon bicarbonate of soda
¼ teaspoon vanilla essence
100 g/4 oz self-raising flour, sifted

Put the fat and syrup into a heavy-based saucepan and warm until the fat has melted. Remove from the heat and mix in the bicarbonate of soda and vanilla essence, then beat in the flour. Cool.

Roll out the mixture until wafer thin and cut into shapes with biscuit cutters. Place on greased baking sheets and bake in a preheated cool oven (150°C/300°F, Gas Mark 2) for 40 minutes or until golden brown. Cool on a wire rack.

Note: This recipe was broadcast over BBC radio in the early months of the war and was recommended by Mrs Neville Chamberlain (then the PM's wife) as a good sugar saver.

Chocolate Biscuits

Makes about 14

75 g/3 oz margarine
50 g/2 oz soft brown
  sugar
1 tablespoon cocoa
  powder
pinch of salt
$\frac{1}{4}$ teaspoon vanilla essence
100 g/4 oz self-raising
  flour, sifted
25 g/1 oz cornflakes,
  crushed
melted plain chocolate to
  ice
blanched almonds to
  decorate

Cream together the margarine and sugar. Beat in the cocoa powder, salt and vanilla essence. Gradually and alternately beat in the flour and cornflakes. Knead well, then shape the mixture into rounds.

Place the rounds on a greased baking sheet and bake in a preheated moderate oven (180°C/350°F, Gas Mark 4) for about 15 minutes.

Cool, then ice with melted chocolate and decorate each biscuit with a blanched almond.

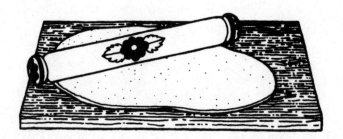

Guernsey Biscuits

Makes 40

450 g/1 lb flour
15 g/$\frac{1}{2}$ oz salt
100 g/4 oz margarine or
  lard
25 g/1 oz fresh yeast
15 g/$\frac{1}{2}$ oz sugar
250 ml/8 fl oz lukewarm
  water or mixed milk
  and water

Sift the flour and salt into a bowl. Rub in the fat. Cream the yeast with the sugar and add the liquid. Leave in a warm place until frothy, then add the yeast mixture to the flour mixture to make a light dough. Knead well. Leave in a warm place to rise for 1$\frac{1}{2}$ hours.

Turn the dough onto a floured board, knock back, knead again and form into balls. Flatten the balls or roll them into biscuit shapes. Place on a greased baking sheet and leave in a warm place for 15 to 20 minutes.

Bake in a preheated moderately hot oven (200°C/400°F, Gas Mark 6) for 20 minutes.

Brandy Snaps
Makes 30

100 g/4 oz golden syrup
90 g/3½ oz caster sugar
100 g/4 oz butter
90 g/3½ oz flour, sifted
1 teaspoon ground ginger
grated rind of ½ lemon
1 teaspoon lemon juice or brandy

Put the syrup, sugar and butter into a heavy-based saucepan and warm, stirring, until the sugar has dissolved and the butter melted. Remove from the heat and tip in the flour, ginger and lemon rind. Add the lemon juice or brandy and mix well.

Drop teaspoonful of the mixture, 7.5 cm/3 inches apart, on greased baking sheets. Bake in a preheated moderate oven (160°C/325°F, Gas Mark 3) for 10 minutes or until golden brown.

Remove from the oven and roll around the greased handle of a wooden spoon whilst hot. Do not allow them to cool as the snaps will become hard and impossible to roll.

Golden Flapjacks
Makes 20

150 g/5 oz butter or margarine
150 g/5 oz demerara sugar
150 g/5 oz porridge oats
3 drops of vanilla essence
2 tablespoons desiccated coconut

Melt the fat in a saucepan. Remove from the heat and mix in the sugar, oats and vanilla. Stir in the coconut. Turn into a greased Swiss roll tin and press into the corners.

Bake in a preheated moderately hot oven (190°C/375°F, Gas Mark 5) for 20 minutes or until golden brown. Cut into fingers, then leave to cool in the tin.

Ginger Biscuits
Makes 35–40

225 g/8 oz flour
2 teaspoons ground ginger
2 teaspoons baking powder
100 g/4 oz margarine
100 g/4 oz sugar
½ teaspoon bicarbonate of soda dissolved in 1 teaspoon hot water
2 large tablespoons golden syrup, warmed

Sift the flour, ginger and baking powder into a bowl. Rub in the margarine. Add the sugar, then mix to a dough with the bicarbonate of soda mixture and syrup.

Roll the mixture into walnut-sized balls and place them on greased baking sheets. Press down the centre of each ball with your thumb. Bake in a preheated moderately hot oven (200°C/400°F, Gas Mark 6) for about 10 minutes.

Almond Shortbread
Makes 30

175 g/6 oz butter
100 g/4 oz sugar
¼ teaspoon almond essence
50 g/2 oz ground almonds
175 g/6 oz flour, sifted
50 g/2 oz ground rice
15 g/½ oz blanched almonds, chopped (optional)

Topping (optional)
1 egg, beaten
75 g/3 oz demerara sugar
65 g/2½ oz desiccated coconut

Cream together the butter and sugar, then beat in the almond essence. Add the ground almonds, flour and ground rice and mix well. Knead in the chopped almonds, if using. Press into an 18 cm/7 inch square baking tin, or roll out the dough and cut into shapes. Put these on greased baking sheets.

Bake in a preheated moderate oven (180 C/350 F, Gas Mark 4) for 35 to 40 minutes if baked in a square tin, or 25 minutes if biscuits. Cool.

To make the topping, beat together all the ingredients and spread over the cooled shortbread. Return to the oven and bake for a further 10 minutes. Cool until almost cold, then cut into fingers if baked in a tin.

Bedfordshire Biscuits
Makes 30

75 g/3 oz margarine
75 g/3 oz caster sugar
75 g/3 oz plain flour
2 tablespoons golden syrup
½ teaspoon vanilla essence
½ teaspoon bicarbonate of soda dissolved in 1 tablespoon hot water
175 g/6 oz porridge oats

Cream together the margarine and sugar. Sift the flour and mix into the creamed mixture. Add the syrup, vanilla essence and soda mixture, then fold in the oats.

Roll out the mixture to 1 cm/½ inch thickness and cut into rounds or other shapes with biscuit cutters. Place on greased baking sheets and bake in a preheated moderately hot oven (190°C/375°F, Gas Mark 5) for 15 minutes.

Yarmouth Biscuits
Makes 30

350 g/12oz flour
225 g/8 oz butter
225 g/8 oz caster sugar
3 eggs, beaten
225 g/8 oz currants

Sift the flour into a bowl. Rub in the butter, then mix in the sugar. Bind with the eggs and mix in the currants.

Drop in rough heaps on to greased baking sheets and bake in a preheated moderately hot oven (190°C/375°F, Gas Mark 5) for 20 minutes.

Golden Shortbread Biscuits
Makes about 30

100 g/4 oz margarine
50 g/2 oz caster sugar
pinch of salt
¼ teaspoon vanilla essence
175 g/6 oz flour
25 g/1 oz ground rice
25 g/1 oz custard powder
caster sugar for
sprinkling

Cream together the margarine and sugar. Beat in the salt and vanilla essence. Sift together the flour, ground rice and custard powder and work into the creamed mixture.

Roll out to 5 mm/¼ inch thickness and cut into shapes with biscuit cutters. Place on greased baking sheets and prick well. Bake in a preheated moderately hot oven (190°C/375°F, Gas Mark 5) for 15 minutes. Dust with caster sugar, then leave to cool.

Maryland Biscuits
Makes 25–30

100 g/4 oz margarine or
half margarine and
half lard
100 g/4 oz sugar
100 g/4 oz flour
1 tablespoon golden syrup
1 tablespoon milk
1 teaspoon bicarbonate of
soda
50 g/2 oz plain chocolate,
finely chopped

Cream together the fat and sugar. Sift in the flour and mix into the creamed mixture. Heat the syrup and milk until the syrup is very liquid, then stir in the bicarbonate of soda. Add to the creamed mixture, then fold in the chocolate.

Roll the mixture into tiny balls and place on greased baking sheets. Press the balls flat with a fork. Bake in a preheated cool oven (150°C/300°F, Gas Mark 2) for 25 to 30 minutes or until golden brown.

Brooke Priory Biscuits
Makes 30–35

225 g/8 oz butter
100 g/4 oz sugar
1 egg yolk
450 g/1 lb flour
25 g/1 oz caraway seeds
egg white to glaze
sugar for sprinkling

Cream together the butter and sugar. Beat in the egg. Sift over the flour, then mix in well. Add the caraway seeds.

Roll out the mixture to 5 mm/¼ inch thickness and cut into shapes with biscuit cutters. Place on greased baking sheets and brush the biscuits with egg white. Dust with sugar. Bake in a preheated moderate oven (180°C/350°F, Gas Mark 4) for 25 minutes.

239

Oatcakes

Makes 20–25

225 g/8 oz flour
1 rounded teaspoon salt
1 rounded teaspoon
  bicarbonate of soda
1 rounded tablespoon
  sugar
450 g/1 lb medium
  oatmeal
100 g/4 oz margarine,
  melted
5 tablespoons lukewarm
  water

Sift the flour, salt and bicarbonate of soda into a bowl. Mix in the sugar and oatmeal, then bind with the margarine and water.

Roll out the mixture to about 3 mm/⅛ inch thickness and cut into rounds. Place on a greased baking sheet. Bake in a preheated moderately hot oven (190°C/375°F, Gas Mark 5) for 20 minutes or until hard to the touch.

Oat Biscuits

Makes 30

100 g/4 oz porridge oats
50 g/2 oz flour, sifted
75 g/3 oz sugar
50 g/2 oz desiccated
  coconut
1 teaspoon baking
  powder
100 g/4 oz butter or
  margarine, melted
1 egg, beaten

Mix together the oats, flour, sugar, coconut and baking powder. Add the butter and egg and blend well. Roll out the mixture to 1 cm/½ inch thickness and cut into shapes with biscuit cutters. Place on a greased baking sheet and bake in a preheated moderate oven (180°C/350°F, Gas Mark 4) for 20 minutes.

Ormskirk Gingerbreads

Makes 20–24

900 g/2 lb flour
1 tablespoon baking
  powder
1½ teaspoons ground
  ginger
225 g/8 oz butter
450 g/1 lb soft brown
  sugar
450 g/1 lb golden syrup

Sift the flour, baking powder and ginger into a bowl. Rub in the butter, then mix in the sugar. Warm the syrup and stir into the ginger mixture. Leave overnight.

The next day, roll out the dough thinly and cut into shapes or gingerbread men with biscuit cutters. Place on greased baking sheets and bake in a preheated moderate oven (180°C/350°F, Gas Mark 4) for 15 minutes. Watch the gingerbreads because they will burn easily.

Gingerbread Men   *Makes 20–25*

*225 g/8 oz butter or
  margarine
75 g/3 oz icing sugar,
  sifted
225 g/8 oz self-raising
  flour
2 teaspoons ground
  ginger
½ teaspoon salt
75 g/3 oz medium
  oatmeal
5 drops of vanilla essence
glacé icing to decorate*

Cream the fat and gradually beat in the sugar. Sift together the flour, ginger and salt and add to the creamed mixture with the oatmeal and vanilla essence. Mix to a stiff dough. Either mould into the shape of little men by hand or roll out the dough and cut into shapes with a biscuit cutter.

Place on a greased baking sheet and bake in a preheated moderate oven (180°C/350°F, Gas Mark 4) for about 20 minutes. Cool on a wire rack, then pipe on faces, features and buttons with glacé icing.

Welsh Cakes   *Makes 24*

*225 g/8 oz flour
½ teaspoon baking powder
pinch of salt
¼ teaspoon mixed spice
100 g/4 oz margarine
75 to 100 g/3 to 4 oz
  sugar
100 g/4 oz currants
1 egg, beaten
little milk*

Sift the flour, baking powder, salt and spice into a bowl. Rub in the margarine, then mix in the sugar and currants. Bind with the egg and a little milk to make a consistency like shortcrust pastry. Roll out to about 5 mm/¼ inch thick and cut into rounds. Cook on a griddle or hot plate until golden brown on both sides.

Grantham Gingerbread   *Makes 35*

*450 g/1 lb flour
1 teaspoon ground ginger
175 g/6 oz butter or
  margarine
450 g/1 lb caster sugar
3 eggs, beaten
3 drams Vol Ammonie
  (bicarbonate of
  ammonia)
milk*

Sift the flour and ginger into a bowl. Rub in the fat, then mix in the sugar. Make a well in the centre of the mixture and add the eggs. Gradually mix the eggs into the flour mixture. Dissolve the Vol Ammonie in a little milk and add to the bowl, with enough additional milk to make a stiff but pliable dough.

Roll out the dough to 5 mm/¼ inch thickness and cut into 6 cm/2½ inch rounds. Place the rounds on a greased baking sheet and bake in a preheated very cool oven (120°C/250°F, Gas Mark ½) for 1 hour.

241

Almond slices
Makes 25

100 g/4 oz flour
75 g/3 oz butter
1½ tablespoons sugar
1 egg yolk
Topping
jam
1 egg white
65 g/2½ oz caster sugar
50 g/2 oz ground
  almonds
few chopped almonds
  mixed with a little
  sugar

Sift the flour into a bowl. Rub in the butter, then add the sugar and egg yolk and work together as for shortbread. Roll out into a long strip 7.5 cm/3 inches wide and place on a baking sheet. Flute the edges.

Bake in a preheated moderate oven (180°C/350°F, Gas Mark 4) for 20 minutes.

Spread the strip with jam. Beat the egg white until stiff and fold in the sugar and ground almonds. Spread this over the jam and sprinkle with the almond sugar mixture. Return to the oven and increase the temperature to moderately hot (190°C/375°F, Gas Mark 5). Bake for a further 15 minutes or until set and firm.

When nearly cool, cut into 2.5 to 4 cm/1 to 1½ inch wide strips.

Teisen Aberffraw (Aberffraw Cakes)
Makes 25-30

175 g/6 oz flour
50 g/2 oz caster sugar
100 g/4 oz butter
caster sugar to dredge

Sift the flour and sugar into a bowl. Add the butter and work together until the mixture binds into a dough. Form into walnut-sized balls. To make the traditional shape that gives these cakes their name, use a floured and sugared shell similar to a flat scallop shell. Press the dough balls in the shell, then remove them carefully and place on a floured baking sheet.

Bake in a preheated moderate oven (180°C/350°F, Gas Mark 4) for 20 minutes or until the cakes are just beginning to colour. Cool slightly, then toss in caster sugar.

Note: The tradition is that when Prince Llywelyn held Court in Aberffraw, his Queen went walking on the beach with her attendants and found a shell. She asked to have cakes baked in the same shape and they were called Teisen Aberffraw.

Goosnargh Cakes
Makes 25

225 g/8 oz flour
200 g/7 oz butter or margarine
25 g/1 oz lard
1 egg white, beaten
½ teaspoon caraway seeds
1 tablespoon caster sugar
caster sugar for dredging

Sift the flour into a bowl and rub in the butter or margarine and lard. Add the egg white, caraway seeds and 1 tablespoon sugar and mix well. Roll out the mixture on a floured board to 5 mm/¼ inch thickness and cut out 4 to 5 cm/1½ to 2 inch rounds.

Place the rounds on greased baking sheets and dredge thickly with caster sugar. Bake in a preheated cool oven (150°C/300°F, Gas Mark 2) for 30 to 40 minutes. Dredge again with sugar, then leave to cool.

Rich Seed Cake

450 g/1 lb butter
450 g/1 lb loaf sugar, crushed and sifted
8 eggs, separated
450 g/1 lb flour
1 nutmeg, grated
1 teaspoon ground cinnamon
50 g/2 oz caraway seeds

Cream the butter and sugar together. Beat the egg yolks until well mixed and add to the creamed mixture. Beat the egg whites until frothy and add to the creamed mixture. Sift the flour with the spices and add to the creamed mixture. Stir in the caraway seeds.

Turn into a greased 20 cm/8 inch cake tin and bake in a preheated moderately hot oven (190°C/375°F, Gas Mark 5) for 2 hours. Cool in the tin.

Banana Cake

2 or 3 very ripe bananas
1 teaspoon lemon juice
100 g/4 oz butter or margarine
100 g/4 oz caster sugar
2 eggs, beaten
225 g/8 oz self-raising flour
lemon icing (optional)

Mash the bananas with the lemon juice. Cream together the fat and sugar, then beat in the eggs followed by the bananas. Sift the flour and mix into the banana mixture.

Turn into a greased 15 × 20 cm/6 × 8 inch cake tin and bake in a moderately hot oven (200°C/400°F, Gas Mark 6) for 40 to 45 minutes. Cool on a wire rack.

If you like, ice the cake with a lemon icing, but it is very nice plain.

Wigs

450 g/1 lb treacle
100 g/4 oz butter
150 ml/¼ pint milk
450 g/1 lb flour
1 teaspoon bicarbonate of soda
2 teaspoons ground ginger
100 g/4 oz sugar
15 g/½ oz caraway seeds

Put the treacle and butter into a saucepan and heat, stirring occasionally, until the mixture is hot and the butter has melted. Stir in the milk.

Sift the flour, bicarbonate of soda and ginger into a bowl and stir in the sugar and caraway seeds. Add the treacle mixture and mix well. Pour into a 21 cm/8 in shallow round tin and bake in a preheated moderate oven (180°C/350°F, Gas Mark 4) for 40 minutes.

Apple Cake

100 g/4 oz butter or margarine
100 g/4 oz caster sugar
2 eggs, beaten
175 g/6 oz self-raising flour
pinch of salt
pinch of ground cinnamon (optional)
2 or 3 tablespoons stewed or grated raw apple

Cream the fat with the sugar, then beat in the eggs. Sift in the flour, salt and cinnamon, if used, and mix together. Stir in the apple. If raw grated apple is used, a little water may be needed to make a dropping consistency.

Turn into a greased 18 cm/7 inch cake tin and bake in a preheated moderate oven (180°C/350°F, Gas Mark 4) for 40 minutes. Alternatively, the mixture may be baked in small bun tins or paper cases, in which case decrease the baking time to about 15 minutes.

Cherry and Almond Cake

225 g/8 oz butter (or half butter and half margarine)
225 g/8 oz caster sugar
3 eggs, beaten
225 g/8 oz flour
pinch of salt
½ teaspoon baking powder
100 g/4 oz ground almonds
100 g/4 oz glacé cherries, quartered
few drops of almond essence

Cream together the butter and sugar. Beat in the eggs. Sift the flour with the salt and baking powder and add to the creamed mixture with the almonds and cherries. Lastly add the almond essence and mix well.

Turn into a greased and lined 20 cm/8 inch cake tin and bake in a preheated cool oven (140°C/275°F, Gas Mark 1) for 3 hours.

Keep for at least 2 weeks before serving.

Rich Christmas Cake

450 g/1 lb butter
450 g/1 lb brown sugar
450 g/1 lb flour
1 teaspoon mixed spice
pinch of salt
8 eggs, beaten
450 g/1 lb currants
450 g/1 lb sultanas
450 g/1 lb seedless
  raisins, chopped
225 g/8 oz chopped
  mixed peel
225 g/8 oz glacé cherries
50 g/2 oz blanched
  almonds
grated rind of 1 lemon
1 tablespoon rose water
5 tablespoons brandy or
  sherry

Cream together the butter and sugar. Sift the flour with the spice and salt. Add to the creamed mixture alternately with the eggs. Add the remaining ingredients and mix well.

Line a 25 cm/10 inch cake tin with three thicknesses of greased greaseproof paper. Turn the cake mixture into the tin. Bake in a preheated cool oven (150°C/300°F, Gas Mark 2) for 5 hours. Cool in the tin until nearly cold, then turn out on to a wire rack. Keep for 2 to 3 weeks before icing.

Walnut Cake

175 g/6 oz butter or
  margarine
175 g/6 oz sugar
100 g/4 oz walnuts,
  chopped finely
50 g/2 oz glacé cherries,
  quartered and floured
½ teaspoon vanilla essence
225 g/8 oz flour
½ teaspoon baking powder
2 eggs, beaten
buttercream to finish
walnut halves to decorate

Cream together the fat and sugar. Add the walnuts, cherries and vanilla essence and mix well. Sift the flour with the baking powder and add to the creamed mixture alternately with the eggs.

Turn into a greased 20 cm/8 inch cake tin and bake in a preheated moderate oven (180°C/350°F, Gas Mark 4) for 1 to 1¼ hours. Cool in the tin.

Turn out and cover the top of the cake with buttercream. Decorate with walnuts.

White Christmas Cake

175 g/6 oz glacé cherries, halved
100 g/4 oz chopped mixed peel
50 g/2 oz walnuts, chopped
50 g/2 oz almonds, chopped
100 g/4 oz sultanas
75 g/3 oz glacé pineapple, chopped
75 g/3 oz crystallized ginger, chopped
3 tablespoons brandy
250 g/9 oz butter
250 g/9 oz caster sugar
4 large eggs, beaten
350 g/12 oz plain flour
1 tablespoon baking powder

Put the cherries, peel, nuts, sultanas, pineapple and ginger in a bowl and sprinkle over the brandy. Leave overnight.

The next day, cream the butter and sugar together, then beat in the eggs. Sift together the flour and baking powder and add to the creamed mixture. Mix well. Stir in the fruit and nuts. If the mixture is too stiff, add a little milk.

Line a 25 cm/10 inch cake tin with greased greaseproof paper. Wrap newspaper around the outside of the tin. Turn the cake mixture into the tin.

Bake in a preheated moderate oven (160°C/325°F, Gas Mark 3) for 1½ hours, then reduce the temperature to cool (150°C/300°F, Gas Mark 2) and bake for a further 1½ to 2 hours.

Shearing Cake

225 g/8 oz flour
1 teaspoon baking powder
pinch of grated nutmeg
100 g/4 oz butter
175 g/6 oz sugar
grated rind of ½ lemon
2 teaspoons caraway seeds
150 ml/¼ pint milk
1 egg, beaten

Sift the flour, baking powder and nutmeg into a bowl. Rub in the butter, then stir in the sugar, lemon rind and caraway seeds. Bind with the milk and egg.

Turn into a greased 18 cm/7 inch cake tin lined with greased greaseproof paper. Bake in a preheated moderate oven (180°C/350°F, Gas Mark 4) for 1 hour.

French Chew

Base
40 g/1½ oz margarine
50 g/2 oz sugar
1 egg yolk
¼ teaspoon vanilla essence
75 g/3 oz self-raising
   flour
pinch of salt

Topping
1 egg white
25 g/1 oz desiccated
   coconut
50 g/2 oz sugar
glacé cherries or chopped
   nuts to decorate

Cream the margarine with the sugar, then beat in the egg yolk and vanilla essence. Sift in the flour and salt and mix well. Press this mixture into a 20 cm/8 inch shallow cake tin lined with greaseproof paper.

Beat the egg white until stiff, then fold in the coconut and sugar. Spread over the base and decorate with cherries or nuts.

Bake in a preheated moderate oven (160°C/325°F, Gas Mark 3) for about 30 minutes. Cool in the tin.

The Versatile Cake and Friends

175 g/6 oz margarine
175 g/6 oz caster sugar
3 eggs, beaten
175 g/6 oz self-raising
   flour, sifted

Cream together the margarine and sugar. Gradually beat in the eggs, then fold in the flour. Divide between two greased and lined 20 cm/8 inch sponge cake tins. Bake in a preheated moderately hot oven (200°C/400°F, Gas Mark 6) for 30 minutes or until golden brown and well risen. Cool on a wire rack.

When cold, sandwich together with buttercream, walnut filling, banana frosting or praline and buttercream (see page 248).

Basic Buttercream

100 g/4 oz unsalted
  butter
175 g/6 oz icing sugar,
  sifted

Cream the butter until soft, then gradually beat in the sugar. Add any required flavouring and colouring during the beating.

Coffee:
Add 2 teaspoons instant coffee dissolved in 1 tablespoon hot water.

Chocolate: Add 50 g/2 oz melted plain chocolate.

Lemon: Add 3 tablespoons lemon curd.

Praline: Add 50 g/2 oz finely crushed almond rock or homemade praline (see below).

Walnut Filling

3 tablespoons apricot
  jam, warmed and
  sieved
3 tablespoons ground
  almonds
1 tablespoon chopped
  walnuts
1 teaspoon vanilla
  essence

Mix together all the ingredients.

Banana Frosting

1 ripe banana
½ teaspoon lemon juice
50 g/2 oz butter
100 g/4 oz icing sugar,
  sifted

Mash the banana with the lemon juice. Cream the butter, then gradually beat in the sugar alternately with the banana and continue beating until light and fluffy.

Praline

75 g/3 oz caster sugar
75 g/3 oz blanched
  almonds

Put the sugar and almonds into a heavy-based saucepan and heat gently, stirring to melt the sugar. Cook until the mixture is golden brown. Pour onto a greased baking sheet and leave to cool and set.

Break the praline into pieces and store in a tin. When required, crush between sheets of greaseproof paper with a rolling pin.

Barley Bread

550 g/18 oz barley flour
175 g/6 oz plain flour
1 teaspoon salt
1 teaspoon bicarbonate of
    soda
2 teaspoons cream of
    tartar
600 ml/1 pint buttermilk

Mix together the dry ingredients, then mix in the buttermilk. Roll out to 2.5 cm/1 inch thickness.

Cook the bread on a hot girdle for 10 minutes on each side or until golden brown. Alternatively, bake in a preheated hot oven (230°C/450°F, Gas Mark 8) for 15 to 20 minutes, without turning.

Yorkshire Bun Loaf

275 g/10 oz self-raising
    flour
100 g/4 oz margarine
75 g/3 oz caster sugar
2 eggs, beaten
2 teaspoons marmalade
75 g/3 oz sultanas
75 g/3 oz currants
little milk
caster sugar for
    sprinkling

Sift the flour into a bowl. Rub in the margarine, then stir in the sugar, eggs, marmalade, sultanas and currants. Bind to a medium stiff mixture with milk, then turn into a greased 500g/1 lb loaf tin. Sprinkle the top with caster sugar and bake in a preheated moderately hot oven (190°C/375°F, Gas Mark 5) for 1 hour.

Chocolate Nut Loaf

225 g/8 oz flour
2 teaspoons baking
    powder
75 g/3 oz margarine
50 g/2 oz caster sugar
50 g/2 oz mixed nuts,
    chopped
75 g/3 oz plain chocolate,
    grated
1 egg, beaten
4 to 5 tablespoons milk

Sift the flour and baking powder into a bowl. Rub in the margarine, then mix in the sugar, nuts and chocolate. Bind with the egg and milk.

Turn into a greased 500 g/1 lb loaf tin and bake in a preheated moderately hot oven (190°C/375°F, Gas Mark 5) for 1 hour.

Apricot Tea Bread

175 g/6 oz dried apricots,
  chopped
250 ml/8 fl oz water
175 g/6 oz caster sugar
75 g/3 oz lard
½ teaspoon ground
  cinnamon
pinch of ground cloves
½ teaspoon salt
225 g/8 oz wholemeal
  flour
1 teaspoon bicarbonate of
  soda
2 eggs, beaten

Put the apricots into a saucepan with the water, sugar, lard, spices and salt. Bring slowly to the boil, stirring, and simmer gently for 5 minutes. Remove from the heat and cool.

Sift the flour and soda into a bowl. Add the apricot mixture and eggs and mix well. Pour into a greased and bottom-lined 1 kg/2 lb loaf tin.

Bake in a preheated moderate oven (180°C/350°F, Gas Mark 4) for about 1 hour or until firm to the touch. Cool on a wire rack. Serve thinly sliced and buttered.

Date and Walnut Loaf

Makes 2 loaves

175 g/6 oz stoned dates,
  chopped
1 teaspoon bicarbonate of
  soda
150 ml/¼ pint boiling
  water
225 g/8 oz flour
1 teaspoon salt
25 g/1 oz margarine
75 g/3 oz caster sugar
3 tablespoons golden
  syrup
1 egg, beaten
50 g/2 oz walnuts,
  chopped

Put the dates in a bowl and stir in the bicarbonate of soda and boiling water. Leave to soak until required.

Sift the flour and salt into a bowl. In another bowl cream together the margarine, sugar and syrup. Beat the egg into the creamed mixture, then add the flour, walnuts and date mixture and mix well.

Divide between two greased and lined 500 g/1 lb loaf tins and bake in a preheated cool oven (150°C/300°F, Gas Mark 2) for 1¼ hours.

Christmas Bread

Makes 4 loaves

1.35 kg/3 lb flour
pinch of salt
50 g/2 oz baking powder
100 g/4 oz lard
100 g/4 oz butter or
margarine
900 g/2 lb moist brown
sugar
450 g/1 lb raisins or
sultanas
100 g/4 oz chopped
mixed peel
3 eggs, beaten
600 ml/1 pint buttermilk
or milk

Sift the flour, salt and baking powder into a bowl. Rub in the fat, then mix in the sugar, fruit and peel. Add the eggs and mix well, then stir in the buttermilk or milk. Divide the mixture between four greased and lined 1 kg/2 lb loaf tins.

Bake in a preheated moderate oven (180 C/350 F, Gas Mark 4) for $1\frac{1}{4}$ hours.

Brioche

Makes 10

225 g/8 oz flour
pinch of salt
100 g/4 oz butter or
margarine
15 g/½ oz caster sugar
3 eggs, beaten

Sponging mixture
15 g/½ oz fresh yeast
5 tablespoons lukewarm
milk
50 g/2 oz flour, sifted

To make the sponging mixture, cream the yeast with the milk, then mix in the flour. Leave to rise in a warm place.

Sift the flour and salt into a bowl. Rub in the fat, then mix in the sugar. Add the eggs and sponging mixture and knead well. Shape into a ball and put into an oiled polythene bag. Leave to rise in a warm place until doubled in bulk.

Turn the dough out of the bag, knock back and knead until firm. Divide the dough into 10 portions and place in small greased fluted brioche tins. Cover loosely with oiled polythene and leave to rise in a warm place. Glaze with beaten egg.

Bake in a preheated hot oven (220°C/425°F, Gas Mark 7) for 10 to 15 minutes.

Variation: For a savoury brioche, bake one large brioche (for 25 to 30 minutes). When it is cool, cut it into thick slices horizontally and spread each slice with a different savoury filling or paste. Reshape the brioche and garnish the outside with hard-boiled egg, tomato, etc.

Irish Fruit Loaf

Makes 1 loaf

15 g/½ oz fresh yeast
150 ml/¼ pint lukewarm
 water
225 g/8 oz flour
¼ teaspoon salt
¼ teaspoon mixed spice
40 g/1½ oz butter.
50 g/2 oz caster sugar
50 g/2 oz raisins
15 g/½ oz chopped mixed
 peel
50 g/2 oz sultanas
50 g/2 oz currants
1 egg, beaten

Cream the yeast with a little of the water and leave in a warm place until frothy. Sift the flour, salt and spice into a bowl and make a well in the centre. Add the yeast and the remaining water and mix to a dough. Turn out and knead for 10 minutes or until smooth, firm and elastic. Shape into a ball and put into an oiled polythene bag. Leave to rise in a warm place for 1 hour.

Cream together the butter and sugar, then beat in the fruit and egg. Turn the dough out of the bag and knock back. Beat in the fruit mixture and add more flour if necessary to make a good consistency. Shape into a loaf and place in a greased 500 g/1 lb loaf tin. Cover loosely with oiled polythene and leave to rise in a warm place until the dough reaches the top of the tin.

Bake in a preheated hot oven (220°C/425°F, Gas Mark 7) for 1 hour. Cool on a wire rack.

Malt Bread

Makes 2 loaves

25 g/1 oz fresh yeast
approx. 150 ml/¼ pint
 lukewarm water
2 tablespoons black
 treacle
4 tablespoons, or 100 g/4
 oz, malt extract
25 g/1 oz butter or
 margarine
450 g/1 lb flour
½ teaspoon salt
50 to 100 g/2 to 4 oz
 sultanas (optional)
honey, or milk and sugar
 syrup to glaze
 (optional)

Cream the yeast with a little of the water and leave in a warm place until frothy. Warm the treacle, malt extract and fat in a saucepan until the mixture is liquid. Cool.

Sift the flour and salt into a bowl. Make a well in the centre and add the yeast, malt mixture and the remaining water. Mix to a dough, then turn out and knead for 10 minutes or until smooth, firm and elastic. Knead in the sultanas, if used.

Divide the dough in half and shape each portion into a loaf. Place in two greased 500 g/1 lb loaf tins. Cover loosely with oiled polythene and leave to rise in a warm place until the dough reaches the top of the tin.

Bake in a preheated moderately hot oven (200°C/400°F, Gas Mark 6) for 45 minutes. Brush the hot loaves with honey, or milk and sugar syrup, if used, and leave to cool.

Milk Bread

25 g/1 oz fresh yeast
approx. 300 ml/½ pint
 lukewarm milk
450 g/1 lb strong plain
 flour
1 teaspoon salt
75 g/3 oz butter or
 margarine
milk to glaze

Cream the yeast with a little of the milk and leave in a warm place until frothy. Sift the flour and salt into a bowl. Rub in the fat, then make a well in the centre of the mixture. Add the yeast and the remaining milk and mix to a dough. Turn out and knead for 10 minutes or until smooth, firm and elastic. Shape into a ball and put into an oiled polythene bag. Leave to rise in a warm place for 1 to 1½ hours or until doubled in bulk.

Turn the dough out of the bag, knock back and knead until firm. Shape into a loaf as described below, or divide into 16 portions and shape into rolls. Place on greased baking sheets. Cover loosely with oiled polythene and leave to rise in a warm place.

Brush the loaf or rolls with the milk and bake in a preheated hot oven (230°C/450°F, Gas Mark 8) for 25 minutes for a loaf and 15 minutes for rolls. To test if a loaf is cooked, tip it out of the tin and rap the bottom with your knuckles: it should sound hollow. Cool on a wire rack.

Vienna loaf: Shape into a long loaf tapered at the ends; make four or five diagonal slashes in the top before the second rising (proving).

Cottage loaf: Divide the dough in two, one portion double the size of the other. Shape into two balls. Dampen the larger ball and using two floured fingers make a firm hole through the centre to the bottom of the ball. Taper the end of the smaller ball slightly and place it on the larger ball with the tapered end in the hole. Push through both balls with the end of a wooden spoon.

Wholewheat Bread

Makes 3 loaves

25 g/1 oz fresh yeast
450 ml/¾ pint lukewarm
  water
650 g/1½ lb strong plain
  wholewheat flour
2 teaspoons salt
15 g/½ oz lard
beaten egg or milk to
  glaze

Cream the yeast with a little of the water and leave in a warm place until frothy. Sift the flour and salt into a bowl. Rub in the lard, then make a well in the centre of the mixture. Add the yeast and the remaining water and mix to a dough. Turn out and knead for 10 minutes or until smooth, firm and elastic. Shape into a ball and put into an oiled polythene bag. Leave to rise in a warm place for 1 to 1½ hours or until doubled in bulk.

Turn the dough out of the bag, knock back and knead until firm. Divide the dough into three and shape into loaves. Place in three greased 500 g/1 lb loaf tins. Cover loosely with oiled polythene and leave to rise in a warm place until the dough reaches the top of the tins.

Brush the tops with beaten egg or milk and bake in a preheated hot oven (230°C/450°F, Gas Mark 8) for 30 to 40 minutes. To test if the loaf is cooked, tip it out of the tin and rap the bottom with your knuckles: it should sound hollow. Cool on a wire rack.

Note: Many other shaped loaves and rolls, etc. can be made from this dough.

Chelsea Buns
Makes 14

450 g/1 lb risen enriched dough (see milk bread, page 253)
50 g/2 oz lard
75 g/3 oz sugar
225 g/8 oz mixed dried fruit
1 teaspoon mixed spice
caster sugar for dredging

Knock back the dough and knead until firm. Roll out to an oblong 30 cm/12 inches long and 5 mm/¼ inch thick.

Melt the lard in a saucepan and stir in the sugar until dissolved. Remove from the heat and stir in the fruit and spice. Allow to cool slightly, then spread the filling over the dough oblong. Roll up tightly like a Swiss roll, then cut into 2.5 cm/1 inch thick slices. Place the slices in a greased tin that is 5 cm/2 inches deep, placing them about 5 mm/¼ inch apart. Cover loosely with oiled polythene and leave to rise in a warm place until the buns are puffy.

Bake in a preheated moderately hot oven (190°C/375°F, Gas Mark 5) for about 20 minutes. Dredge with caster sugar and leave to cool.

Lardy Cake

225 g/8 oz flour
¼ teaspoon salt
¼ teaspoon mixed spice
¼ oz fresh yeast
150 ml/¼ pint lukewarm milk
50 g/2 oz lard
50 g/2 oz sugar
50 g/2 oz mixed dried fruit
sugar and water glaze

Sift the flour, salt and spice into a bowl and warm in the oven. Cream the yeast with a little of the milk and leave in a warm place until frothy. Add to the flour mixture with enough of the remaining milk to make a soft dough. Beat well, then cover and leave in a warm place until doubled in bulk.

Roll out the dough on a well-floured board to an oblong 5 mm/¼ inch thick. Spread on half the lard and sprinkle with half the sugar and half the fruit. Fold in three, turn to the left as for flaky pastry and roll out again. Cover with the rest of the lard, sugar and fruit. Fold in three again, turn and roll out to an oblong 2.5 cm/1 inch thick. Place in a deep baking tin and leave in a warm place until well risen.

Score the top of the cake with a knife and brush with sugar and water glaze. Bake in a hot oven (220°C/425°F, Gas Mark 7) for 30 minutes.

Croissants
Makes 12

15 g/¼ oz fresh yeast
approx. 300 ml/½ pint
lukewarm milk
275 g/10 oz strong plain
flour
pinch of salt
15 g/½ oz sugar
150 g/5 oz butter or
margarine
beaten egg to glaze

Cream the yeast with a little of the milk and leave in a warm place until frothy. Sift the flour and salt into a bowl. Stir in the sugar, then make a well in the centre. Add the yeast and the remaining milk and mix to a dough. Turn out and knead for about 10 minutes or until smooth, firm and elastic. Shape into a ball and put into an oiled polythene bag. Leave to rise in a warm place for about 1 hour or until doubled in bulk.

Turn the dough out of the bag, knock back and knead until firm. Press out into an oblong. Add the fat as for flaky pastry, rolling out and folding five times in all. Allow to rest in the refrigerator for 20 minutes (or overnight).

Divide the dough in half and roll out each portion into a 30 cm/12 inch round. Leave for 5 minutes to relax, then cut each round into 6 triangles. The triangles should be about 15 cm/6 inches on the two long sides with a 10 cm/4 inch base. Roll up the triangles towards the point and press firmly. Curve into a crescent and place on a baking sheet with the point underneath. Cover loosely with oiled polythene and leave to rise in a warm place for 20 to 30 minutes.

Brush the croissants with egg and bake in a preheated hot oven (220°C/425°F, Gas Mark 7) for 15 to 20 minutes.

Hot Cross Buns

Makes 12 buns

15 g/½ oz fresh yeast
approx. 150 ml/¼ pint
  lukewarm milk
350 g/12 oz flour
pinch of salt
50 g/2 oz butter or lard,
  softened
40 g/1½ oz caster sugar
50 g/2 oz currants
50 g/2 oz chopped mixed
  peel
pinch of ground cinnamon
pinch of grated nutmeg
1 egg, beaten

To Glaze
2 teaspoons caster sugar
1 teaspoon hot milk

Cream the yeast with a little of the milk and leave in a warm place until frothy. Sift the flour and salt into a bowl. Add the yeast and the remaining milk and mix to a dough. Knead lightly until elastic, then shape into a ball and put into an oiled polythene bag. Leave to rise in a warm place for about 1 hour or until doubled in bulk.

Turn the dough out of the bag and knock back. Beat in the fat, sugar, currants, peel, spices and egg. Divide the dough into 12 portions and shape into buns. Cut a cross in the top of each bun with a sharp knife. Place on a greased and floured baking sheet. Cover loosely with oiled polythene and leave to rise in a warm place for 20 to 30 minutes.

Bake in a preheated hot oven (230°C/450°F, Gas Mark 8) for about 15 minutes or until golden brown. Dissolve the sugar in the milk for the glaze and brush over the buns. Bake for a further 2 minutes. Cool on a wire rack.

Note: This dough may also be baked in a tin to make a bun loaf. Bake for 35 minutes.

French Muffins

Makes 20

40 g/1½ oz fresh yeast
600 ml/1 pint mixed
* lukewarm milk and*
* water*
2 eggs, beaten
900 g/2 lb flour
7 g/¼ oz salt
25 g/1 oz baking powder
150 g/5 oz fat
175 g/6 oz sugar
beaten egg to glaze

Cream the yeast with a little of the liquid and leave in a warm place until frothy. Add the rest of the liquid and the eggs and mix well.

Sift the flour, salt and baking powder into a bowl. Rub in the fat, then mix in the sugar. Add the liquid and mix to a dough. Knead well. Shape into a ball and put into an oiled polythene bag. Leave to rise in a warm place until doubled in bulk.

Turn the dough out of the bag, knock back and knead until firm. Divide into 275 g/10 oz portions. Roll out each portion into a 2.5 cm/ 1 inch thick round and cut into quarters. Put the quarters on floured baking sheets. Cover loosely with oiled polythene and leave to rise in a warm place.

Brush with beaten egg and bake in a preheated moderate oven (180°C/350°F, Gas Mark 4) for 30 minutes or until lightly brown and just firm. Turn the muffins over and brush with beaten egg again. Bake for a further 10 minutes.

Pikelets

Makes 25

225 g/8 oz flour
1 teaspoon salt
20 g/¾ oz fresh yeast
approx. 300 ml/½ pint
* lukewarm milk*
1 egg, beaten

Sift the flour and salt into a bowl and warm thoroughly. Cream the yeast with a little of the milk and leave in a warm place until frothy. Make a well in the centre of the flour and add the yeast, remaining milk and the egg. Beat to a smooth, thin batter, adding more warm milk if necessary. Leave to rise in a warm place for about 30 minutes or until doubled in bulk.

Heat a gridle or hot plate and grease lightly. Pour a small cupful of the yeast batter onto the hot girdle and cook for 5 minutes on each side or until golden brown. Keep hot while you cook the remaining pikelets in the same way and serve hot.

Rye Bread

Makes 4 loaves

25 g/1 oz fresh yeast
450 ml/¾ pint mixed lukewarm milk and water
675 g/1½ lb rye flour
450 g/1 lb plain flour, sifted
1 teaspoon salt
25 g/1 oz butter
beaten egg to glaze
caraway seeds to finish

Cream the yeast with a little of the liquid and leave in a warm place until frothy. Mix together the flours and salt and rub in the butter. Make a well in the centre and add the yeast and the remaining liquid. Mix to a dough. Turn out and knead for 10 minutes or until smooth, firm and elastic. Shape into a ball and put into an oiled polythene bag. Leave to rise in a warm place for 1 to 1½ hours or until doubled in bulk.

Turn the dough out of the bag, knock back and knead until firm. Divide into four portions and shape into loaves. Place in four greased 500 g/1 lb loaf tins. Alternatively, shape into cob loaves and place on greased baking sheets. Cover loosely with oiled polythene and leave to rise in a warm place until the dough reaches the top of the tin.

Bake in a preheated hot oven (230 C/450°F, Gas Mark 8) for 30 minutes. Brush with beaten egg and sprinkle with caraway seeds. Bake for a further 10 minutes. To test if a loaf is cooked, tip it out of the tin and rap the bottom with your knuckles: it should sound hollow. Cool on a wire rack.

Picnic Pittas
Makes 6

*approx. 750 g/1½ lb risen
  white or brown bread
  dough*
oil

Filling
*6 slices of cooked ham,
  tongue, beef or salami,
  etc.*
*2 to 3 hard-boiled eggs,
  sliced*
2 tomatoes, sliced
few lettuce leaves
few onion rings
few stuffed olives, sliced

Knock back the dough and divide into six portions. Roll each to an oval shape about 20 × 10 cm/8 × 4 inches. Place on a dampened and oiled baking sheet and brush the tops liberally with oil. Do not put to rise again. Cook under a hot grill for about 2 minutes or until golden brown, then turn over, brush again with oil and grill for a further 2 minutes.

Quickly slit open each pitta along one long side to let out the steam. Cool on a wire rack.

Fill each with a folded slice of meat, a few egg and tomato slices, lettuce, onion rings and olive slices.

Scotch Baps
Makes 10

25 g/1 oz fresh yeast
*approx. 300 ml/½ pint
  mixed lukewarm milk
  and water*
*450 g/1 lb strong plain
  flour*
2 teaspoons salt
*50 g/2 oz butter or
  margarine*
1 egg, beaten

Cream the yeast with a little of the liquid and leave in a warm place until frothy. Sift the flour and salt into a bowl. Rub in the fat, then make a well in the centre of the mixture. Add the yeast, the remaining liquid and the egg and mix to a dough. Turn out and knead for 10 minutes or until smooth, firm and elastic. Shape into a ball and put into an oiled polythene bag. Leave to rise in a warm place until doubled in bulk.

Turn the dough out of the bag, knock back and knead until firm. Divide into small portions about the size of a duck egg and shape into baps. Place on a greased and floured baking sheet. Cover loosely with oiled polythene and leave to rise in a warm place until doubled in size.

Bake in a preheated moderately hot oven (200°C/400°F. Gas Mark 6) for 15 to 20 minutes.

Note: These should not be glazed, but floury on top.

Preserves

Gage Plum Jam
Makes 4.5 kg/10 lb

2.5 kg/6 lb gages
600 ml/1 pint water
2.75 kg/6 lb warmed
  sugar
liquid pectin, if
  necessary

Put the fruit and water in a saucepan and simmer until the skins are tender and the total volume has decreased by one-third. Take a pectin test, and add liquid pectin if necessary to obtain a satisfactory result.

Add the sugar and stir to dissolve, then bring back to the boil and boil until setting point is reached (108°–109°C/220°–222°F). Skim off any scum if necessary, then pot as usual.

Rhubarb Jam
Makes 4.5 kg/10 lb

3.5 kg/8 lb peeled
  rhubarb
juice of 4 lemons or
  750 ml/1¼ pints
  redcurrant or
  gooseberry juice
2.75 kg /6 lb sugar

Make as for gage plum jam, cooking the rhubarb with the lemon or redcurrant or gooseberry juice, but no water, until they are pulpy.

Blackcurrant Jam
Makes 4.5 kg/10 lb

2 kg/4 lb blackcurrants
1.8 litres/3 pints water
2.75 kg/6 lb sugar

Make as for gage plum jam.

261

Fresh Apricot Jam
Makes 4.5 kg/10 lb

*2.75 kg/6 lb ripe
  apricots, stoned
600 ml/1 pint water
2.75 kg/6 lb sugar
liquid pectin*

Make as for gage plum jam.

Dried Apricot Jam
Makes 4.5 kg/10 lb

*1 kg/2 lb dried apricots,
  chopped
3.25 litres/6 pints water
2.75 kg/6 lb sugar
liquid pectin*

Soak the apricots in the water for 24 hours,
then proceed as for gage plum jam.

Raspberry Jam
Makes 4.5 kg/10 lb

*2.75 kg/6 lb raspberries
2.75 kg/6 lb sugar
liquid pectin*

Make as for gage plum jam, cooking the
raspberries, without any water, until they are
pulpy.

Dark Thick Marmalade
Makes 4.5 kg/10 lb

*1 kg/2 lb Seville oranges
1 small lemon
2.75 to 4 litres/5 to 7
  pints water
2.75 kg/6 lb sugar
25 g/1 oz dark treacle
225 g/8 oz crystallized
  ginger, chopped
  (optional)*

Scrub the fruit, then cut it in half and squeeze
out the juice into a preserving pan. Remove the
pips and fibrous membranes and tie these in a
piece of muslin. Add to the pan. Finely shred
the peel without removing any of the white pith
and add to the pan with the water. Bring to the
boil and simmer gently for about 2 hours or
until the peel is very soft and the contents of the
pan are well reduced. Remove the muslin bag,
squeezing out the juice against the side of the
pan.

Add the sugar and treacle and stir to dissolve, then return to the boil and boil until setting point is reached. Add the ginger, if using.
Skim off the scum and leave to stand for 4 to 5
minutes for the peel to settle. Pot as usual.

Pressure Cooker Marmalade
Makes 2.25 kg/5 lb

750 g/1½ lb Seville oranges
900 ml/1½ pints water
juice of 1 lemon
1.5 kg/3 lb warmed sugar

Scrub the oranges and peel thinly. Shred the peel and put into a pressure cooker. Remove the white pith and all the pips from the oranges and tie in a piece of muslin. Add to the cooker. Cut up the fruit roughly and put in the cooker with the water and lemon juice. Do not overfill the cooker. Put on the cover, bring to 7 kg (15 lb) pressure and cook steadily for 20 minutes

Reduce the pressure at room temperature, then remove and discard the muslin bag. Add the sugar and stir to dissolve. Return the cooker to the heat, without the cover, and boil until setting point is reached. Pot as usual.

Rhubarb and Blackberry Jam
Makes 4.5 kg/10 lb

3.5 kg/8 lb blackberries
900 ml/1½ pints water
2 kg/4½ lb rhubarb, chopped
warmed sugar

A few slightly under-ripe blackberries may be added to help the pectin content, but not too many. Put the blackberries and water in a preserving pan and bring to the boil. Simmer until tender, then sieve. Return to the pan and add the rhubarb. Simmer until pulpy.

Measure the pulp and add 450 g/1 lb sugar to each 450 g/1 lb pulp. Stir to dissolve the sugar, then bring back to the boil. Boil until setting point is reached, then pot as usual.

Apple and Pineapple Jam
Makes 4.5 kg/10 lb

2.75 kg/6 lb cooking apples, peeled, cored and chopped
juice of 2 lemons
750 g/1 lb 8 oz canned pineapple pieces
approx. 1 litre/1¾ pints pineapple juice
2.75 kg/6 lb sugar

Put the cooking apples and lemon juice in a preserving pan. Drain the syrup from the can of pineapple pieces and make it up to 1.2 litres/2 pints with the pineapple juice. Add to the pan and bring to the boil. Simmer until the mixture is pulpy, then add the sugar. Stir until dissolved. Add the pineapple pieces and continue simmering until setting point is reached. Pot as usual.

Gooseberry Mint Jelly   *Makes about 450 g/1 lb*

*1 kg/2 lb green
    gooseberries
warmed sugar
12 mint sprigs*

There is no need to top and tail the gooseberries. Put them in a preserving pan with water to cover and simmer until pulpy. Strain through a jelly bag, then measure the liquid: to each 600 ml/1 pint add 450 g/1 lb sugar. Stir to dissolve the sugar, then add the mint, tied in a bundle, and boil until setting point is reached. Remove the mint and pot as usual.

Serve with hot or cold lamb.

Note: This is not a clear jelly. Frozen gooseberries may be used.

Variation: Sage leaves may be used instead of mint.

Apple Curd   *Makes about 1.25 kg/2½ lb*

*750 g/1½ lb cooking
    apples, peeled, cored
    and quartered
juice of 1 lemon
350 g/12 oz sugar
2 eggs, beaten
100 g/4 oz butter
good pinch of ground
    ginger*

Put the apples and lemon juice in a preserving pan with a very little water. Cover and cook until pulpy. Sieve and return to the pan. Add the sugar, eggs and butter and cook very gently (preferably in a double saucepan) until the mixture thickens. Do not boil. Add the ginger and pot as usual.

Green Grape Jelly

*green grapes
warmed sugar*

Use the small, green, unripe grapes thinned from the bunches (they are usually about the size of a pea). Put the grapes in a preserving pan with water to cover and simmer until pulpy. Strain through a jelly bag, then measure the liquid: to each 600 ml/1 pint add 450 g/1 lb sugar. Stir to dissolve the sugar, then boil until setting point is reached. Pot as usual.

Note: The jelly will be red in colour.

Rowan or Mountain Ash Jelly

*1.5 kg/3 lb ripe rowan
berries
1.5 kg/3 lb crabapples,
quartered
warmed sugar*

Put the berries in a preserving pan, just cover with water and cook gently until pulpy. Strain through a jelly bag. Do the same with the crabapples, then measure, both strained juices and mix together in the pan. To each 600 ml/1 pint of mixed juices add 450 g/1 lb sugar. Stir to dissolve the sugar, then boil until setting point is reached. Pot as usual.

Note: If you prefer, make this jelly with 1 kg/2 lb of rowans and 2 kg/4 lb of crabapples; this will produce a less acid result.

Spiced Redcurrant Jelly

*1.5 kg/3 lb redcurrants
600 ml/1 pint water
150 ml/¼ pint white
vinegar
3 cloves
½ cinnamon stick
warmed sugar*

Put the redcurrants, water and vinegar into a preserving pan. Tie the cloves and cinnamon in a piece of muslin and add to the pan. Bring to the boil and simmer until the redcurrants are pulpy. Strain through a jelly bag, then measure the liquid: to each 600 ml/1 pint add 450 g/1 lb sugar. Stir to dissolve the sugar, then boil until setting point is reached. Pot as usual.

Note: The quantity of spices may be varied to suit individual taste.

Spiced Peaches

*450 g/1 lb peaches
(about 4), peeled,
halved and stoned
225 g/8 oz sugar
1 teaspoon ground
allspice
1 teaspoon whole
coriander seeds
½ teaspoon ground cloves
pinch of grated nutmeg
300 ml/½ pint white wine
vinegar*

Put the peaches in a pan. Mix together the sugar and spices and sprinkle over the peaches. Pour over the vinegar. Bring slowly to the boil, making certain all the sugar has dissolved before boiling point is reached. Simmer gently for 5 minutes. Lift out the peach halves with a slotted spoon and pack them into jars. Simmer the syrup for a further 10 minutes or until it starts to thicken. Pour it over the peaches and cover as usual. Serve with ham, pork, cold duck or pheasant.

Pear and Ginger Preserve
Makes about 750 g/1½ lb

450 g/1 lb sugar
scant 300 ml/½ pint water
450 g/1 lb pears (not
  over-ripe), peeled,
  cored and sliced
50 g/2 oz preserved
  ginger, chopped
juice of 2 lemons

Dissolve the sugar in the water, then add the remaining ingredients. Cook very gently until the pears are tender. Remove the pears from the pan with a slotted spoon and pack into prepared jars. Boil the syrup for a further 5 to 7 minutes, then pour it over the pears. Finishing sterilising in the usual way. Serve this preserve as a sweet with ice cream and meringues.

Apple Ginger
Makes 3.75 kg/8 lb

2 kg/4½ lb sugar
1.8 litres/3 pints water
2 kg/4½ lb apples, peeled,
  cored and thinly sliced
50 g/2 oz ground ginger

Dissolve the sugar in the water and bring to the boil. Simmer until a thick syrup is formed. Add the apples and simmer until transparent. Stir in the ginger and simmer for a further 5 minutes. Pot as usual.

Serve as a preserve or use as a tart filling.

Spiced Orange Rings

8 to 10 firm medium
  oranges, thinly sliced
  (not peeled)
900 ml/1½ pints white
  distilled vinegar
750 g/1½ lb sugar
1 teaspoon ground cloves
2 pieces of cinnamon
  stick
1 teaspoon whole cloves

Layer up the orange slices in a saucepan. Cover with water, bring to the boil, cover the pan and simmer gently for about 45 minutes or until the orange rind is really tender. Drain off the liquid into another saucepan.

Add the vinegar, sugar, ground cloves and cinnamon to the liquid and heat, stirring to dissolve the sugar. Bring to the boil and boil for 10 minutes. Add the orange rings to the liquid a few at a time and simmer gently until the rind becomes clear. As the rind clears, transfer the orange rings to warmed jars with a slotted spoon, packing neatly.

Continue boiling the syrup until it starts to thicken. Cool slightly, then strain it and pour over the orange rings in the jars to cover completely. Add a few whole cloves to each jar and cover with a vinegar-proof top. Store for several weeks before using.

Sweet Pickled Pears

1 kg/2 lb sugar
600 ml/1 pint spiced
vinegar (see page 268)
to which ½ teaspoon
coriander seeds has
been added
1 teaspoon lemon juice
2 kg/4½ lb pears, peeled,
quartered and cored

Dissolve the sugar in the vinegar, then add the lemon juice and pears. Simmer very gently until the pears are tender, then remove the pears from the pan with a slotted spoon and pack them into hot jars. Keep hot.

Boil the liquid until it is thick and syrupy. Pour it over the pears and cover with a vinegar-proof top. Store for 3 months before using.

Variations: Quinces, peaches, apricots, damsons and apples may be pickled in the same way.

Kentish Pickled Cherries

1 kg/2 lb dark red
cherries, stoned
450 g/1 lb sugar
3 cloves
½ teaspoon ground
allspice
pinch of ground mace
pinch of ground cinnamon
pinch of grated nutmeg
300 ml/½ pint malt
vinegar

Make alternate layers of cherries, sugar and spice in a pan. Add the vinegar and bring to the boil. Simmer for 5 minutes. Remove the cherries from the pan with a slotted spoon and pack into hot jars. Boil the syrup until it starts to thicken, then strain it over the fruit. Cover as usual with a vinegar-proof top.

Apricot Chutney

Makes 1.25 kg/2½ lb

450 g/1 lb large dried
apricots, soaked for 6
hours
1 large onion, sliced
1 tablespoon coarse salt
350 g/12 oz demerara
sugar
75 g/3 oz sultanas
2 teaspoons whole mixed
spices
300 ml/½ pint white
vinegar

Drain the apricots and put into a preserving pan with the onion, salt, sugar and sultanas. Tie the spices in a piece of muslin and add to the pan with the vinegar. Simmer gently, stirring occasionally, for about 50 minutes or until the mixture has reduced to the consistency of jam, the apricots remaining whole. Discard the bag of spices and pot as usual.

267

Piccalilli

Makes 3.5 kg/8 lb

*1 kg/2 lb marrow, peeled,
seeded and chopped
1 large cauliflower,
broken into florets
1 kg/2 lb small onions
1 large cucumber, cut
into 1 cm/½ in pieces
450 g/1 lb French beans,
halved
225 g/8 oz cooking salt
2.25 litres/4 pints water
60 g/2½ oz flour
100 g/4 oz dry mustard
25 g/1 oz turmeric
2.25 litres/4 pints vinegar*

Put the vegetables in a deep bowl. Dissolve the salt in the water and pour over the vegetables. Leave for 24 hours, then drain well.

Put the flour, mustard, turmeric and vinegar in a saucepan and stir well. Bring to the boil and simmer, stirring, until thickened. Add the vegetables and heat through but do not boil. Pot, using ceresin discs and screw tops.

Tomato and Orange Chutney

Makes 1.5 kg/3 lb

*750 g/1½ lb sugar
300 ml/½ pint vinegar,
preferably tarragon
1 kg/2 lb firm tomatoes,
skinned and sliced
2 small oranges, thinly
sliced and pipped
good pinch of salt*

Dissolve the sugar in the vinegar then boil to a thin syrup. Add the tomatoes, oranges (except the end slices) and salt and simmer for about 45 minutes or until setting point is reached. Pot as usual.

Best Spiced Vinegar

*7 g/¼ oz cinnamon bark
7 g/¼ oz whole cloves
7 g/¼ oz whole mace
blades
7 g/¼ oz whole allspice
berries
6 peppercorns
vinegar*

Tie the spices loosely in muslin and drop into a bottle of vinegar. Leave for 2 months, shaking the bottle daily. Allow to settle for 1 week before straining.

Drinks

Economical Lemonade
Makes approx. 600 ml/1 pint

2 lemons
25 g/1 oz citrus or
 tartaric acid
450 g/1 lb sugar
1.2 litres/2 pints boiling
 water

Peel the lemons thinly and put the peel in a bowl. Add the acid and sugar and pour over the boiling water. Stir well, then cover and leave to cool.

Squeeze the juice from the lemons. Strain the lemon rind mixture and stir in the lemon juice. Pour into clean bottles and cap.

The lemonade will keep for at least 2 weeks in the refrigerator, but for longer storage it should be sterilized as for blackberry syrup (see page 271). To serve, dilute with water or soda water to taste.

Variations: Add a couple of cloves when making, or add a little chopped mint when serving.

Orange Refresher
Serves 6

150 ml/¼ pint orange
 squash
900 ml/1½ pints water
juice of ½ orange
1 tablespoon sugar
mint sprigs
Garnish
orange slices
cucumber peel

Pour the squash into a 1.75 litre/3 pint jug and stir in the water, orange juice, sugar and mint. Chill.

Float orange slices on top and slide strips of cucumber peel down the side of the jug before serving.

Cider Punch (cold)

Serves 6–8

1.2 litres/2 pints cider
1.2 litres/2 pints soda
   water
1 miniature bottle whisky
1 miniature bottle gin
½ teaspoon lemon juice
½ tablespoon caster sugar
few thin strips lemon rind

Chill the cider and soda water for 30 minutes. Mix together the whisky, gin, lemon juice, sugar and lemon rind in a jug or bowl. Add the cider and soda and serve.

Punch (hot)

Serves 3–4

900 ml/1½ pints pale ale
1 miniature bottle whisky
1 miniature bottle rum
spice and sugar to taste,
   e.g. cinnamon stick,
   root ginger, etc.
lemon juice

Put all the ingredients into a saucepan and bring nearly to the boil. Pour into mugs and drink hot.

Apple Toddy

1.2 litres/2 pints

2 large apples, chopped
600 ml/1 pint water
1 tablespoon honey
½ teaspoon bicarbonate of
   soda

Put the apples in a saucepan with the water. Cover and simmer gently until the apples are thoroughly softened. Sieve, then stir in the honey and bicarbonate of soda. Sip slowly while hot.
Note: This is a children's drink, and the bicarbonate of soda is added to make the drink fizz.

Tea Julep

Serves 4

600 ml/1 pint freshly
   made tea, strained
sugar
6 mint sprigs, lightly
   crushed
1 orange
1 lemon
300 ml/½ pint ginger ale

Sweeten the tea with sugar to taste. Add the mint sprigs. Cut two thin slices from the orange and lemon, then squeeze the juice from the rest of the fruit. Add to the tea and stir well. Chill for 1 hour.
   Strain the julep and add the ginger ale just before serving. Garnish with the orange and lemon slices.
Variation: Add a dash of your favourite spirit.

Cider Toddy
Serves 1

200 ml/⅓ pint dry cider
7 g/¼ oz root ginger,
  bruised
twist of lemon rind
1 tablespoon honey

Put the cider, ginger and lemon rind in an aluminium, stainless steel or enamelled saucepan and heat until bubbles just begin to rise in the liquid. Remove from the heat, stir in the honey and strain into a warmed glass.

Lamb's Wool
Serves 6

1.75 litres/3 pints ale
2 baked apples
few cloves
sugar
grated nutmeg
ground ginger
3 eggs

Warm the ale in a saucepan. Stick the apples with the cloves and add to the pan with sugar to taste and the spices.

Beat the eggs in a bowl until smooth. Strain the hot but not boiling spiced ale on to the eggs and stir until a smooth, creamy mixture is obtained. Drink hot.

Blackberry Syrup

2.75 kg/6 lb blackberries
300 ml/½ pint water
sugar
15 g/½ oz whole cloves
  (optional)
60 ml/2 fl oz brandy or
  fruit liqueur (optional)

Put the blackberries and water in a double saucepan and stew gently for 1 hour. Strain and measure the juice: to each 600 ml/1 pint add 450 g/1 lb sugar. Stir to dissolve the sugar, then bring to the boil. If using the cloves, tie them in a piece of muslin and add to the pan. Simmer for 10 minutes.

Remove the cloves, if used, and cool. If using the brandy or liqueur, add it now, then pour the syrup into hot bottles, leaving about 5 cm/ 2 inches between the syrup level and the base of the cork or screw stopper. Put the bottles into a deep pan fitted with a false bottom and pour in enough water to come to the bases of the corks. Bring the water to simmering point, then maintain for 20 minutes. Remove the bottles to a wooden board and cool. Dip the tops in melted paraffin wax or brush with melted beeswax.

To serve, dilute with hot or iced water to taste.

271

Cherryade
Serves 7–8

*225 g/8 oz cherries,
  stoned
600 ml/1 pint boiling
  water
piece of lemon rind
50 g/2 oz caster sugar
1 tablespoon brandy
  (optional)*

Put the cherries in a bowl, bruise them with a spoon and pour over the boiling water. Add the lemon rind. Leave for 4 to 5 hours. Strain.

Stir in the sugar until dissolved. Add the brandy, if using.

Grape Syrup

*7.25 kg/16 lb well-
  coloured grapes
sugar*

Put the grapes into a saucepan and cover with water. Bring to the boil, then simmer until the juice is well extracted. Stir frequently and replace any water that evaporates. Pour into a jelly bag and leave to drain overnight; do not squeeze the bag or the syrup will be cloudy.

Measure the juice and add 450 g/1 lb sugar to each 1.2 litre/2 pints. Stir to dissolve the sugar, then boil for 30 minutes. Skim and add more boiling water if necessary, then pour into heated bottles. Seal with sterilized corks immediately and then sterilize as for blackberry syrup (see page 271).

To serve, dilute with three parts hot or iced water.

Apple Quencher
Makes 1.2 litres/2 pints

*450 g/1 lb apple skins
  and cores
600 ml/1 pint water
pinch of ground ginger or
  cinnamon, or juice and
  grated rind of ½ lemon
2 tablespoons sugar
green, yellow or red food
  colouring (optional)*

Put the apple skins and cores in a saucepan with the water and simmer gently for 10 minutes. Add the spice or lemon juice and rind and the sugar and remove from the heat. Allow to cool, then strain. If the colour is dingy, add a little food colouring.

Store in the refrigerator, but do not keep for long.

Mixed Fruit Punch

Serves 7–8

1 dessert pear, cored and chopped
1 peach, skinned, stoned and chopped
1 dessert apple, cored and chopped
2 small oranges or 3 tangerines, peeled and segmented
few grapes, seeded if necessary
1 small cucumber, thinly sliced
sugar
juice of 1 lemon
white wine, fruit juice, lemonade or weak tea
soda water

Put the fruit and cucumber in a bowl and sprinkle with sugar to taste. Add the lemon juice. then pour over enough wine, fruit juice, lemonade or tea to cover. The fruit must be submerged to prevent browning, so put a plate on top if necessary. Leave in a cool place for at least 6 hours.

To serve, ladle into wine glasses and top up with a dash of soda water.

Red Reviver

1 part blackcurrant syrup
2 parts bottled lime juice and soda
3 or 4 parts water
minted ice cubes
marachino cherry (optional)

Mix together the syrup, lime juice and soda and water just before serving. Pour into tall glasses over minted ice cubes and add a cherry on a stick to each glass, if liked.

Rhubarb Cordial

1.8–2.2 litres/3–4 pints

1 kg/2 lb rhubarb, chopped
100 g/4 oz sugar
2 whole cloves
7 g/¼ oz root ginger, bruised
1.2 litres/2 pints water
mint leaves to garnish

Put the rhubarb, sugar, cloves, ginger and water in a saucepan and bring to the boil, stirring to dissolve the sugar. Simmer gently until the rhubarb is soft, replacing any water that evaporates.

Strain well and serve in a warmed glass jug, garnished with mint leaves.

273

Prizewinners

Low Calorie Tomato and Lettuce Soup

450 g/1 lb tomatoes, finely chopped
100 g/4 oz lettuce, finely chopped
225 g/8 oz onions, finely chopped
2 beef stock cubes
2 litres/3½ pints water
1 tablespoon fresh marjoram, chopped
salt
pepper
natural yogurt to serve

Put the tomatoes, lettuce and onions in a saucepan. Crumble in the stock cubes, then add the water and marjoram. Bring to the boil and simmer for 30 minutes. Cool, then blend the soup to a smooth purée. Add salt and pepper and strain through a fine sieve.

Reheat and serve with a spoonful of yogurt in each serving bowl.

Note: Over-ripe tomatoes and mis-shapen lettuce leaves may be used. The soup may be frozen.

Courgette Soup

3 tablespoons oil
450 g/1 lb young courgettes, cut into 5 mm/¼ inch slices
225 g/8 oz canned tomatoes
1 tablespoon tomato purée
good pinch of garlic salt
salt
pepper
600 ml/1 pint water
1 stock cube, crumbled

Garnish
thin lemon slices
chopped parsley

Heat the oil in a saucepan. Add the courgettes and toss to coat with the oil. Stir in the tomatoes, then the garlic salt, salt and pepper. Cover and cook gently for 5 minutes, stirring occasionally.

Add the water and stock cube and bring to the boil. Simmer until the courgettes are tender. Blend to a smooth purée.

Serve hot or cold, garnished with lemon slices and parsley.

Summer Soup

Serves 4–6

1 lettuce, shredded
heart of a Savoy
  cabbage, cored and
  shredded
2 tomatoes, halved
1 leek, chopped
2 or 3 small onions,
  chopped
225 g/8 oz green beans,
  shredded
2 potatoes, chopped
225 g/8 oz shelled fresh
  peas
50 g/2 oz butter
1.2 litres/2 pints water
salt
300 ml/½ pint milk
pepper

Put the lettuce, cabbage, tomatoes, leek, onions, beans, potatoes and peas in a saucepan. Add the butter, water and salt and bring to the boil. Simmer gently until the potatoes are tender.

Stir in the milk and heat through gently. Add pepper and serve hot.

Spanish Summer Soup

Serves 4

1 kg/2 lb canned
  tomatoes
1 green pepper, cored,
  seeded and chopped
100 g/4 oz mushrooms,
  chopped
½ cucumber, chopped
1 garlic clove
2 onions, chopped
100 ml/3 fl oz dry white
  wine
½ teaspoon dried oregano
1 tablespoon lemon juice
salt
pepper

Garnish
twist of lemon
chopped chives
ice cubes

Put all the ingredients into a blender goblet and blend until a smooth purée. (You may have to do this in two batches.) Chill well.

Serve garnished with a twist of lemon, chives and ice cubes.

Batchelor Soup

Serves 6

450 g/1 lb stewing steak, cubed
450 g/1 lb potatoes, quartered if large
225 g/8 oz carrots, diced
225 g/8 oz frozen mixed vegetables
600 ml/1 pint chicken stock
100 ml/3 fl oz white wine
1 teaspoon dried mixed herbs
salt
pepper
freshly boiled potatoes to serve

Put all the ingredients except the freshly boiled potatoes in a saucepan and bring to the boil. Cover and simmer for 45 minutes.

Pour the soup into the blender goblet and blend until smooth. Reheat and serve with freshly boiled potatoes floating in the soup.

Crème Verde

Serves 6

450 g/1 lb potatoes
salt
1 cucumber
1 bunch of watercress
2 to 3 parsley sprigs
600 ml/1 pint chicken stock
pepper
pinch of grated nutmeg
150 ml/¼ pint milk
100 g/4 oz cooked shelled shrimps
1 tablespoon cream

Cook the potatoes in boiling salted water until tender. Meanwhile, cut 6 thin slices of cucumber for the garnish. Peel the remaining cucumber thinly, cut it in half lengthways and scrape out the seeds. Chop the cucumber and put it into a saucepan with the watercress, parsley and stock. Bring to the boil and simmer gently for about 10 minutes or until just tender. Do not overcook or the colour of the finished soup will be spoiled.

Drain the potatoes, then blend them with the cucumber mixture to a smooth purée. Return the purée to the rinsed-out pan and add salt and pepper to taste and enough of the milk to make the soup the desired consistency. Stir in the shrimps and reheat gently without boiling.

Stir in the cream and serve, garnished with the cucumber slices.

Note: Canned shrimps may be used, in which case, add the can liquor to the stock.

Tomato and Almond Soup   *Serves 4*

*2 tablespoons oil,
  preferably olive*
*2 medium onions, thinly
  sliced*
15 g/½ oz flour
*600 ml/1 pint chicken
  stock*
150 ml/¼ pint milk
*450 g/1 lb tomatoes,
  skinned, chopped and
  softened in 5
  tablespoons stock*
*5 drops of almond
  essence*
*finely pared rind of ½
  lemon*
*40 g/1½ oz ground
  almonds*
salt
pepper

Garnish
cream
*borage flower (sepals
  removed) or chopped
  parsley*

Heat the oil in a saucepan and fry the onions until softened. Stir in the flour and cook for 2 minutes, then gradually stir in the stock followed by the milk. Bring to the boil and simmer for 3 minutes. Stir in the tomato mixture.

Blend the soup to a smooth purée, then strain it into a bowl. Add the almond essence, lemon rind and ground almonds and stir well. Add salt and pepper, then cover and chill overnight.

Remove the lemon rind before serving, garnished with a swirl of cream and a borage flower or chopped parsley.

Cucumber and Mint Soup   *Serves 4*

*1 medium cucumber,
  peeled and chopped*
*1.2 litres/2 pints chicken
  or beef stock*
1 bunch of mint
2½ tablespoons cornflour
2 tablespoons water

Garnish
cream or top of milk
*1 tablespoon chopped
  fresh mint*

Put the cucumber in a saucepan with the stock and mint. Bring to the boil and simmer gently until the cucumber is soft. Discard the bunch of mint.

Dissolve the cornflour in the water and add to the pan. Simmer, stirring, until thickened. Serve, hot or cold, garnished with a swirl of cream or top of the milk and chopped mint.

Harvester's Love-Apple Soup
Serves 6

1 kg/2 lb ripe tomatoes, skinned
1 handful of mint leaves
50 g/2 oz wheat germ
25 g/1 oz seedless raisins or sultanas
stock if necessary
salt
pepper

Blend the tomatoes and mint to a purée. Alternatively, pulp the tomatoes in a Mouli-légumes or sieve and stir in the finely chopped mint.

Stir the wheat germ and raisins or sultanas into the tomatoes with enough stock to make the mixture up to 1 litre/1¾ pints. Tip into a saucepan and bring to the boil. Add salt and pepper and serve hot.

Pauline's Prawns
Serves 4

175 g/6 oz cooked shelled prawns
175 g/6 oz button mushrooms, sliced
4 tablespoons olive oil
2 tablespoons lemon juice
salt
pepper
chopped parsley to garnish

Put the prawns and mushrooms in a bowl. Mix together the oil, lemon juice, salt and pepper and pour over the prawns and mushrooms. Toss well together, then leave to marinate for 1 hour.

Sprinkle with parsley before serving.

Garlic Mushrooms
Serves 4–6

150 g/5 oz butter
450 g/1 lb mushrooms, sliced
2 garlic cloves, crushed
salt
pepper
75 g/3 oz Cheddar cheese, grated

Melt 100 g/4 oz of the butter in a frying pan. Add the mushrooms and fry quickly until just tender. Stir in the garlic, salt and freshly ground black pepper. Divide between 6 small ovenproof dishes.

Divide the remaining butter into 6 portions and place one in each dish. Top with the cheese.

Bake in a preheated moderately hot oven (200°C/400°F, Gas Mark 6) for 15 minutes. Serve hot with wholemeal bread or toast fingers.

Secret Salad

Serves 4

*1 Webb's Wonder
 lettuce, shredded*
100 g/4 oz croûtons
Dressing
150 ml/¼ pint oil
*150 ml/¼ pint malt
 vinegar*
2 eggs
*50 g/2 oz canned anchovy
 fillets with oil*
4 garlic cloves
1 teaspoon dry mustard
juice of ½ lemon
1 tablespoon soy sauce
*1 tablespoon
 Worcestershire sauce*
salt
pepper

Put all the dressing ingredients in the blender goblet and blend to a smooth purée.

Mix together the lettuce and croûtons in a salad bowl. Pour over about one-quarter of the dressing and toss well. Serve. The remainder of the dressing will keep in a covered container in the refrigerator for about 2 weeks.

Kate's Surprise

Serves 4

15 g/½ oz gelatine
300 ml/½ pint water
1 teaspoon lemon juice
*1 teaspoon anchovy
 essence*
salt
pepper
4 thin tomato slices
*150 g/5 oz cooked shelled
 prawns*
*1 tablespoon chopped
 parsley*
*50 g/2 oz cottage cheese,
 sieved*

To serve
lettuce leaves
tomato slices

Dissolve the gelatine in the water, then mix in the lemon juice, anchovy essence, salt and pepper.

Arrange the tomato slices on the bottom of a 600 ml/1 pint mould and pour over a thin layer of the gelatine mixture. Chill until set.

Fold the prawns and parsley into two-thirds of the remaining gelatine mixture. Spoon into the mould on top of the tomato slices and chill until set.

Mix the cottage cheese with the remainder of the gelatine mixture and spoon into the mould. Chill until set.

Line a serving plate with lettuce leaves and tomato slices and turn out the jelly on to it.

Stuffed Steak

Serves 4

4 × 175 g/6 oz rump or fillet steaks, cut about 1.5 cm/¾ inch thick
100 g/4 oz mushrooms, diced
1 green pepper, cored, seeded and diced
5 tomatoes, diced
25 g/1 oz butter
1 garlic clove, crushed
2 small onions, thinly sliced
300 ml/½ pint red wine
225 g/8 oz canned tomatoes
salt
pepper

Make a cut in each steak, not all the way through, then open it like a book and beat with a rolling pin or steak mallet to flatten it.

Mix together the mushrooms, green pepper and diced tomatoes. Put 1 to 2 tablespoons of the vegetables on one half of each steak and reshape them. Secure with wooden cocktail sticks.

Melt the butter in a frying pan and fry the garlic and onions until softened. Add the steak parcels to the pan and brown quickly on both sides. Transfer the steaks and pan juices to a casserole.

Put the wine, canned tomatoes, salt and pepper in the pan and bring to the boil. Pour this over the steaks and add any remaining vegetable mixture. Bake in a preheated moderate oven (180°C/350°F, Gas Mark 4) for 45 minutes. Remove the cocktail sticks before serving.

Tomato Fondue

Serves 6

3 garlic cloves
1 teaspoon salt
298 g/10½ oz canned condensed tomato soup
225 g/8 oz Stilton cheese, crumbled or grated
225 g/8 oz Red Leicester cheese, grated
1 tablespoon tomato purée
120 ml/4 fl oz sweet sherry

To Serve
chunks of French bread
carrot sticks
celery sticks

Crush the garlic with the salt and put into a heavy saucepan with the remaining ingredients. Heat very gently, stirring, until the cheese has melted and the mixture is just below boiling point. Do not allow it to boil.

Transfer the mixture to a fondue pot, or wrap the base of the saucepan in a thick towel or several table napkins and rush it to the table. Serve with chunks of French bread, carrot and celery sticks and any other vegetables of your choice for dipping.

Huddersfield Hash
Serves 3–4

50 g/2 oz butter
1 large Spanish onion,
finely chopped
1 bay leaf
pinch of paprika
pinch of cumin seed
pinch of ground coriander
pinch of garlic powder
450 g/1 lb minced beef
100 g/4 oz canned
tomatoes
225 g/8 oz courgettes,
sliced
450 ml/¾ pint thick
cheese sauce
1 large egg, beaten

Melt 25 g/1 oz of the butter in a frying pan and fry the onion until lightly browned. Stir in the bay leaf and spices, adding more if you wish, then crumble in the beef. Fry until the beef is well browned.

Meanwhile, melt the remaining butter in another pan. Add the courgettes and brown on all sides.

Add the courgettes to the meat mixture with the tomatoes. Simmer gently for 15 minutes until the mixture is thick.

Mix together the cheese sauce and egg.

Turn the meat mixture into a baking dish and cover with the cheese sauce. Bake in a preheated moderate oven (180°C/350°F, Gas Mark 4) for 30 minutes or until the top is golden brown. Serve with a green vegetable.

Tropical Mackerel
Serves 4

25 g/1 oz butter
1 medium onion, finely
chopped
200 g/7 oz canned
crushed pineapple,
drained
25 g/1 oz diced red
pepper
2 garlic cloves, crushed
few drops of
Worcestershire sauce
pinch of dried mixed
herbs
salt
4 medium whole
mackerel, cleaned

Melt the butter in a frying pan and fry the onion until softened. Stir in the pineapple, red pepper, garlic, Worcestershire sauce, herbs and salt and leave to cool.

When the stuffing is cool, use it to fill the cavities in the mackerel. Secure the fish closed with wooden cocktail sticks. If there is any stuffing left over, spread it on the bottom of a greased ovenproof dish. Place the fish on top, cover the dish and cook in a preheated moderate oven (180°C/350°F, Gas Mark 4) for 45 minutes or until the fish is done.

Remove the cocktail sticks before serving, hot or cold, with French bread and a green salad.

281

Kidneys in a Nest

Serves 4

75 g/3 oz noodles
salt
5 sheep kidneys, skinned,
* halved and cored*
flour for coating
75 g/3 oz butter
1 small onion, chopped
50 g/2 oz button
* mushrooms, halved*
150 ml/¼ pint white wine
2 teaspoons flour
pepper
chopped parsley to
* garnish*

Cook the noodles in boiling salted water until they are tender.

Meanwhile, coat the kidney pieces with flour. Melt 50 g/2 oz of the butter in a frying pan, add the kidney pieces and brown on both sides. Add the onion and fry until softened. Stir in the mushrooms and fry for a further 2 minutes. Add the wine, stir well and bring to the boil. Leave to simmer gently.

Drain the noodles and arrange in a warmed serving dish. Keep hot.

Blend the remaining butter with the 2 teaspoons flour to make a paste. Add to the kidney mixture and simmer, stirring, until thickened. Add salt and pepper.

Pour the kidney mixture over the noodles and sprinkle with parsley.

Spicy Barbecue Sauce

Serves 6

50 g/2 oz butter or
* margarine*
1 large onion, chopped
175 g/6 oz canned
* mushrooms, drained*
3 tablespoons vinegar
1 tablespoon tomato
* paste*
1 tablespoon dry mustard
3 tablespoons
* Worcestershire sauce*
3 drops Tabasco sauce
3 tablespoons
* evaporated milk*
150 ml/¼ pint water
175 ml/6 fl oz dry white
* wine*
herbs and spices to taste
* (optional)*

Melt the butter or margarine in a saucepan and fry the onion until softened. Stir in the remaining ingredients and bring to the boil. Simmer for 20 minutes, stirring occasionally. Serve with chicken, sausages, hamburgers or chops.
Note: This sauce may be reheated.

Chicken in Brandy

Serves 4–6

*1 × 1.5 kg/3 lb chicken,
  jointed
salt
pepper
100 g/4 oz butter
225 g/8 oz mushrooms,
  sliced
1 tablespoon brandy,
  warmed
1 tablespoon flour
1½ teaspoons tomato
  purée or sauce
450 ml/¾ pint cream*

Rub the chicken joints with salt and pepper. Melt the butter in a heavy pan, add the chicken joints and brown on all sides. Continue cooking for about 30 minutes or until tender.

Add the mushrooms and cook for a further 5 minutes.

Pour in the brandy and set it alight. When the flames have died down, remove the chicken and mushrooms from the pan. Arrange on a warmed serving dish and keep hot.

Stir the flour into the cooking juices in the pan, then stir in the tomato purée, cream and salt and pepper. Simmer gently for 10 minutes, stirring frequently. Pour this sauce over the chicken and serve.

Kidneys with Red Wine

Serves 4

*50 g/2 oz butter
8 lamb's kidneys, skinned
  and halved
1 large onion
  thinly sliced
1 large carrot, thinly
  sliced
1 tablespoon flour
1 teaspoon tomato purée
100 ml/3 fl oz red wine
250 ml/8 fl oz stock
1 bouquet garni
175 to 225 g/6 to 8 oz
  flat mushrooms
browned breadcrumbs
chopped parsley to
  garnish*

Melt 40 g/1½ oz of the butter in a flameproof casserole. Add the kidneys and brown quickly on both sides. Remove them from the pot. Add the onion and carrot to the casserole and fry until they are golden brown. Sprinkle over the flour and stir in well, then stir in the tomato purée. Stir in the wine, bring to the boil and boil until reduced by about one-quarter.

Add the stock and return to the boil. Replace the kidneys in the casserole and add the bouquet garni. Cover the casserole and transfer to a preheated moderately hot oven (200°C/400°F, Gas Mark 6). Cook for 20 minutes.

Discard the bouquet garni and turn the kidney mixture into a baking dish. Lay the mushrooms on top, stalks up, and sprinkle generously with breadcrumbs. Dot with the remaining 15 g/½ oz butter. Return to the oven and bake for a further 15 minutes or until the top is browned. Serve garnished with parsley.
Note: Ox or pig kidneys may also be used, but allow a longer cooking time.

Adam's Lamb
Serves 4

2 breasts of lamb, cut
  into 'riblets'
600 ml/1 pint water
6 tablespoons malt
  vinegar
3 tablespoons plum jam
3 tablespoons tomato
  purée or sauce
1 tablespoon honey
2 tablespoons lemon juice
1 teaspoon made mustard
3 tablespoons soy sauce
1 tablespoon
  Worcestershire sauce
salt
pepper
saffron rice to serve

Put the lamb riblets in a saucepan with the water and 4 tablespoons of the vinegar. Bring to the boil, then cover and simmer for 20 minutes. Drain the lamb.

Put the remaining ingredients, including the rest of the vinegar, in a saucepan and heat gently, stirring, until well combined.

Arrange the lamb riblets in a roasting tin and pour over the sauce. Roast in a preheated moderately hot oven (200°C/400°F, Gas Mark 6) for 40 minutes, basting the riblets with the sauce every 15 minutes. Increase the heat to hot (230°C/450°F, Gas Mark 8) and roast for a further 10 minutes to crisp the coating.

Serve hot on a bed of saffron rice.

Savoury Sausage Casserole
Serves 6

2 tablespoons oil
1 large green pepper,
  cored, seeded and
  chopped
450 g/1 lb tomatoes,
  skinned and chopped
450 g/1 lb courgettes,
  peeled and chopped
450 g/1 lb cooking
  apples, peeled, cored
  and chopped
1 tablespoon chopped
  fresh thyme
salt
pepper
450 g/1 lb sausagemeat
1 large onion, sliced
100 g/4 oz Cheddar
  cheese, grated

Heat the oil in a frying pan. Add the green pepper and fry gently for 2 to 3 minutes. Add the tomatoes, courgettes, apples, thyme, salt and pepper and stir well. Cover and simmer gently for 20 minutes.

Meanwhile, press the sausagemeat into a 20 cm/8 inch square baking tin. Scatter the onion rings on top. Pour over the vegetable mixture and sprinkle with the cheese.

Bake in a preheated moderately hot oven (190°C/375°F, Gas Mark 5) for 45 minutes. Serve hot with baked potatoes or crusty rolls and a salad.

Seafood Suprême

Serves 4

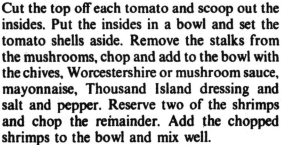

4 medium firm tomatoes
2 large flat mushrooms
1 tablespoon chopped chives
2 teaspoons Worcestershire or mushroom sauce
2 tablespoons mayonnaise
3 tablespoons Thousand Island dressing
salt
pepper
50 g/2 oz cooked shelled shrimps
50 g/2 oz frozen peas, thawed
50 g/2 oz frozen sweetcorn, thawed
150 g/5 oz butter
2 thick coley fillets, skinned
25 g/1 oz flour
150 ml/¼ pint milk
watercress or parsley to garnish

Cut the top off each tomato and scoop out the insides. Put the insides in a bowl and set the tomato shells aside. Remove the stalks from the mushrooms, chop and add to the bowl with the chives, Worcestershire or mushroom sauce, mayonnaise, Thousand Island dressing and salt and pepper. Reserve two of the shrimps and chop the remainder. Add the chopped shrimps to the bowl and mix well.

Fill two of the tomatoes with peas and the other two with sweetcorn. Place the tomatoes in a small baking dish and sprinkle them with salt and pepper. Dot the tops with 25 g/1 oz of the butter. Bake in a preheated moderate oven (160°C/325°F, Gas Mark 3) while you prepare the fish.

Melt half the remaining butter in a frying pan. Add the fish and cook until firm and tender. Transfer the fish to a warmed flat serving dish and keep hot.

Cook the mushroom caps in the remaining fat until tender. Remove them from the pan and keep warm.

Add the remaining butter to the pan. When it has melted, stir in the flour and cook for 2 minutes. Gradually stir in the milk and bring to the boil. Simmer, stirring, until thickened. Add the shrimp mixture from the bowl and simmer gently, stirring frequently, for 5 minutes.

Pour the sauce over the fish and garnish each with a mushroom cap. Place a whole reserved shrimp in each mushroom cap. Arrange the stuffed tomatoes at alternate corners of the dish and garnish with watercress or parsley.

Chicken Montreal
Serves 4

4 chicken breasts,
  skinned and boned
2 tomatoes, halved
1 garlic clove, finely
  chopped
salt
pepper
4 back bacon rashers,
  rinded
425 g/15 oz canned
  tomatoes
300 ml/½ pint chicken
  stock
1 tablespoon arrowroot
100 g/4 oz mozzarella
  cheese, sliced
½ teaspoon dried
  marjoram

Beat each chicken breast with a mallet to flatten. Place a tomato half on each breast and sprinkle with garlic, salt and pepper. Roll up the breasts, then wrap a bacon rasher around each and secure with a wooden cocktail stick.

Arrange the chicken in a baking dish and pour over the tomatoes and stock. Bake in a preheated moderate oven (180°C/350°F, Gas Mark 4) for 40 minutes or until the chicken is tender.

Drain off the cooking liquid into a saucepan. Mix the arrowroot with a little water and add to the pan. Cook, stirring, until thickened. Pour this sauce back over the chicken. Cover with the cheese slices and sprinkle with the marjoram. Return to the oven and bake for a further 10 minutes or until the cheese has melted.

Ground Nut Stew
Serves 6

large knob of fat or
  dripping
1 kg/2 lb shin of beef, cut
  into chunks
2 large onions, sliced
1 garlic clove, crushed
1½ tablespoons flour
salt
pepper
½ teaspoon chilli powder
1 teaspoon Bovril
1 teaspoon Marmite
300 ml/½ pint hot water
1 heaped tablespoon
  tomato purée
3 tablespoons chunky
  peanut butter

Melt the fat or dripping in a saucepan. Add the beef and fry until the chunks are browned on all sides. Remove them from the pan.

Add the onions and garlic to the pan and fry until lightly browned. Stir in the flour, salt, pepper and chilli powder, then return the beef to the pan.

Mix the Bovril and Marmite into the hot water and stir half of this stock into the pan. Add the tomato purée and peanut butter, then the remaining stock and mix well. If necessary, add more water so that the meat is covered.

Bring to the boil, then simmer gently for 1½ to 2 hours or until the meat is tender.

Hasty Fish Pie

Serves 4–6

450 g/1 lb coley fillet,
  skinned
300 ml/½ pint water
salt
pepper
25 g/1 oz butter
2 onions, sliced
75 g/3 oz mushrooms,
  sliced
3 hard-boiled eggs, sliced
1 teaspoon dried mixed
  herbs
600 ml/1 pint parsley
  sauce
750 g/1½ lb mashed
  potato

Put the coley in a saucepan with the water, salt and pepper. Bring to a simmer, then poach gently until tender. Drain the fish, reserving the liquid to make the parsley sauce (half milk, half water), if you like. Flake the fish.

Melt the butter in a frying pan and fry the onions until softened. Stir in the fish and remove from the heat.

Make alternate layers of the fish mixture, mushrooms, eggs, herbs, sauce and potatoes, ending with potatoes, in a baking dish. Bake in a preheated moderately hot oven (200°C/400°F, Gas Mark 6) for 30 minutes or until the top is golden brown.

Note: Mash the potatoes with lots of butter.

Variation: Grated cheese and sliced tomatoes may be put on the top before baking.

Chiltern Country Pie

Serves 6

100 g/4 oz dried apricots
1 medium onion
350 g/12 oz minced beef
100 g/4 oz pork
  sausagemeat
100 g/4 oz streaky bacon
  or bacon pieces, rinded
2 teaspoons dried Italian
  seasoning
100 ml/3 fl oz port
shortcrust pastry made
  with 225 g/8 oz flour,
  50 g/2 oz lard and
  50 g/2 oz margarine
parsley sprig to garnish

Finely chop the apricots or put them through the mincer. Mince together the onion, beef, sausagemeat and bacon. Add the apricots, herbs and port and mix well.

Roll out two-thirds of the pastry and use to line a 1 kg/2 lb loaf tin. Press in the meat filling. Roll out the remaining pastry for the lid and crimp the edges together to seal. Make three slits in the lid.

Bake in a preheated moderately hot oven (200°C/400°F, Gas Mark 6) for 10 minutes, then lower the temperature to moderate (180°C/350°F, Gas Mark 4) and bake for a further 30 minutes.

Loosen the pie with a knife, then leave in the tin to cool. Turn out to serve, garnished with parsley.

Pork Chops in Cream Sauce

Serves 4

4 pork chops
1 small egg, beaten
crushed wheatflakes or
* breadcrumbs to coat*
75 g/3 oz butter or
* margarine*
1 medium onion, sliced
1 garlic clove, crushed
50 g/2 oz mushrooms,
* chopped*
½ red or green pepper,
* cored, seeded, sliced*
* and blanched*
300 ml/½ pint béchamel
* sauce*
5 tablespoons medium
* sherry*
5 tablespoons single
* cream*
good pinch of grated
* lemon rind*
salt
pepper

Garnish
1 red apple, cored, cut
* into 4 rings and fried*
* in butter*
2 spiced prunes, halved
chopped parsley

Dip the chops in beaten egg, then coat with wheatflakes or breadcrumbs. Melt 40 g/1½ oz of the fat in a frying pan and fry the chops until they are crisp and brown on both sides. Transfer them to a baking dish with the fat from the pan and cook in a preheated moderate oven (180°C/350°F, Gas Mark 4) for 45 minutes to 1 hour or until tender.

Meanwhile, melt half of the remaining fat in the cleaned-out frying pan and fry the onion and garlic until softened. In another pan, melt the remaining fat and fry the mushrooms until tender. Drain all the vegetables.

Heat up the béchamel sauce and stir in the sherry, cream, lemon rind, salt, pepper and mushrooms.

Arrange the chops on a warmed serving platter. Surround with the onion and green pepper and pour around the sauce. Place an apple ring on each chop and put half a prune in the centre. Sprinkle with parsley and serve.

Note: If no spiced prunes are available, soak prunes in cold tea until they are plump, then drain and simmer with a little sherry and sugar until the prunes are nicely glazed.

Calf's Liver with Orange

Serves 4

2 to 3 tablespoons flour
salt
pepper
pinch of dry mustard
pinch of cayenne pepper
6 to 8 slices of calf's liver
50 g/2 oz butter
1 onion, finely chopped
2 garlic cloves, crushed
100 ml/3 fl oz red wine
450 ml/¾ pint stock
1 tablespoon chopped
  parsley
1 teaspoon chopped fresh
  thyme

Pilaff
25 g/1 oz butter
1 onion, thinly sliced
150 g/5 oz long-grain rice
salt
pepper
pinch of saffron powder
  (optional)
450 to 600 ml/¾ to 1 pint
  stock
25 g/1 oz cheese, grated

Garnish
15 g/½ oz butter
sugar
1 orange, thinly sliced

First make the pilaff. Melt two-thirds of the butter in a flameproof casserole. Add the onion and fry until softened. Stir in the rice and fry for a few minutes. Add salt, pepper and the saffron, if using. Stir in 450 ml/¾ pint of stock and bring to the boil. Cover and transfer to a preheated moderate oven (180°C/350°F, Gas Mark 4). Cook for 20 to 30 minutes or until the rice is tender and the stock has been absorbed.

Meanwhile, mix the flour with salt, pepper, the mustard and cayenne. Use to coat the liver slices. Melt 25 g/1 oz of the butter in a frying pan. Add the liver slices and fry quickly until brown and firm. Arrange the slices in a warmed serving dish and keep hot.

Add the rest of the butter to the frying pan. When it has melted, add the onion and garlic and fry until golden. Stir in the wine, bring to the boil and boil until reduced by half. Add the stock and herbs, return to the boil and simmer for 1 minute. Spoon this sauce over the liver.

Wipe out the pan. Add the butter for the garnish, melt it and sprinkle with sugar. Add the orange slices and brown quickly on both sides. Arrange them around the liver. Keep hot.

Stir the pilaff with a fork. Add the rest of the butter, the cheese and the remaining stock if necessary, mix well and serve with the liver.

Swedish Meatballs
Serves 6

450 g/1 lb minced beef
225 g/8 oz minced pork
25 g/1 oz fresh
  breadcrumbs
1 onion, finely chopped
1 teaspoon sugar
½ teaspoon ground
  allspice
salt
pepper
1 egg, beaten
250 ml/8 fl oz milk
100 g/4 oz butter
450 ml/¾ pint stock

Mix together the beef, pork, breadcrumbs, onion, sugar, allspice, salt and pepper, using your hands to combine the ingredients thoroughly. Bind together with the egg and milk. Shape into walnut-sized balls.

Melt the butter in a frying pan and fry the meatballs, in batches, until they are brown on all sides. As they brown, transfer them to a saucepan.

Pour the stock over the browned meatballs and bring to the boil. Cover and simmer for 30 minutes.

Corned Beef Mould
Serves 4

4 tablespoons raw swede,
  shredded
1½ tablespoons made
  mustard
1½ tablespoons vinegar
100 g/4 oz corned beef
100 g/4 oz soaked bread
175 g/6 oz carrots,
  cooked and mashed
1 tablespoon parsley,
  chopped

Mix together the swede, mustard and vinegar, then add the remaining ingredients and combine well. Press into a 500 g/1 lb pudding basin. Put a plate on top and then a weight and leave for 4 hours.

Turn out of the basin and cut into slices. Serve with potato salad.

Rhubarb Semolina Pudding
Serves 4

350 g/12 oz rhubarb,
  chopped
150 ml/¼ pint water
90 g/3½ oz sugar
25 g/1 oz margarine
½ teaspoon ground ginger
50 g/2 oz semolina
2 tablespoons milk
1 egg, beaten

Put the rhubarb in a saucepan with the water and sugar and simmer gently until tender. Stir in the margarine and ginger.

Mix the semolina with the milk and add to the rhubarb. Combine thoroughly. Cool slightly, then mix in the egg. Turn into a greased pie dish and bake in a preheated moderate oven (180°C/350°F, Gas Mark 4) for 35 to 40 minutes. Serve hot.

Honey Orange Soufflés
Serves 6

thinly pared rind and juice of 2 medium oranges
150 ml/¼ pint milk
15 g/½ oz gelatine
2 tablespoons water
2 teaspoons lemon juice
3 large eggs, separated
2 tablespoons English honey
1 tablespoon caster sugar
150 ml/¼ pint double cream, whipped

Put the orange rind and milk in a saucepan and bring to just below boiling point. Remove from the heat and set aside to infuse.

Meanwhile, dissolve the gelatine in the water. Stir in the orange and lemon juices. Keep the gelatine mixture warm so that it does not set.

Put the egg yolks, honey and sugar in a heatproof bowl over a pan of hot water and whisk until the mixture is pale and frothy. Strain the milk, reserving the orange rind, and add to the egg yolk mixture. Continue whisking until the mixture thickens. Place the bowl in another bowl of cold water and leave to cool for 5 minutes, stirring constantly. Stir in the gelatine mixture and chill until thick.

Whisk the egg whites until stiff and fold into the orange custard. Turn into 6 individual glasses and chill until set. Serve decorated with whipped cream and a few shreds of the reserved orange rind.

Strawberry and Blackcurrant Snow Cream Delight
Serves 4–6

1 packet blackcurrant jelly
350 g/12 oz strawberries, hulled
2 egg whites
150 ml/¼ pint whipping cream

To Decorate
1 chocolate flake bar, crushed
2–3 glacé cherries, halved

Put the jelly in a measuring cup and make up to 300 ml/½ pint with water. Tip into a saucepan and heat gently until melted. Do not boil. Pour into a bowl and leave to cool until it begins to thicken.

Blend the strawberries to a purée. Whisk the jelly mixture until foamy, then gradually whisk in the strawberry purée. Whisk the egg whites until stiff. Whip the cream until thick. Fold the cream into the strawberry mixture followed by the egg whites. Divide between 4 to 6 sundae dishes and chill until firm and set.

Decorate each serving with a little crushed chocolate and half a glacé cherry.

Orange and Chocolate Yog-Torte
Serves 6

20 g/¾ oz gelatine
5 tablespoons water
2 large eating apples,
  peeled, cored and
  sliced
200 ml/⅓ pint orange
  juice, unsweetened
175 g/6 oz caster sugar
25 g/1 oz cocoa powder,
  sifted
2 eggs, separated
150 g/5 oz Jaffa orange
  yogurt
175 g/6 oz double cream
1 tablespoon Cointreau
  (optional)
75 g/3 oz fresh brown
  breadcrumbs

To Decorate
150 ml/¼ pint double
  cream
1 tablespoon icing sugar
dash of Cointreau
  (optional)
chocolate curls

Dissolve the gelatine in the water. Rinse and chill an 18 cm/7 inch non-stick or stainless steel cake tin. Arrange the apple slices on the bottom of the tin.

Put the orange juice and sugar in a saucepan and heat gently, stirring to dissolve the sugar. Stir in the gelatine. Spoon enough of this mixture over the apples in the tin just to cover them and chill until set.

Add the cocoa powder to the rest of the orange juice mixture and bring to the boil, stirring. Cool.

Beat the egg yolks with the yogurt, cream and Cointreau, if used. Whisk the egg whites until stiff. Mix the orange juice mixture and breadcrumbs into the yolk mixture, then fold in the egg whites. Pour over the apples in the tin and chill until set.

Turn out the torte on to a chilled serving dish. Whip the cream with the icing sugar and Cointreau, if used, and pipe in roses around the top and bottom edges of the torte. Decorate with chocolate curls.

Pineapple Cheese Cream
Serves 6

275 g/10 oz canned
  crushed pineapple
1 packet lime jelly
75 g/3 oz Philadelphia
  cream cheese
½ sachet Dream Topping,
  made up as directed
50 g/2 oz nuts, crushed
50 g/2 oz celery, diced
grated rind of 1 lemon
¼ small green pepper,
  cored, seeded and diced

Drain the pineapple and reserve the syrup. Make up the jelly according to the directions on the packet, using the pineapple syrup and hot water. Allow to cool, then mix in the remaining ingredients. Pour into 6 individual ramekin dishes or a serving dish about 3.5 cm/1½ inches deep. Chill until set.

Lemon Ice Box
Serves 4–6

4 trifle sponge cakes
100 g/4 oz unsalted
  butter, melted
100 g/4 oz caster sugar
4 large eggs, separated
grated rind and juice of 2
  medium lemons
pinch of salt

To Decorate
whipped cream
glacé cherries
chocolate flakes
nuts
orange and lemon slices

Split each sponge cake into three slices. Cream together the butter and sugar. Beat in the egg yolks, followed by the lemon rind and juice. Whisk the egg whites with the salt until stiff and fold into the creamed mixture.

Make alternate layers of sponge cake and lemon mixture in a 500 g/1 lb loaf tin lined with bakewell or greaseproof paper. Start and finish with sponge cake. Cover and leave in the coldest part of the refrigerator (not the freezer) for at least 6 hours or overnight.

Turn out on to a serving plate and cover with whipped cream.

Cinnamon Apple Slice
Serves 4–6

100 g/4 oz self-raising
  flour
pinch of salt
50 g/2 oz shredded suet
5 tablespoons cold water

Filling
225 g/8 oz cooking
  apples, peeled, cored
  and chopped
25 g/1 oz sultanas
25 g/1 oz demerara sugar
1 teaspoon ground
  cinnamon
milk
25 g/1 oz granulated
  sugar

Sift the flour and salt into a bowl. Mix in the suet, then bind to a dough with the water. Chill for 10 minutes.

Meanwhile, mix together the apple, sultanas, demerara sugar and cinnamon.

Roll out the dough to a 34 × 23 cm/13 × 9 inch rectangle. Spoon the apple filling down the centre of the rectangle. Dampen the dough edges, then fold the long sides over the filling followed by the short sides. Transfer to a baking sheet. Brush with milk and sprinkle with the granulated sugar.

Bake in a preheated moderately hot oven (200°C/400°F, Gas Mark 6) for 30 minutes or until firm and golden brown. Serve hot, cut into diagonal slices, with rum sauce or cold with cream.

Apple Surprise

Serves 4

*4 dessert apples, peeled
and cored
4 tablespoons mincemeat
4 egg whites
225 g/8 oz caster sugar
hot chocolate sauce to
serve*

Put the apples in a saucepan with a little water and poach gently until they are tender, but not mushy. Drain and arrange in a baking dish. Fill the hollows with the mincemeat.

Whisk the egg whites until stiff. Add 4 teaspoons of the sugar and continue whisking for 1 minute, then carefully fold in the remaining sugar. Pile this meringue on the apples and swirl around to cover them.

Bake in a preheated hot oven (220°C/425°F, Gas Mark 7) for 10 minutes or until the meringue is golden brown. Serve with hot chocolate sauce.

Nutty Bars

Makes 25–30

*50 g/2 oz butter, melted
225 g/8 oz soft brown
sugar
1 egg, beaten
¼ teaspoon vanilla essence
100 g/4 oz plain or self-
raising flour
1 heaped teaspoon baking
powder
½ teaspoon salt
100 g/4 oz walnuts,
almonds, hazelnuts or
cashews, chopped*

Mix together the butter and sugar, then beat in the egg and vanilla essence. Sift the flour with the baking powder and salt and stir into the sugar mixture. Fold in the nuts.

Turn the mixture into a greased and lined Swiss roll tin. Bake in a preheated moderate oven (180°C/350°F, Gas Mark 4) for 30 minutes, or until a skewer inserted into the centre comes out clean.

Cut into bars while still hot, then leave to cool in the tin.

Note: If you prefer, use a mixture of the nuts suggested.

Nutty Cheese Biscuits

Makes 20

*100 g/4 oz Cheddar
cheese, grated
100 g/4 oz soft margarine
100 g/4 oz flour
½ teaspoon mustard
powder
75 g/3 oz porridge oats
100 g/4 oz peanuts,
chopped*

Cream together the cheese and margarine. Sift the flour and mustard into a bowl and mix in the oats and nuts. Add this to the creamed mixture and knead together lightly.

Pull off walnut-sized pieces and shape them into balls. Arrange on a greased baking sheet and flatten the balls. Bake in a preheated moderate oven (180°C/350°F, Gas Mark 4) for 15 to 20 minutes.

Eggless Cake

225 g/8 oz self-raising
    flour
1 teaspoon baking
    powder
1 teaspoon bicarbonate of
    soda
pinch of grated nutmeg
100 g/4 oz sugar
50 g/2 oz margarine
50 g/2 oz raisins
50 g/2 oz currants
25 g/1 oz candied citron,
    chopped
150 ml/¼ pint milk

Sift the flour, baking powder, bicarbonate of soda and nutmeg into a bowl. Stir in the sugar, then rub in the margarine. Add the dried fruit and citron and bind together with the milk. Cover and leave overnight.

The next day, turn into a greased 18 cm/7 inch tin and bake in a preheated moderate oven (180°C/350°F, Gas Mark 4) for 2 hours.

Cornish Splits or Tuffs
Makes 28

2 teaspoons dried yeast
300 ml/1 pint lukewarm
    milk
450 g/1 lb self-raising
    flour
1 teaspoon caster sugar
1 teaspoon salt
50 g/2 oz lard

Mix the yeast with the milk and leave in a warm place until frothy. Sift the flour, sugar and salt into a bowl and rub in the lard. Add the yeast mixture and mix to a soft workable dough. Leave to rise in a warm place for about 1 hour.

Divide the dough into 28 portions and shape them into balls. Arrange them on baking sheets and flatten them slightly. Leave to prove for 5 to 10 minutes.

Bake in a preheated moderately hot oven (200°C/400°F, Gas Mark 6) for 15 to 20 minutes.

Note: All ingredients should be at room temperature.

Walnut Crispies

Makes 35–40

100 g/4 oz margarine
100 g/4 oz sugar
175 g/6 oz dates, stoned
  and chopped
50 g/2 oz sultanas
50 g/2 oz glacé cherries,
  chopped
50 g/2 oz walnuts,
  chopped
50 g/2 oz Rice Krispies
100 g/4 oz plain or milk
  chocolate, melted

Put the margarine, sugar, dates, sultanas and cherries in a saucepan and bring to the boil, stirring well. Simmer until the dates are soft and tender. Remove from the heat and fold in the walnuts and Rice Krispies.

Turn into a greased Swiss roll tin and spread out evenly. Cool slightly, then cover with the melted chocolate. Cool completely before cutting into pieces.

Paradise Cakes

Makes 25–30

175 g/6 oz margarine
150 g/5 oz caster sugar
3 eggs, beaten
100 g/4 oz ground rice
75 g/3 oz ground
  almonds
50 g/2 oz sultanas
50 g/2 oz glacé cherries
75 g/3 oz currants
shortcrust pastry, made
  with 100 g/4 oz flour
caster sugar to dredge

Cream the margarine and sugar together until pale and fluffy. Gradually beat in the eggs, then mix in the ground rice and almonds. Fold in the fruit.

Roll out the dough and use to line a Swiss roll tin. Spread the fruit mixture over the dough. Bake in a preheated moderate oven (180°C/350°F, Gas Mark 4) for 45 minutes.

Cool, then cut into fingers and dredge with caster sugar.

Vinegar Cake

225 g/8 oz self-raising
  flour
½ teaspoon salt
100 g/4 oz caster sugar
75 g/3 oz margarine
50 g/2 oz currants
50 g/2 oz raisins
25 g/1 oz chopped mixed
  peel
1 tablespoon vinegar
9 tablespoons milk

Sift the flour, salt and sugar into a bowl. Rub in the margarine, then mix in the dried fruit and peel. Mix to a dropping consistency with the vinegar and milk.

Turn into a greased 18 cm/7 inch cake tin. Bake in a preheated moderate oven (180°C/350°F, Gas Mark 4) for about 1½ hours.

Brooklyn Cake

300 ml/½ pint boiling water

1¼ teaspoons bicarbonate of soda

175 g/6 oz dates, stoned and finely chopped

175 g/6 oz butter or margarine

350 g/12 oz granulated or brown sugar

3 eggs

300 g/11 oz flour, sifted

Dissolve the bicarbonate of soda in the water. Add the dates and leave to cool.

Cream together the fat and sugar, then beat in the eggs. Alternately, fold in the flour and the date mixture. Turn into a greased and lined 25 cm/10 inch baking tin and bake in a preheated moderate oven (180°C/350°F, Gas Mark 4) for 50 minutes or until the top of the cake is firm.

Variations: For a chocolate cake, add 25 g/1 oz cocoa powder and 1 teaspoon instant coffee powder or ½ teaspoon vanilla essence with the flour. Make an icing with 225 g/8 oz icing sugar, 25 g/1 oz cocoa powder and a little coffee or vanilla essence.

For a coffee walnut cake, add 2 to 3 tablespoons coffee essence and 75 g/3 oz chopped walnuts with the flour. Make an icing with 225 g/8 oz icing sugar and coffee essence to taste, and decorate with walnut halves or chopped walnuts.

For a ginger and orange cake, add the grated rind of 2 oranges, 2 tablespoons concentrated frozen orange juice (undiluted), 100 g/4 oz chopped mixed peel and 2 teaspoons ground ginger with the flour. Make an icing with 225 g/8 oz icing sugar and orange juice.

For a lemon and cherry cake, add the grated rind and juice of 2 large lemons, 75 g/3 oz chopped glacé cherries and 75 g/3 oz desiccated coconut with the flour. Make an icing with 225 g/8 oz icing sugar and lemon juice.

Hot Apple Muffins

225 g/8 oz flour
1 teaspoon baking powder
75 g/3 oz lard
50 g/2 oz dark brown sugar
3 large cooking apples, peeled, cored and minced
1 egg, beaten
milk
To Serve
butter
caster sugar

Sift the flour and baking powder into a bowl. Rub in the lard, then stir in the sugar. Mix together the apples and egg and add to the flour mixture with a little milk if the mixture seems too dry.

Turn into a greased Swiss roll tin and bake in a preheated moderately hot oven (200°C/400°F, Gas Mark 6) for 35 minutes or until evenly browned.

Cut into 7.5 cm/3 inch rounds for traditionally shaped muffins or cut into squares. Split open and spread with butter. Dredge with caster sugar and serve hot.

Claremont Gingerbread

450 g/1 lb flour
2 teaspoons bicarbonate of soda
2 teaspoons ground ginger
2 teaspoons ground rice
225 g/8 oz butter
225 g/8 oz demerara sugar
2 tablespoons dark treacle
1 egg, beaten
1 tablespoon milk

Sift together the flour, bicarbonate of soda and ginger. Stir in the ground rice.

Put the butter, sugar and treacle in a saucepan and heat gently, stirring until the butter has melted and the sugar has dissolved. Remove from the heat and stir in the flour mixture. Beat in the egg and milk.

Turn into a greased 20 cm/8 inch square tin and spread into the corners. Bake in a preheated moderately hot oven (200°C/400°F, Gas Mark 6) for 30 minutes.

Index

NOTES

NOTES